W0415117

# English Phrasal Verbs in Use

## Advanced

60 units of vocabulary reference and practice

Self-study and classroom use

Michael McCarthy
Felicity O'Dell

CAMBRIDGE
UNIVERSITY PRESS
www.cambridge.org

CAMBRIDGE
UNIVERSITY PRESS

University Printing House, Cambridge CB2 8BS, United Kingdom

Cambridge University Press is part of the University of Cambridge.

It furthers the University's mission by disseminating knowledge in the pursuit of education, learning and research at the highest international levels of excellence.

www.cambridge.org
Information on this title: www.cambridge.org/9780521684187



First published 2007
10th printing 2015

Printed in Dubai by Oriental Press

*A catalogue record for this publication is available from the British Library*

ISBN 978-0-521-68418-7 Edition with answers

# Contents

## Work, study and finance



## Personal life



## The world around us



## Key verbs

# Acknowledgements

The authors wish to thank their editors at Cambridge University Press, especially Martine Walsh and Caroline Thiriau who have provided invaluable professional expertise and guidance throughout the project. We very much appreciate the importance of their input at every stage of our work. We also thank Alyson Maskell for all the highly valued experience and skills she brought to the preparation of the manuscript for production and printing.

We must also thank the lexicographers and electronic team at Cambridge University Press. We are particularly grateful for their analysis of phrasal verbs in the Cambridge International Corpus in their development of the Cambridge Dictionary of Phrasal Verbs. Our selection of phrasal verbs for this book is firmly based on this work.

The book has also benefited enormously from the very useful feedback we have received from teachers and students. In particular we would like to thank the following teachers who reviewed and piloted the material throughout its development:

David Matley, Germany
Rui da Silva, South Korea
Colin Mackenzie, France
Gillian Davidson, Russia
Barbara Gardner, UK
Marie Bojarová, Czech Republic
Magdalena Kijak, UK
Dennis Akers, Spain
Kevin Rutherford, Poland

Also, as always, we are grateful to our domestic partners for their patience and support during the writing of this book.

Michael McCarthy and Felicity O'Dell

*Development of this publication has made use of the Cambridge International Corpus (CIC). The CIC is a computerised database of contemporary spoken and written English, which currently stands at over one billion words. It includes British English, American English and other varieties of English. It also includes the Cambridge Learner Corpus, developed in collaboration with the University of Cambridge ESOL Examinations. Cambridge University Press has built up the CIC to provide evidence about language use that helps to produce better language teaching materials.*

*The publisher has used its best endeavours to ensure that the URLs for external websites referred to in this book are correct and active at the time of going to press. However, the publisher has no responsibility for the websites and can make no guarantee that a site will remain live or that the content is or will remain appropriate.*

Produced by Kamae Design, Oxford
Illustrations by Mark Duffin, David Shenton, Lisa Smith and Yane Christensen

# Using this book

## Why was this book written?

It was written to help you take your knowledge of phrasal verbs to a more advanced level. It is intended for students who already have at least an upper intermediate level of English. Many of you will have already worked with *English Phrasal Verbs in Use Intermediate* and this book builds on the work done there. However, it does not matter if you have gained your knowledge of phrasal verbs in a different way. We do not assume that you have used *English Phrasal Verbs in Use Intermediate*, although we do present and practise either different phrasal verbs in this book or, occasionally, more advanced uses of verbs that were presented in the lower level book.

## How were the phrasal verbs in this book selected?

The approximately 1,000 phrasal verbs and related nouns and adjectives which are presented in this book were all selected from those identified as significant by the CANCODE corpus of spoken English developed at the University of Nottingham in association with Cambridge University Press, and the Cambridge International Corpus of written and spoken English. The phrasal verbs selected are accordingly also to be found in the *Cambridge Phrasal Verbs Dictionary*, where you can find additional usage notes and examples. You can search this dictionary online by going to the following website: www.dictionary.cambridge.org.

## How is the book organised?

The book has 60 two-page units. The left-hand page explains the phrasal verbs that are presented in the unit. You will usually find an explanation of the meaning of the phrasal verb, an example of it in use and, where appropriate, some comments on when and how it is used. The exercises on the right-hand page check that you have understood the information on the left-hand page and give you practice in using the material presented.

The units are organised into different sections.

First we start with important information about phrasal verbs in general (Units 1–4): what they are, how their grammar works and so on. We strongly recommend that you do these units first.

The next section looks at some interesting aspects of more advanced phrasal verbs, dealing with such important issues as collocation, register and metaphor. As these are themes that are returned to throughout the book, it is a good idea to work through these units before progressing to other more specific units.

After these two introductory sections, there is a section dealing with some of the most common particles used in forming phrasal verbs. Working on these units will help you to gain a feeling for the force of these particles and will help you have a feeling for the meaning of a phrasal verb you are meeting for the first time.

The next two sections deal with Concepts (e.g. Change) and Functions (e.g. Arranging things). These sections are followed by a large number of topic-based units focusing on different aspects of Work, Personal life and The world around us.

The final section looks at some of the most common verbs which are used to form phrasal verbs.

The book has a key to all the exercises so that you can check your answers. At the back of the book you will also find a useful Mini dictionary. This provides clear definitions of all the phrasal verbs and related noun and adjective forms that appear in this book. The Mini dictionary also indicates the unit number where you can find a particular phrasal verb.

## How should I use this book?

It is strongly recommended that you work through Units 1–4 first so that you become familiar with the way phrasal verbs (and their associated nouns and adjectives) operate and with the terminology that is used in the rest of the book. Then we suggest that you move on to Units 5–9 and after that you may work on the units in any order that suits you.

## What else do I need in order to work with this book?

You need a notebook or file so that you can write down the phrasal verbs that you study in the book as well as any others that you come across elsewhere.

You also need to have access to a good dictionary. We strongly recommend the *Cambridge Phrasal Verbs Dictionary* as this gives you exactly the kind of information that you need to have about phrasal verbs. Your teacher, however, may also be able to recommend other dictionaries that you may find useful.

So all that remains is to say **Go for it!** (Unit 31). We hope you'll find this an enjoyable as well as a useful way to keep up and extend your knowledge of English phrasal verbs in use.

# 1 Phrasal verbs: what are they and how are they used?

## A What are phrasal verbs?

Phrasal verbs are verbs that consist of a verb and a particle (a preposition or adverb) or a verb and two particles (an adverb *and* a preposition, as in **get on with** or **look forward to**). They are identified by their grammar (more about that in Unit 2), but it is probably best to think of them as individual vocabulary items, to be learnt in phrases or chunks. They often – but not always – have a one-word equivalent. For example, you can **come across** a new phrasal verb or you can **encounter** it. You can **pick up** a language or you can **acquire** it. **Come across** and **pick up** sound less literary or formal than **encounter** or **acquire**.

## B Why are phrasal verbs important?

Phrasal verbs are extremely common in English. They are found in a wide variety of contexts. You may have noticed them in songs, for example the Beatles' *I'll get by with a little help from my friends* or *Roll over Beethoven*, Bob Marley's *Get up, stand up* and Red Hot Chili Peppers' *Knock me down*. You find them in film titles such as *The Empire Strikes Back*, *Spirited Away*, *Along Came Polly* or *Cast Away*. They are very frequent in newspaper headlines. Here are just a few examples:

**Country's misplaced pride holds back its democracy**

**Cricket: England holds out for a draw**

**Cover-up** raises fears over bird flu

**Turner adds up likely cost of pensions**

Phrasal verbs are common in less formal English but you will also hear or see and need to use them in more formal contexts. Register is discussed in more detail in Unit 6.

## C Which phrasal verbs does this book deal with?

This book is based on information gained from the Cambridge International Corpus (a huge computerised database of present-day English) about phrasal verbs and how they are used in contemporary English. It focuses on phrasal verbs more advanced students need to know – but in general does not deal with the verbs in the lower level *English Phrasal Verbs in Use Intermediate*. It includes phrasal nouns like **standby** or **onset** (see Unit 3) and phrasal adjectives such as **outgoing** or **worn out** (see Unit 4).

## D What can I do to help myself master phrasal verbs?

Try to think positively about them! And, now you are at a more advanced level, try not just to understand them, but also to use them in your own speaking and writing.

Keep an eye open for them whenever you are reading anything in English and make a note of any interesting ones you find. Write them down in a complete phrase or a sentence to fix in your mind how they are used.

Be aware that one of the special features of phrasal verbs is that some of them have many different meanings – for example, you can **pick** something **up** from the floor, you can **pick up** a language or bad habits, the weather can **pick up**, you can **pick up** a bargain, a radio can **pick up** a signal, the economy can **pick up**, you can **pick up** a story where you left it, you can **pick** someone **up** in your car. Sometimes the meanings are clearly related, some being more literal and some more metaphorical. Unit 7 deals with this in more detail.

In this book we may not present all the meanings of the verbs that are included. You may find others in *English Phrasal Verbs in Use Intermediate* and there are still more in the *Cambridge Phrasal Verbs Dictionary*.

# Exercises

**1.1 Underline the phrasal verbs in these texts. Remember the particle or preposition may not be immediately next to the verb.**

1 I decided to take up gardening, so I went to the library, took a book out and read up on the subject. I found out so many interesting things, such as the best time to plant flowers out for the summer and how to grow vegetables. I've really got into it now and spend hours in the garden every weekend.

2 The other day we went off on a hike in the mountains. We put our wet-weather gear on as the weather forecast wasn't good. We set off early to avoid the rush hour and soon reached the starting point for our walk. The whole walk took about four hours and when we got back we were exhausted.

3 I have to catch up on my coursework this weekend as I've fallen behind a bit. I worked on till midnight last night but I still have loads to do. I have to hand one essay in on Tuesday and another one on Friday. I'm not sure whether I'll make it, but I'll try.

**1.2 Choose the correct particle to finish these song titles.**

1 Can't get you *off from* / *out of* / *away from* my head (Kylie Minogue)
2 Hold you *against* / *down* / *at* (Jennifer Lopez)
3 We can work it *with* / *across* / *out* (The Beatles)
4 Send *from* / *in* / *with* the clowns (Barbra Streisand)

**1.3 Complete the sentences in the right-hand column with a phrasal noun or adjective based on the phrasal verbs in the left-hand column. Use a dictionary if necessary, and remember that the particle may come at the beginning or end of the noun or adjective.**

| | | |
|---|---|---|
| 1 | The school took in some outstanding students last year. | Last year's .............................. included some outstanding students. |
| 2 | Some prisoners broke out of the local prison last night. | There was a(n) .............................. at the local prison last night. |
| 3 | It was an experience that put everyone off. | It was a(n) .............................. experience. |
| 4 | She always speaks out and gives her opinion. | She is very .............................. . |
| 5 | A lorry which had broken down was blocking the road. | A .............................. lorry was blocking the road. |

**1.4 Match the headlines with the sentences from the stories.**

1 BIG SHAKE-UP EXPECTED IN EDUCATION

2 MINISTER DENIES COVER-UP

3 LOCKOUT CONTINUES AT AVIATION PLANT

4 BREAKAWAY GROUP TO FORM NEW PARTY

5 POWER PLANT SHUTDOWN LEAVES 5,000 HOMES IN DARKNESS

a) The dispute is now in its fifth week.
b) Unity was no longer possible, a spokesperson said.
c) The event happened at 7.45 pm with no warning.
d) There will be major changes at all levels.
e) There was no attempt to hide the truth, claimed Pamela Harding.

# 2 Grammar of phrasal verbs

## A Phrasal verbs with and without objects

Some phrasal verbs take an object (transitive); others do not take an object (intransitive).

| *with object (transitive)* | *no object (intransitive)* |
|---|---|
| They're **knocking down** the old hotel. | The path **branched off**[1] to the river. |
| The plumber soon **sorted out** the shower problem. | The noise of the train **died away**. |
| She **tied** her hair **back** so she could work better. | In the winter the lake **froze over**. |

[1] if a road or path branches off, it goes in another direction

Some verbs can be used both with and without an object, but the meaning may change. Use the context to decide if the verb has a different meaning from the one you are familiar with.

Tina and Jo were so clever the teacher **moved** them **up** to a higher class. (with object)
Tina and Jo **moved up** to a higher class. (no object = same meaning)
I can **drop** you **off** at the station. (with object = drive you somewhere and leave you there)
I was sitting in the armchair and I **dropped off.** (no object = fell asleep, different meaning)

Some verbs must have two objects, one after the verb and one after the particle.

I always **associate** that song **with** our holiday in Jamaica.
Playing tennis for three hours every evening after school **deprived** her **of** her youth.

## B Position of the object

In many cases, the particle may come before or after the object.

The teacher **marked** two students **down** / **marked down** two students because they answered the wrong questions in the exam.

Very long objects usually come after the particle.

The accident **cut off** domestic and industrial water and electricity supplies.

When the object is a personal pronoun, the pronoun always comes before the particle.

| *noun object* | *personal pronoun object* |
|---|---|
| I **picked** my parents **up** / **picked up** my parents and drove them to the airport. | I'll **pick** you **up** at 5.30. (Not: ~~I'll **pick up** you at 5.30~~.) |

Some verbs (sometimes called prepositional verbs) must have the object after the particle, even if it is a pronoun. A good dictionary will tell you if this is so.

We've had to **contend with** a lot of problems lately. (Not: ~~**contend** a lot of problems **with**~~) [deal with a difficult or unpleasant situation]

You probably already know some of these verbs (**look for, look after, cope with**).

## C Three-part verbs

Some phrasal verbs have three parts, the verb and two particles. The object comes last.

I will not **put up with** such bad behaviour. [tolerate]

Other examples include **look forward to, look down on, get on with, catch up on** [do something you did not have time to do earlier], **face up to** [accept that a difficult or unpleasant situation exists].

# Exercises

**2.1** **Look at A. Do these sentences need an object? If they do, add an appropriate one in the correct place.**

EXAMPLE Last summer we knocked down.

Yes. *Knock down* is transitive; it needs an object.
Last summer we knocked down the old shed in our garden.

1 The sound of the violin slowly died away.
2 If you're ready to leave now I can drop off at your office.
3 The river in St Petersburg freezes over for several months each year.
4 My son is so good at English that I think the teachers should move up to the class above.
5 I associate with that evening we spent together in Rome.
6 I was so tired that I dropped off in front of the TV.

**2.2** **Put the words in the correct order to make sentences. If you can do it in two different ways, then do so.**

1 pick / off / you / work / the / I / and / can / at / you / from / airport / up / drop / then
2 from / that / put / teacher / she / The / not / would / said / with / such / up / class / rudeness / her
3 villages / The / off / several / have / mountains / in / cut / the / floods
4 your / doesn't / the / improve / down / If / will / handwriting / mark / examiners / you
5 always / Margot / to / with / all / seems / her / cheerfully / problems / cope

**2.3** **Rewrite each sentence using the verb in brackets in an appropriate form.**

1 I'll have to ask my nephew to get my Internet connection working. (SORT)
2 I was so tired after work that I fell asleep in the train on the way home. (DROP)
3 I was given a lower mark because my essay was far too long. (MARK)
4 Bill has no right to despise me – I'm no worse than he is. (LOOK)
5 Lisa doesn't have a good relationship with one of her flatmates. (GET)
6 You have to accept the fact that you will probably never see each other again. (FACE)
7 Maria has got a new job taking care of an old lady. (LOOK)
8 If you don't let the children get enough sleep, they won't be able to concentrate at school. (DEPRIVE)
9 In Lapland we had to manage in some difficult driving conditions. (CONTEND)
10 The road to our house leaves the main road just after the petrol station. (BRANCH)

**2.4** **Write answers to these questions using the phrasal verb in brackets.**

1 What are your plans for the summer holidays? (LOOK FORWARD TO)
2 What homework have you got to do this weekend? (CATCH UP ON)
3 If you've been away somewhere by train and arrive back late, how do you usually get home from the railway station? (PICK UP)
4 What is your favourite album and why do you like it? (ASSOCIATE WITH)
5 What sorts of things make you feel stressed? (CONTEND WITH)
6 How easy do you find it to fall asleep at night? (DROP OFF)

**FOLLOW UP**

Look up these verbs in your dictionary: *associate with*, *deprive of*, *contend with* and *face up to*. How does your dictionary give information about the structures that these verbs require? What nouns do these verbs typically combine with according to the examples in your dictionary?

# 3 Phrasal nouns

## A What are phrasal nouns?

Like phrasal verbs, phrasal nouns consist of a verb combined with a particle. The particle may come before or after the verb.

| *phrasal noun* | *example* | *meaning* |
|---|---|---|
| **standby** | My wife's a pilot and she's on **standby** over the weekend. We're keeping the old equipment as a **standby**, in case of emergencies. | ready to be used if necessary |
| **letdown** | I had been looking forward to the concert for weeks but it turned out to be a terrible **letdown**. | disappointment |
| **back-up** | Neil can provide technical **back-up** if you need it. | support |
| **warm-up** | The comedian who did the **warm-up** for the studio audience before the TV programme started was excellent. | preparation |
| **onset** | The match was halted by the **onset** of rain. | start (of something unpleasant) |
| **input** | Try to come to the meeting – we'd value your **input**. | contribution |
| **overkill** | Shall I add some more decorations to the cake or would that be **overkill**? | more of something than is needed |

Some such nouns have a corresponding phrasal verb but some don't. For example, there is no phrasal verb ~~to kill over~~. The phrasal verb **set on** exists but it means attack. The verb related to **onset** is **set in**: We couldn't continue playing after the rain **set in**.

If the particle is in first place, then the phrasal noun is never written with a hyphen. If the particle comes second, then there is sometimes a hyphen between the two parts of the phrasal noun, particularly if that particle is *in* or *up* or if the phrasal noun is relatively infrequent e.g. **walk-on** [small part, with no words, in a play], **stand-off**.

## B When are phrasal nouns used?

Phrasal nouns are used frequently in newspapers and informal conversation.

**STOWAWAY**[1] FOUND ON PLANE

**STAND-OFF**[2] IN TRADE TALKS

**WALKOUT**[3] AT CAR FACTORY

SINGER STAGES A **COMEBACK**

**BREAKDOWN** IN STRIKE TALKS

MANAGEMENT **BUYOUT** FOR HIGH STREET CHAIN

HELP FOR BUSINESS **START-UPS**

MILITARY **BUILD-UP**[4] CONTINUES

1 person hiding in order to travel
2 failure to reach agreement
3 strike
4 increase in size or strength

Anna: Who do you think will get the job – Paul or Lisa?
Bill: I don't know. It's a **toss-up**. [(informal) both seem equally likely]

Carla: Did you have a good time at squash last night?
Dave: Yes, but we didn't have a real game, just a **knockabout** with the ball.

**TIP** The stress is on the first syllable in these nouns, regardless of whether this is the verb or the particle.

# Exercises

**3.1** **Complete these sentences, using a phrasal noun from A opposite.**

1 The .................... of winter meant that there was less food for the animals and birds.
2 I thought having a 45-piece orchestra at their wedding really was .................... , personally.
3 The police officer radioed for .................... before entering the bank.
4 Let's ask Joel what he thinks. I always find his .................... very useful in these matters.
5 TV producers find that studio audiences react better if they have a .................... to watch before a live programme.
6 Our holiday in the Mediterranean was a bit of a .................... . The hotel was second-rate and the food was awful.
7 Although Tim usually rides his new mountain bike to school now, he's kept his old bike as a .................... .

**3.2** **Rewrite these sentences, starting with the cues given, using phrasal nouns from the opposite page instead of the underlined words.**

1 Two men who had stowed away in the container were arrested when police opened it.
The police opened the container and ..........................................................................
2 Negotiations with union members broke down after a couple of hours.
There was a ..........................................................................
3 The management bought out the company in 2003.
There was a ..........................................................................
4 Last night all the workers walked out and the factory was forced to close.
There was a ..........................................................................
5 Military forces are continuing to build up on both sides of the border.
The military ..........................................................................

**3.3** **Correct the mistakes with the phrasal nouns in these sentences.**

1 There has been a stand-up for several days now in the talks between the government and the rebels. Neither side will make any concessions.
2 Last year there were 15,000 new Internet business start-offs, most of which only survived for a few months.
3 After years without releasing a CD, Sonia Flame has staged a comeagain with her new collection of love songs.
4 Jess: Have you decided where you're going this summer?
Kelly: Not really. It's a toss-over whether it'll be Italy or Greece.
5 I met Chris and we just had a knockover on the tennis courts for half an hour.

**3.4** **Choose the correct phrasal noun in each sentence. Use a dictionary if necessary.**

A–Z

1 *Putout / Output* has increased this year and the factory is doing well.
2 One of the robbers acted as *lookout / outlook* while the others robbed the bank.
3 There was a sudden *pourdown / downpour* and we all got very wet.
4 The *breakout / outbreak* of war in 1914 changed Europe for ever.
5 *Lift-off / Off-lift* is scheduled for 07.00 on Friday and the shuttle will arrive at the space station later that day.
6 There was *a break-in / an in-break* at our office last night. Two computers were stolen.

# 4 Phrasal adjectives

Some phrasal verbs have related adjectives. Make a note of these as you meet them.

| *phrasal verb* | *adjective* | *example* | *meaning* |
|---|---|---|---|
| **go on** | **ongoing** | We've had an **ongoing** problem with the computer system. | one which continues |
| **wear out** | **worn out** | She was wearing old, **worn-out** shoes. | weak, damaged through much use |
| **break down** | **broken-down** | In our garage we've got an old **broken-down** fridge. | one that has stopped working |

However, this is not the case for all such adjectives. We can say 'that way of thinking is very **outdated**', but there is no related verb ~~to date out~~; we can say 'the restaurant was really **overpriced**', but there is no phrasal verb ~~to price over~~ (the verb is 'to overprice').

Note the phrasal adjectives in these extracts from people talking about their dreams and ambitions.

I'm an **outgoing** sort of person, so I want a career where I mix with people. To be honest, I find the idea of a desk job quite **off-putting**[1]; I just don't think I'd like it at all. I'd love to do something new, something completely different.

[1] makes you not like it or not want to do it

I've always been very **outspoken**. I'm never afraid to express my opinion, so I think a job campaigning for an environmental organisation would suit me. I would never accept any **watered-down**[2] proposals and would make some very direct demands of our political leaders.

[2] made less strong in order to make more people agree with them

I always feel completely **tired out** at the end of the day in my present job and just want to sleep. Instead of feeling cheerful after a good weekend, I always feel quite **downcast**[3] every Monday when the new week starts, so I want something new and more stimulating, preferably with a more **go-ahead** company which will bring interest and excitement into my work.

[3] sad and depressed

Here are some more examples in small advertisements and announcements.

**Forthcoming**[4] events at the City Stadium

[4] happening in the near future

**Live-in** nanny wanted for 3-year-old.

**Fold-up** picnic chair for sale. As new.

Caravan for sale: **built-in** fridge, freezer and satellite TV

For rent, cosy one-room flat with **foldaway** bed. Ideal for student.

**TIP** When you come across a phrasal adjective, check to see whether it has a 'matching' verb and, if so, learn the two together.

# Exercises

**4.1** **Replace the adjective in each sentence with a phrasal adjective with the opposite meaning.**

1 There was a new carpet on the stairs.
2 The newsletter has a list of recent activities at the tennis club.
3 What's happened? You're looking very cheerful!
4 Unlike her sister, Emily is very introverted.
5 I find the cover of this novel very attractive, don't you?
6 It doesn't matter what time of day it is, Tilly always looks fresh.
7 We are not in the habit of going to such cheap restaurants.
8 When you meet my boss I think you'll find him surprisingly uncommunicative.

**4.2** **What do these pictures show?**

1 a ................................ chair
2 a ................................ car
3 a ................................ oven
4 a ................................ bed

**4.3** **Answer these questions about the words on the opposite page.**

1 Can you think of one advantage and one disadvantage for parents of having a live-in nanny?
2 In what kind of room might it be particularly useful to have a foldaway bed?
3 What kind of job would not be suitable for a very outspoken person?
4 When might you want to give a watered-down version of something that happened to you?
5 What kind of job requires you to be outgoing?
6 What kind of problem tends to be ongoing?
7 What might you find off-putting if you are having a meal in a restaurant?
8 What sorts of things do you think are often overpriced?

**4.4** **Match the pairs of synonyms in the box below.**

| | | | | | |
|---|---|---|---|---|---|
| broken-down | candid | continuing | diluted | downcast | dynamic |
| exhausted | extrovert | forthcoming | future | go-ahead | miserable |
| not working | obsolete | off-putting | ongoing | outdated | outgoing |
| outspoken | repellent | shabby | tired-out | watered-down | worn out |

**4.5** **Here are some more phrasal adjectives. Work out from the context what they mean and rewrite the sentences replacing the underlined words with a word or phrase that means the same.**

1 If the union doesn't accept our terms, what should we have as <u>our fallback position</u>?
2 Clare always feels <u>left out</u> when her brother's friends come round to play.
3 Sophie is usually chatty but her brother is not very <u>forthcoming</u>.
4 You shouldn't get <u>so worked up</u> about every little thing.
5 Zak met me at the airport with <u>outstretched</u> arms.

# 5 Collocation and phrasal verbs

## A Why is collocation important?

Collocation means the way words combine with one another. When learning a phrasal verb it is important to note what kinds of words the verb is typically used with. For example, can it be used for both people and things, or only for people, or only for things? Is it typically used with negative things or can it be used for both positive and negative things?

Look at this chart for the verb **pore over** [study or look carefully at something] and note how the objects it is used with refer especially to books or documents.

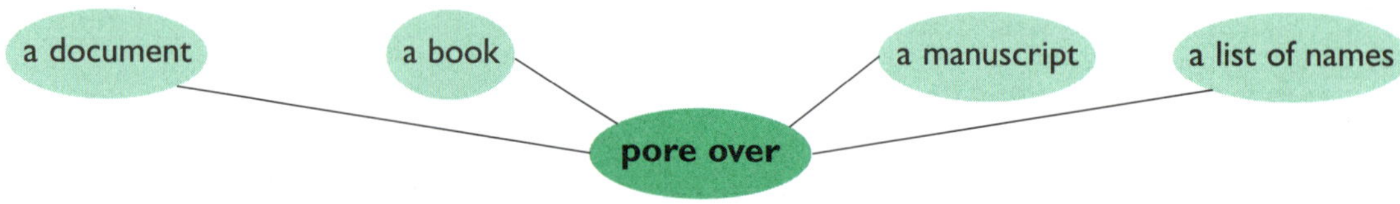


Making a note of collocations in this way will help you remember the meaning of the phrasal verb. It is a good idea to learn the verb and its typical collocations as chunks of language. This will help you to speak and write more fluently.

## B Collocations with positive or negative/problematic things

Make a note if a phrasal verb collocates especially with positive or negative things.

☑ typical/correct collocation ☒ untypical/wrong collocation

The plan was **riddled with** problems ☑ good ideas ☒.
The rain ☑ The traffic ☑ The fine weather ☒ has **eased off** now.
After hours of discussion, we **hit upon** a good idea ☑ the solution ☑ a stupid plan ☒.

## C Collocations with objects denoting people or things

Make a note if a phrasal verb collocates especially with objects denoting people or things, or both.

She **flirted with** the idea ☑ the good-looking guy ☑ for a while but then got bored.
I've really **gone off** Hilary ☑ cheese ☑ recently.
I'd advise you to **keep in with** the boss ☑ James ☑ the exam system ☒.

## D Collocations with subjects denoting people or things

Make a note if a phrasal verb collocates especially with subjects denoting people or things, or both.

As we opened the door, **water streamed into** the room. ☑
**People were streaming into** the meeting. ☑
**I have to dash off**. I have a meeting in ten minutes. ☑
**The car dashed off** along the motorway. ☒ [**headed off / drove off at high speed** would be more typical]

## E Collocations with particular situations

Make a note of particular situations a phrasal verb typically refers to.

He just **sailed through** his exams ☑ the interview ☑ his breakfast ☒. [**sail through** is used with challenging things and situations]
I was always **hankering after** an easier life ☑ sweet food while I was on a diet ☑ passing my exams ☒. [**hanker after** is most often used with things we cannot or should not have]

# Exercises

**5.1** **Answer the following questions.**

1 What does the word *collocation* mean?
2 Which of these are correct collocations?
a) pore over a book
b) pore over a view
c) pore over a manuscript
d) pore over a flower
e) pore over a list of names
3 What do the nouns that collocate with *pore over* have in common?
4 Why is it helpful to learn phrasal verbs in collocations?
5 What sorts of things might you note down about what a phrasal verb collocates with?

**5.2** **Do the sentences below show appropriate collocations or not?**

1 When we took our old dog to the vet, she discovered he was riddled with disease.
2 The pain in his leg seems to be beginning to ease off now.
3 You can always rely on Joe to hit upon an idea that will never work.
4 Although she now has very conservative opinions, in her youth she flirted with left-wing politics.
5 I used to enjoy that TV series but I've gone off it a bit now.
6 It's usually a good idea to keep in with your bank account.

**5.3** **Complete these sentences using the correct particles.**

1 There is no point in hankering ................ your lost youth.
2 When Mary noticed that water was streaming ................ the basement, she dashed ................ to the station, hoping to catch her father before he boarded his train.
3 I always find job interviews really difficult but my brother seems to sail ................ them.
4 We'll have to cut down that tree – it's riddled ................ disease.
5 When my sister was pregnant she drank a lot of milk but she completely went ................ tea and coffee.
6 Harry was bullied a bit when he started school but it seems to have eased ................ now.
7 You should apologise to Jane's mother. It's sensible to keep ................ ................ your future in-laws.
8 I'm flirting ................ the idea of retraining to become a police officer.

**5.4** **Rewrite each sentence using the verb in brackets in an appropriate form.**

1 Helena easily passed her driving test. (SAIL)
2 I really don't like coffee any more. (GO)
3 The wind is less strong than it was now. (EASE)
4 If I have a problem, I find a walk by the sea often helps me to find a solution. (HIT)
5 Masses of people entered the shop as soon as it opened, hoping to find a bargain in the sale. (STREAM)
6 There are a lot of holes in his argument. (RIDDLE)

**FOLLOW UP**

Look back at any other phrasal verbs you have recently written in your vocabulary notebooks. Write them down in some typical collocations. You will find these in the example sentences of a good dictionary e.g. the *Cambridge Phrasal Verbs Dictionary*.

# 6 Register

## A Phrasal verbs in the English lexicon

The word *register* is often used to refer to whether a word is formal or informal. It can also be used to refer to the language associated with a particular job or interest.

English vocabulary is particularly rich because it combines a large vocabulary originating from Anglo-Saxon roots with a large vocabulary originating from Latin or French. This means that English often has words with very similar meanings from each of these sources. To give a phrasal verb example, you can **put forward** or **propose** an idea, where **put forward** (like the majority of phrasal verbs) has a typical Anglo-Saxon etymology, whereas **propose** is of Latin origin. It is interesting to note that **propose** comes from the Latin prefix pro- [= forward] added to the Latin root -pose [= put]; there are many other examples of where the Latin etymology parallels the etymology of its phrasal verb equivalent. Words of Latin or French origin tend to be more formal and so 'proposing an idea' is found more frequently in formal written English than in informal spoken English.

Although phrasal verbs are typical of more informal English, many – like **put forward,** for example – will also be found in neutral or formal as well as informal contexts. Most phrasal verbs are like this. Some phrasal verbs, however, are only used in either informal or formal situations. We indicate throughout the book when this is the case.

## B Informal phrasal verbs

Serge: How's things, Jessie? Is work OK these days?
Jessie: Not really. Sophie's **gunning for**[1] me. I think she's after my job. I **mucked up**[2] an important deal yesterday and she was so thrilled!
Serge: Don't pay any attention to her.
Jessie: I know, but the trouble is Tim's **ganged up with**[3] her now too. So it's got much worse. They **hang around**[4] together in every break and after work too. If Sophie doesn't **shoot down**[5] one of my ideas, Tim does.
Serge: Well, they're **asking for**[6] trouble, aren't they? You know your boss respects you.
Jessie: Yes, I **couldn't ask for**[7] a better boss, that's for sure. But he's got more important things on his plate than sorting out petty office squabbles.

1 (only used in continuous) trying to cause trouble for
2 did very badly with
3 formed a group to act against me
4 spend time together
5 criticise strongly
6 (only used in continuous) behaving in a way that is sure to create problems for them
7 couldn't ever find, because this person (or thing) is the best of their kind

## C Formal phrasal verbs

In the first five examples below, the base verb is in itself formal. The base verb here is of Latin rather than Anglo-Saxon origin. In the final three examples it is the specific usage rather than the base verb which is formal.

The authorities finally **acceded to** his request for a work permit. [agreed to]
We will **attend to** your request in due course. [deal with]
He **ascribes** his success **to** hard work in his youth. [explains]
The presence of the gene may **predispose** a person **to** heart disease. [make more likely]
James Hansen is to **preside over** the government inquiry. [be in charge of]
Some new facts have emerged which **bear upon** the Smith case. [are connected to]
The castaways had to **call upon** all their strength to survive. [use]
All her life the Princess had never **wanted for** anything. [needed]

# Exercises

**6.1** **Replace the phrasal verbs in the letter with verbs from the box to make it more formal.**

| | | | | | | |
|---|---|---|---|---|---|---|
| meet | continue | complain | respond | remedy | investigate | achieve |

> Dear Mr Janes,
>
> Thank you for your letter of 23 May 2005 going on about the bad service you experienced at this hotel. I promise you we will look into the problem at once and get back to you as soon as possible. We always try to go for the highest standards of service, and if we have failed to live up to those standards we will immediately seek to sort out the situation. Meanwhile we hope you will go on making Miromana Hotels your first choice for all your business and leisure travel.
>
> Yours sincerely,
>
> G. H. Logan (General Manager)

**6.2** A–Z **Now do the opposite with these sentences. Use phrasal verbs from the box to make the sentences less formal. Use a dictionary if necessary.**

| | | | | |
|---|---|---|---|---|
| go into | fall through | put out | go over to | look after |
| call in on | buy up | get by | take on | ask out |

1 Will you attend to Aunt Elsie while I go and get the children's supper ready?
2 He explored the subject in great detail in his lecture.
3 When the President died his son assumed the title of Great Leader.
4 I like her. Do you think I should invite her to go out with me?
5 During the war he defected to the enemy side and was killed in action.
6 She purchased all the shares in the company in 2004.
7 The local newspaper published a story about a strange animal seen in the city park.
8 I think I'll visit my grandmother on the way home from work.
9 The deal collapsed at the last minute.
10 I managed to survive on about €50 a day when I was travelling.

**6.3** A–Z **Which professional registers are these phrasal verbs associated with? Put each of them into one of the three categories below. Use a dictionary if necessary.**

| | | | | | |
|---|---|---|---|---|---|
| sell up | sum up | log in | take over | put forward | back up |
| gloss over | boot up | scroll down | base upon | hack into | |
| turn over | bail out | carry forward | square up | print off | |

| computers and technology | academic lectures/writing | money and business |
|---|---|---|
| | | |

**6.4** **Rewrite each sentence using the word in brackets in an appropriate form.**

1 Despite his family's poverty, Alan always has everything he needs. (WANT)
2 You must inform the police if you have evidence relating to the case. (BEAR)
3 Jack will have to use all his ingenuity to resolve the situation. (CALL)
4 The president believes his party's victory is due to his leadership. (ASCRIBE)
5 The manager will deal with your enquiry without delay. (ATTEND)

# 7 Meaning and metaphor

## A Multiple meanings

Many phrasal verbs have more than one meaning. Often, the basic meaning relates to some physical action, while other meanings are metaphorical (i.e. they are figurative, not literal). For example, the meanings in the grey boxes below are literal and the others are figurative.

| *phrasal verb* | *example* | *definition of phrasal verb* |
|---|---|---|
| **run over** | I **ran over** a rabbit as I was driving home. It really upset me. | hit sth/sb with a moving vehicle and injure or kill them |
| | The meeting **ran over** so I missed my train. | go on after its expected time |
| | Could we just **run over** the schedule again to make sure it's all going to work? | read quickly to make sure something is correct |
| **brush** sth/sb **off** | I **brushed off** the dust from my shoes. | use a brush (or hand) to remove something |
| | The boss just **brushed** him **off** and told him to get back to work. | refuse to listen to what someone says, or refuse to think about something seriously |

## B Examples of metaphors based on quick or violent actions

The price of petrol has **shot up** this year. [gone up rapidly and sharply]

I don't want to just **dive into** a new job without carefully considering it. [start doing something suddenly and energetically without thinking about it]

The leader of the opposition party has **hit out at** the government's new proposals on tax. [strongly criticised, typical of journalism]

My success in the exam **spurred** me **on** to study even harder. [spurs are worn on the ankle and are used to make a horse go faster; here the meaning is 'encouraged me']

## C Metaphors and context

The context will usually tell you that a verb is being used in a metaphorical way. Look at these horoscopes. They show phrasal verbs being used metaphorically rather than literally.

Don't just **stand by** and let others have all the fun. It's time to **strike out** and do something completely different. **Sweep aside** all your inhibitions and start living life to the full. It all **boils down** to whether you are prepared to take control of life or let life control you.

You find it difficult to **drag** yourself **away** from domestic responsibilities this month, and you feel **sandwiched between** your family and your career. All this is **eating into** your free time. However, **soldier on** for now because next month will bring an exciting new development which will change everything.

## D More examples of phrasal verbs used metaphorically

She searched in her handbag and **fished out** an old photograph.
We wandered round the old market, just **drinking in** the atmosphere.
He spends hours **glued to** the TV every evening.
We found this vase when we were just **nosing around** in a bric-a-brac shop.
People were **flooding into** the stadium two hours before the concert.

# Exercises

**7.1** **Look at A and B opposite. Read the email and then answer the questions below, using your own words rather than the phrasal verbs in the email.**

> Hi Bill
>
> Sorry to miss you this morning – the budget meeting ran over and I just couldn't leave. We had to try to find some ways to cope with the way that our transport costs have shot up over the last few months. Dave was finding fault with all my ideas and I had to stay and try to defend them as best I could. He always takes any opportunity to hit out at me – I don't know why. Anyway, could we meet later today to run over the agenda for tomorrow's meeting? My problems today have spurred me on to succeed tomorrow. We mustn't just dive into our proposal without preparing the ground carefully. It'd be a disaster if the boss just brushed us off after all that work!
>
> Ray

1 When did the budget meeting end?
2 What has happened to transport costs recently?
3 How does Dave usually behave towards Ray?
4 What does Ray want to do with Bill this afternoon regarding tomorrow's agenda?
5 Has today's meeting made Ray more or less determined about tomorrow's meeting?
6 What does Ray not want to do with their proposal at tomorrow's meeting?
7 What is he afraid that the boss might do to them?

**7.2** **Rewrite the underlined parts of these sentences, using a phrasal verb from C or D opposite.**

1 It's not good for children to spend too much time just watching TV.
2 Choosing a university course is a matter of deciding what you want to do with your life.
3 I arrived at the stadium early and watched the other spectators entering in large numbers.
4 Laura reluctantly left the window and returned to her desk.
5 Sam was staring at Fiona, listening intently to every word she said.
6 George dismissed all objections to his plan, saying they were unimportant.

**7.3** **Complete these sentences with a phrasal verb from the opposite page.**

1 It is terrible how the world just ................ ................ and lets such terrible things happen!
2 Despite all his difficulties, Douglas does his best to bravely ................ ................ .
3 William reached into his pocket and ................ ................ his passport.
4 When I go to a new town I love ................ ................ the back streets.
5 You mustn't let your social life ................ ................ your study time.
6 The politician simply ................ ................ the allegations being made against him.
7 When he was 30 Mark left his uncle's business and ................ ................ on his own.
8 Our little house is .................................... ................ a bank and a supermarket.

**7.4** **Here are some more phrasal verbs which can be used metaphorically. How are their literal and metaphorical meanings connected? Use a dictionary if necessary.**

1 I've left you some soup which you can **warm up** when you get home.
A fantastic singer **warmed up** the audience before the main programme started.
2 The boy wasn't looking where he was going and **fell into** a hole in the ground.
Kevin **fell into** his first job as soon as he had left university.
3 The cat got up the tree but didn't seem able to **climb down**.
Paul always wants to win an argument – you'll never get him to **climb down**.

# 8 Idioms using phrasal verbs

## A Problems at work and home

Hi Milly,

How's your awful new boss? Still planning a total reorganisation of the office or have you persuaded her not to **throw the baby out with the bathwater**[1]? Let me know if you need an evening out to **let off steam**[2] – it's about time we met up again.

We've been told at our company that we won't be getting a salary increase this year. They **took the sting out of it**[3] by giving us a Christmas bonus but people are not happy.

My boss is still as difficult as ever. Her secretary's resigned but I think that might be **cutting off her nose to spite her face**[4] as she'll find it hard to find anything else as well-paid. She can usually **run rings round**[5] anyone so it must have been a shock for her to get a boss she couldn't manipulate.

I badly need your advice. Joe's beginning to **turn up the heat** in our relationship – he's dropping hints about marriage. He invited me to meet his parents last weekend. We **got on like a house on fire**[6] but I just don't feel ready to **put down roots** yet. Should I stop seeing him? I don't want to but maybe it'd be kinder? I can't **make up my mind**. Let me know what you think.

Tara

1 get rid of the good parts of something as well as the bad parts
2 talk or act in a way that helps get rid of strong feelings
3 make something that is unpleasant less so
4 doing something because you are angry though it may cause you more problems
5 outwit, be cleverer than
6 immediately liked each other

## B Progress meeting

Bruno: Well, Anna, you've been here for a month now and it's time we had a little chat.

Anna: OK. Well, I know I **got off on the wrong foot**[1] by deleting all last year's client information but I hope you'll agree I've **got my act together**[2] now?

Bruno: Erm, not exactly. I've tried my best to show you where you're going wrong but I just seem to **be going round in circles**[3]. Nothing ever seems to get any better. You **dig your heels in**[4] and don't make any effort to change.

Anna: Oh, I don't think that's fair. I'm sure Geoff would **put in a good word for me**[5]. I've helped him out with one of his projects.

Bruno: Hmm, well Geoff needs to **clean up his act**[6] too. If you don't start **making up for lost time**[7] soon, we're going to have to let you go.

Anna: Oh, no, please. Just give me a bit more authority and I'll **come into my own**[8].

Bruno: Oh, Anna. **Wake up and smell the coffee**[9]! You won't get any more authority unless you **pull out all the stops**[10] and your work improves significantly.

1 started badly
2 (informal) organised myself more effectively
3 using a lot of time and effort with no results
4 refuse to do what others try to persuade you to do
5 say good things about me to someone in authority
6 (informal) start to behave better
7 doing something to compensate for not doing it previously
8 be very successful
9 (informal) be realistic
10 do all you can

# Exercises

**8.1** **Answer these questions.**

1 What should you not throw out with the bathwater?
2 What expression uses a burning house as a metaphor for a good relationship?
3 What expression uses steam as a metaphor for strong feelings?
4 According to the idiom, why might people cut off their own nose?
5 What idiom means 'ease an unpleasant situation' and refers to what bees can do?
6 Which two phrasal verb idioms refer to circular motion?

**8.2** **Complete these sentences using expressions from 8.1.**

1 Refusing that job offer just because you're annoyed about the interview would be cutting ................ your ................ to ................ your ................ .
2 When she reached 30 Estelle decided it was time she ................ down ................ and she bought a little cottage not far from here.
3 The robbers ................ ................ round the police. It took two years to catch them.
4 The extra day's holiday we offered should take the ................ out ................ the pay cut.
5 I felt as if I was just going ................ in ................ and getting nowhere.
6 We should keep the better parts of the old system when we move over to the new system. We don't want to ................ the ................ out with the bathwater.
7 Jim and Steve ................ on like a ................ on fire; they're great friends.
8 I don't think he was really angry with you; he was just ................ ................ steam.

**8.3** **Cross out the five mistakes in this text and write the correct form in the box next to that line.**

After a year of travelling, I decided to ~~put~~ my act together and get a job. A friend who worked for a bank put in some good words for me. In fact he pushed in all the stops and arranged for me to have lunch with the CEO. I got on the wrong feet by saying I wasn't ready to plant down roots yet; I think they were looking for someone to make a long-term commitment. I should have kept quiet!

| | |
|---|---|
| 1 | get |
| 2 | ................................ |
| 3 | ................................ |
| 4 | ................................ |
| 5 | ................................ |

**8.4** **Complete these dialogues using phrasal verbs from the opposite page so that the second speaker agrees with and repeats more or less what the first speaker says.**

1 Greg: Hilary seems determined not to agree to the new plan.
Juan: Yes, she really seems to be digging ................................................................ .

2 Karen: Wow, my old Uncle Josh is 75 and he's getting married for the first time!
Helen: Really? He's obviously trying to make up ................................................................!

3 Luis: James lives in a fantasy world. He thinks he can make a living writing poetry.
Ana: Poets never make any money! He should wake up and ..........................................!

4 Eva: Ted has been very successful in his new career.
Gabriel: Yes, he really seems to have come into ................................................................ .

5 Alan: The boss seems to be getting very serious about the new sales campaign lately.
Dan: Yes, he's really turning up ................................................................ .

6 Franck: I think it's time I made a decision.
Cindy: Yes, it's time for you to make up ................................................................ .

# 9 New phrasal verbs

## A Why are more phrasal verbs needed?

Firstly, social change demands new words. For example, developments in technology have given us the phrasal verb **top up** [pay money onto a **top-up** card (see below) which you spend when you use your mobile phone] and the expression **top-up card** [a card you buy for a mobile phone which allows you to make calls up to the value of the card]. Computers have given us **scroll up/down** [move up or down a computer screen] and **copy** somebody **in** [send someone a copy of an email that you are sending to another person]. Trends in the world of work also provide us with new phrasal verbs such as **skill up** [provide someone with the skills they need to be better at their job, by providing training, for example].

Secondly, phrasal verbs have specific stylistic qualities and for this reason are particularly popular with journalists. They simplify and enliven language in a very flexible way. For instance, it is more interesting to use the expression **dumb up** [opposite of **dumb down**] than 'raise one's intellectual and cultural values'. For the same reason **sex up** was an attractive addition to English and, more recently, **sex down** [make something less exciting].

Finally, young people invent and use new phrasal verbs as a way of making their language different from that of their elders. Phrasal verbs like **chill out** [relax] and **zone out** [stop thinking about anything] for example, are strongly associated with young people.

## B How are new phrasal verbs formed?

New phrasal verbs are formed in a way that allows hearers or readers to understand them. Particles play an important role in making the new meaning immediately clear (see Units 10–16 for more on particles).

Sometimes coining a new phrasal verb is a matter of extending the range of an existing one:

I got **bumped/thrown off** the Internet after five minutes online. [lost my connection]

If you don't give Toby what he wants, he'll **kick off**. [start making trouble]

The older meanings of **bump off** [(informal) kill], **throw off** [get rid of, remove quickly] and **kick off** [start a football match] are not lost; the new meanings are simply added to them.

It is much more unusual for a new word to provide the basis for a phrasal verb, however it does happen. For example, a new word in the computer domain is *phish* [fraudulently obtain people's financial details through dishonest websites – in other words, fish for financial information]. This has led to **phish for** as in:

He was charged with **phishing for** credit card information.

Sometimes a familiar word joins a particle to make a new combination and sometimes a new part of speech. For example, the word poodle is familiar as a type of dog but it is now also a phrasal verb – **poodle around** [wander around in a relaxed way]. Advertisers may talk about their **click-through rate** [a way of measuring the response to an Internet advert by expressing the number of people who click on an online ad to get to the target site as a percentage of all the people who look at the ad]. Phrasal nouns can also be formed like this; an account of a new TV programme reports that, after the show, the team were so pleased with their performance that they had a 'sort of mass **hug-in**' [everyone embraced each other]. Another example is **melt-up** [overheating a financial market, causing prices to rise].

Finally, many 'new' phrasal verbs come from American English, where they may have existed for many years before becoming standard British English. For example:

Ladies and gentlemen, can you **give it up for** Mr Tommy McGee! [applaud him].

People get **weirded out** by my films. [(usually passive) feel uncomfortable or shocked].

# Exercises

**9.1** **Complete the sentences describing the pictures below.**

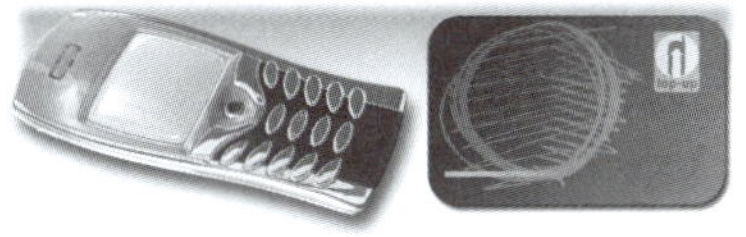

1 I have a ...................... card for my phone.

3 The team always has a ...................... before leaving the changing room.

2 He ...................... the Marketing Manager ...................... on his email.

4 Use your mouse to ...................... up or down the screen.

**9.2** **Complete each sentence using a phrasal verb from the box. Use each phrasal verb twice.**

| chill out | kick off | bump off |
|---|---|---|

1 The robbers threatened to ................ ................ the bank manager's wife if he didn't help them steal the money.
2 It was great to go on holiday and have time to just ................ ................ .
3 The game ................ ................ at 2.30, so should finish soon after 4 o'clock.
4 Juan was getting really stressed so I told him to ................ ................ .
5 I got ................ ................ the website and couldn't get back on for an hour.
6 If the fans are not allowed in to the concert, they are sure to ................ ................ .

**9.3** **Match the headlines (1–4) with the sentences from the stories (a–d).**

1 MARKET MELT-UP FORECAST

2 SOMEONE IS PHISHING FOR YOUR BANK DETAILS

3 RECORD CLICK-THROUGH RATE FOR NEW ONLINE STORE

4 SCIENTISTS SEX DOWN LATEST 'BREAKTHROUGH'

a) Just one day after the site went live, 600,000 people had visited it.
b) They said they wanted to counteract the sensationalism that had surrounded the event.
c) The Treasury is discussing how the potential crisis may be kept under control.
d) Identity theft is the fastest-growing crime, according to a report published today.

**9.4** **Answer the questions.**

1 If you're at a concert and you are asked to 'give it up for the singer', what do you do?
2 If you zone out, are you (a) reading (b) daydreaming or (c) sleeping?
3 What phrasal verb means 'make something more intellectually demanding'?
4 If a manager says that his workforce will need some skilling up, what does he mean?
5 Rewrite these sentences in your own words. Use a dictionary if necessary.

a) The company intend to roll out the new version of the software in April 2012.
b) We lucked out and got the last flight out before the hurricane struck.
c) We drilled down into the data and found some very interesting statistics.

# 10 Around and about

*Around* and *about* are often (but not always) interchangeable in phrasal verbs. A good dictionary will tell you whether they can both be used. The only verbs on this page where both are not possible are marked *.

## A Basic meaning of *around* and *about* in phrasal verbs

*Around* and *about* keep a lot of their basic meaning in many phrasal verbs. They often indicate activities and situations taking place in various locations, often without having a clear direction or order.

There were books **lying around** everywhere in the room.
The children were **running about** in the garden.

Phrasal verbs with *around* and *about* are often informal. Look at this conversation between two teachers.

Sally: Rumours have been **flying around** the staffroom lately that you're leaving. Is it true?

Jake: It amazes me how news **gets around** in this place! I did say to one or two people that I was tired of being **bossed around** by you-know-who, and, I have **asked around*** here and there to see if they need any full-time teachers, but I haven't made a decision yet.

Sally: Oh, right. I heard the other day that you-know-who's secretary is sick of **running around* after** him sorting out problems he's caused. So she might leave too. By the way, do you have a copy of that new grammar book? I want to show it to my students. My copy's **floating about** here somewhere but I just can't find it.

Jake: Yes, I think I have a copy **lying around** here somewhere ... Yes, here you are.

Sally: Thanks very much. So, what are you up to this weekend?

Jake: Nothing much, just **pottering about** at home, really. Oh goodness! Is that the time? I have a class now.

Sally: Ok, see you later. Don't forget that we **switched** our classrooms **around** this afternoon. You're in Room 2.

Note that in **boss around**, around emphasises the fact that the person is *frequently* being bossed by someone else, not the fact that this occurs in different places.

## B Other uses of *around* and *about*

Here are some other phrasal verbs which use *around* and *about*.

Children! Stop **playing around**! Sit politely. [behaving stupidly]

The neighbours have been **banging about** next door all morning. I wonder what they're doing. [making loud noises, for example hammering or moving heavy objects]

Peter was **clowning around** at the party last night. It got very irritating. [acting in a silly way]

Politicians often **skirt around*** the truth and don't give direct answers to questions. [avoid discussing a difficult subject or problem]

It's a problem, but I'm sure we can **work around*** it in some way. [organise our activities to ensure that the problem does not prevent us from doing what we want to do]

# Exercises

## 10.1 Choose the correct word to complete these sentences.

1 I couldn't get to sleep because of Owen ...................... around upstairs.
a) banging b) lying c) switching
2 Wait a moment – the letter you need is ...................... about here somewhere.
a) flying b) floating c) running
3 I think we should stop the car and let the children ...................... around for a bit.
a) get b) lie c) run
4 The room looks different. Have you ...................... the furniture around?
a) pottered b) switched c) banged
5 If you ...................... around, you might be able to find someone with a car for sale.
a) ask b) boss c) play
6 I hate the way rumours ...................... around the office.
a) run b) fly c) lie
7 You really shouldn't leave such important papers ...................... about.
a) clowning b) lying c) playing
8 Tom made the children laugh by ...................... around with pieces of fruit.
a) banging b) getting c) clowning

## 10.2 Complete each dialogue using a verb from the box with *around* or *about*.

| boss | get | ask | clown | lie |
|---|---|---|---|---|

1 Melissa: I need to find a flat to rent in London. Do you know of anything available?
Kate: No, but I'll ...................................... .
2 Sue: Do you know where the London street atlas is?
Roberto: Yes, I think it might be ...................................... in my study somewhere.
3 Adam: How did Hugh know we're getting married?
Tanya: Well, news like that ...................................... very quickly.
4 Diana: Do you get on well with your sister?
Linda: Yes, on the whole, though she ................ me ................ a bit too much.
5 Anna: What do you think of Rick?
Nick: I find the way he ...................................... all the time a bit childish.

## 10.3 Complete these sentences with phrasal verbs from the opposite page. Put the verb in the correct form. Sometimes more than one verb is possible.

1 I thought Alex was just ................................ in his bedroom today but in fact he's been really busy. He's tidied up all the books and papers that were ................................ on the floor. He's also ................................ his bed and his desk, which makes the room feel bigger.
2 When I was a child I used to hate visiting Great Uncle Wilfred. He wouldn't allow us children to ................................ in case we broke anything and he was always ...................... us ......................, getting us to ................................ after him, doing odd jobs for him.
3 Do you think we could find a way to ................................ the problem of having to get written permission from everyone to use the photographs in our book?
4 I think we should be honest with everyone and not try to ................................ the issue.
5 We hear people ................................ every night in the flat upstairs. All sorts of rumours have been ................................ among the neighbours as to what is going on up there.

**FOLLOW UP** Look up these words in your dictionary: *crowd around, knock* sth *about/around, turn around, turn* sth *around, roll about/around, blunder about/around.* Make a note of the meanings of these words and record them with an example sentence.

# 11 Down

## A *Down* meaning lower

Tom: Well, did he **come down**[1] on the price?
Suzie: I **knocked** him **down**[2] by £20 but he wouldn't go any lower.
Tom: Oh, so that's why you **slammed** the phone **down**[3]?
Suzie: No, that was because I was annoyed with you and the TV. Why didn't you **turn** it **down**[4] when I asked? I could hardly hear a word he was saying!

1 suggest or agree to a lower price
2 persuaded him to reduce the price
3 put down with a lot of force
4 reduce the amount of sound

## B *Down* suggesting preventing or restraining

| *phrasal verb* | *example* | *definition of phrasal verb* |
|---|---|---|
| **shout down** sb or **shout** sb **down** | I couldn't hear what the Prime Minister was saying because some people at the front were **shouting** him **down**. | shout in order to prevent someone who you disagree with from being heard |
| **pin down** sb or **pin** sb **down** | Two police officers **pinned** the robber **down** while the third handcuffed him. | force someone to stay in a horizontal position by holding them |
| **tie down** sth/sb or **tie** sth/sb **down** | Make sure you **tie** the suitcase **down** carefully on the top of the car. | use ropes to fasten someone or something in a particular position |
| **tie** sb **down** | My brother prefers to take temporary work because he hates the idea of being **tied down**. | (metaphorical meaning of the previous verb) prevent someone from having the freedom to do what they want to do |

## C Other meanings of *down*

Not working
The computers are always **going down**. We need some new ones. [stopping working]
Don't forget to save your documents before you **shut** the computer **down**. [turn off]

Depressed or sad
This rain is **getting** me **down**. [making me feel depressed]

On a piece of paper
Katie asked me to **put** her **down** for two tickets to the school play. [put on a list to arrange for her to have something]
You can **put** me **down** to organise the refreshments. [put on a list to arrange for me to do something]

Killed/injured
The terrorists mercilessly **gunned down** their victims. [shot and killed or seriously injured]
We had to have our poor old dog **put down** last week; she was very sick. [put to death]

Surviving through time
The legend has **come down** to us from the ancient records of the Quilhoa people. [passed from generation to generation]

Be considered or remembered
This will **go down** in history as the most important event of the century. [be remembered]
My workshop **went down** really well. [was well-received]

# Exercises

**11.1 Read these sentences and then answer the questions below by writing the correct name in the box.**

Harry Irving felt he had lost his freedom when he and Jean had their first baby.
Joe Reece was forced to the ground and held there by two security guards.
People protested so loudly that no one could hear what Linda Trotsky had to say.
Freda Calvo persuaded the man to reduce the price by £50.
Peter Hind was shot dead yesterday by terrorists.

| | |
|---|---|
| 1 Who was shouted down? | |
| 2 Who was gunned down? | |
| 3 Who felt tied down? | |
| 4 Who was pinned down? | |
| 5 Who managed to knock someone down? | |

**11.2 Rewrite the underlined parts of these sentences, using a phrasal verb from the opposite page. Make any other necessary changes.**

1 The computers suddenly <u>stopped working</u> this morning, so we're doing everything manually at the moment.
2 I'm sorry I'm so irritable. Things have been <u>depressing me</u> lately.
3 Shall I <u>write your name on my list</u> to sponsor me for the charity walk?
4 This event will <u>be remembered</u> in history as the worst catastrophe this country has ever suffered.
5 The company had to <u>stop</u> all their machines during the 24-hour strike at the factory.
6 The salesman <u>agreed to a lower price</u>, and after that we even managed to <u>persuade him to reduce the price</u> by a further 10%.
7 Many everyday remedies for minor ailments have <u>reached us over time</u> from our ancestors.

**11.3 Answer the following questions, using a phrasal verb from the opposite page.**

1 What might someone do if they get very angry during a phone call?
2 What might you do to a very old and sick dog or cat?
3 What would you do to stop a suitcase from falling off the roof rack of a car?
4 If housework gets you down, how does it make you feel?
5 If your radio was too loud, what would you do?

**11.4 Which of the meanings given are possible or likely interpretations of the phrasal verbs in these sentences? More than one interpretation may be possible. Use a dictionary if necessary.**

1 I think you should take this down.
a) write it  b) drink it  c) dismantle it
2 The house has come down.
a) has been rebuilt  b) is for sale at a lower price  c) has been demolished
3 She turned it down.
a) reduced the heat  b) refused the offer
c) put the collar of her coat in its normal position
4 They watered it down.
a) extinguished a fire using water
b) added water to make a liquid less strong
c) made an idea, opinion or argument less strong

# 12 In

The particle *in*, when used with phrasal verbs, keeps a lot of its basic meaning, often referring to things which move towards being, or are already, 'within something' or are 'included in something'.

Look at this transcript of a meeting at a computer software company. Gareth, the Chief Executive, who chairs the meeting, speaks first. Note the phrasal verbs with *in*.

Chair: Well, I think we should begin. One of our colleagues from Manchester has been delayed but I've asked David to **show** her **in** when she gets here, so she'll join us later, I hope. Now, first item is the *Musicmatch* software suite, which, I like to think, has helped to **usher in**[1] a new era in music production. It's been **bringing in** good profits, and we've certainly been able to **cash in on** the recent crash of one of our major rivals, as we all know, but with an economic recession **setting in** now, we may want to rethink our pricing so that it **fits in** better **with** the rest of our range. We also need to **factor in**[2] the loss of a major client – we lost the *Popmaster* contract this year.

Hilary: Can I **come in** here, Gareth? Tim and I are already looking at this and we'll have something to report next week. Basically we hope to **build in** an automatic upgrade system so that customers will find it easier to stay with us. Tim's looking at the cost. I said I'd **pitch in**[3] so that we can get it moving faster.

Chair: Okay, well, maybe we can leave that. But I'd just like to say, remember, we need flexibility – we don't want to become **boxed in**[4] by our own systems. We'll come back to it.

David: Sorry to **cut in**, Gareth. Mary Peckham is here.

Chair: Ah, good. Our colleague from Manchester has arrived. Hello, Mary. You're very welcome. Can you **squash in** there somewhere? Sorry the room is a bit small. Mary Peckham, everyone. Some of you know her already. Right, I suggest we move to Rita's presentation. I believe you're going to use the projector, Rita?

Rita: Yes. Could we close those blinds? Thanks. Oh dear, they're still **letting** a lot of light **in**. Never mind. I'll begin. I'd like to use this presentation as a **lead-in**[5] to our general discussion about the future.

1 (formal) begin or cause a period in which new things or changes happen
2 include something when making a calculation or when trying to understand something
3 (informal) help with work that needs to be done
4 restricted
5 something that introduces something else

**TIP**

Take note of the context when you meet new phrasal verbs. For example, the context on this page is a fairly informal business meeting. Spoken business English is often less formal than the spoken language of business in some other languages and cultures. The same is often true for other contexts such as spoken academic language.

# Exercises

**12.1** **Find phrasal verbs or phrasal adjectives from the opposite page which mean the following:**

1 benefit from
2 interrupt (two answers)
3 help
4 introduce
5 unable to act freely
6 introduction
7 take into consideration
8 find a space
9 include
10 start

**12.2** **Correct the mistakes with the phrasal verbs in these sentences.**

1 My new curtains are excellent – they don't bring any light in.
2 Tina, can you pitch Mr Hill in as soon as he arrives, please?
3 Having the meeting on the 28th would squash in better with our plans than the 30th.
4 Our office in Buenos Aires has cashed in a lot of new business this year.
5 When you are planning the course, make sure you set in enough free time.
6 It's rude to factor in when someone else is in the middle of speaking.
7 If everyone shows in, we'll soon get the job done.
8 If I move up, then Rachel should be able to box in at the end of the bench.

**12.3** **Complete this paragraph with verbs from the opposite page.**

My ten-year-old daughter Rosie had some friends to sleep over last night. Eight of them managed to sleep on her bedroom floor. I don't know how they ............................ (1) themselves in as it is a very small room. Rosie's birthday had been the previous week, but we had her party yesterday as that ............................ (2) in better with other plans. In the evening we had a barbecue and we made lots of different salads and puddings. Rosie and her friends all ............................ (3) in, and they enjoyed helping as much as eating. Later in the evening rain ............................ (4) in, so they went indoors and watched a DVD. I was afraid the girls would wake up ridiculously early, but we've had new blinds fitted and they don't ............................ (5) any light in, so no one stirred till half past eight.

**12.4** **Cross out the item which does not normally collocate with the phrasal expression in bold. Use a dictionary if necessary.**

A–Z

1 **bring in** customers / profits / a loss / business
2 a **lead-in** to a discussion / a bargain / a lesson
3 a recession / rain / a new product **sets in**
4 **usher in** a price increase / a new era / changes

**FOLLOW UP**

What other phrasal verbs with *in* do you have in your vocabulary notebook? Do they also have a connection with the basic meaning of *in*? As you learn other new ones think about how the idea conveyed by *in* might help you remember the meaning of the phrasal verb.

# 13 Off

## A Off suggesting get rid of

My feet were hot, so I **kicked off** my shoes. [removed with my feet]
The robbers drove faster and faster to try and **shake off** the police car. [lose]
I went for a long walk to **work off** my frustation. [get rid of a feeling (often unpleasant) by doing something energetic]
Tony doesn't worry about anything – he'll **shrug off** any problem. [treat something as unimportant]

## B Off suggesting separation

| *phrasal verb* | *example* | *definition of phrasal verb* |
|---|---|---|
| **be cut off** | My office is in a different building from my colleagues so I am quite **cut off**. | be unable to see many other people |
| **cut off** sth/sb or **cut** sth/sb **off** | They **cut off** our electricity / **cut** us **off** because we hadn't paid the bill. | stop providing something, e.g. aid, electricity, supplies |
| **split off** | Two of the climbers **split off** from the group and went off on their own. | form a separate group |
| **back off** | She was interfering so I told her to **back off** and let me deal with it on my own. | (slightly informal) stop being involved in a situation, especially in order to allow other people to deal with it themselves |
| **have** sth **off** | I **had** a week **off** last June. | spend time away from work |
| **cordon off** sth or **cordon** sth **off** | The police have **cordoned off** the area the President will be visiting. | put something, e.g. a rope, a barrier, around an area in order to stop people from entering it |

## C Off suggesting starting or finishing

I'll fill in the first line of this spreadsheet to **start** you **off**, then you can do the rest yourself. [help you to start]

The weekly meeting usually **kicks off** around 2 pm. [(informal) starts]

We **rounded off** the meal with freshly brewed coffee. [finished]

That boring meeting just **finished** me **off**. I think I'll go home; I've had enough for one day. [made me feel so weak, tired or unhappy that I couldn't continue]

It's nice to just **switch off** at the weekend and forget about work. [stop giving your attention to someone or something]

## D Other verbs with off

Ben told his little brother to **leave off** playing his new guitar. [(informal) stop]

Wilma told her younger sister to **shove off** out of her room. [(informal) something that you say when you are angry to tell someone to go away.]

Ray wanted to **show** his new bike **off** to his friends. [show someone or something that you are proud of to a group of people]

The boss gave the receptionist a **ticking off** for making private calls to friends. [telling someone that you are angry with them because they have done something wrong]

# Exercises

**13.1 Replace the underlined words in these statements with a phrasal verb from the opposite page.**

1 Kersty's mother to Kersty's father: Kersty's 21 now and should make her own decisions. I think we should stop getting involved and let her run her own life.
2 Newsreader: The Prime Minister has treated as unimportant leadership threats from within his party, saying that they are only rumours.
3 Mother to father: I think we should let the kids run round in the garden for a bit, let them get rid of some of their energy so that they sleep tonight.
4 Father to Petra: Petra, you MUST pay your electricity bill. If you don't, they'll stop providing it and you won't have any heating.
5 Ken to Nick: Oh no! Dave wants to come back with us to Pete's house. He's such a drag! How can we get away from him?
6 Chairperson: I'd like to just conclude the meeting by giving a vote of thanks to the committee for all their work this year.
7 The last 100 metres to the top of the hill just made me so tired I couldn't continue. I had to sit down and rest for an hour.
8 I don't want you in my room any more, so just leave!

**13.2 Cross out the five mistakes in this text and write the correct form in the box next to that line.**

When I come home from work, I love to just kick ~~away~~ my shoes and relax for the evening. It's great to let off worrying about work and round up the day with a nice meal. If I have off a couple of days it's even better. I usually go off to our country cottage. I can just light off completely. I love it. I never stay there long because after a while I feel a bit stood off from all my friends and social life back in the city.

| |
|---|
| ..........off.......... |
| 1 .............................. |
| 2 .............................. |
| 3 .............................. |
| 4 .............................. |
| 5 .............................. |

**13.3 Complete the word puzzle.**

Across
1 The boss ...................... me off with a simple task to get me used to the job.
3 The police decided to ...................... off the scene of the crime.
4 What time does the meeting ...................... off?
5 She always loves to ...................... off her latest technological gadget.
6 Look, just ...................... off playing with my phone, will you? You're getting on my nerves.

Down
2 The director gave him a ...................... off for arriving late at the meeting.
5 A group of youths ...................... off from the rest of the demonstrators and started causing trouble.

# 14 On

Some phrasal verbs with *on* share a meaning of dependence/reliance e.g. **depend on***, **rely on***, **count on***, **hinge on***, **hang on***, **ride on.**

**REFERENDUM RESULT CRUCIAL, SAYS PM**

The Prime Minister said, 'Everything **hinges on** the result of next week's referendum. The future prosperity of the nation **hangs upon** this crucial day of decision.' Politicians of all parties agree that everything **rides on** the government securing a Yes vote.

*On* can also convey the idea of continuing in an irritating or boring way. for example, **harp on** [talk repeatedly about something in a way that others find boring or irritating], **keep on, go on (and on), ramble on** [talk or write for a very long time in a boring way] and **drone on** [talk for a long time in a very boring way and in a monotonous voice].

Don't **keep on** about the garden! I'll mow the lawn tomorrow.
We had a tedious lecture from the boss. She just **went on and on** about punctuality.
He **droned on** for hours about ancient civilisations; everyone fell asleep.

**Read on, press on, live on** and **dwell on*** [(transitive) think or talk about a particular subject for too long] also emphasise continuation over time.

**HOUSING MINISTER HONOURS CHAMPION OF THE POOR**
'Her death is a great loss to society, but her memory will **live on**', said the Minister.

Grouping verbs in this way can help you to remember them.

Now look at these news items which contain some of these and other examples of phrasal verbs with *on*.

**CURATOR FINDS LOST MEDIEVAL MANUSCRIPT**

The curator, Mr Willis Bedgrove, **happened upon*** the lost manuscript while searching the museum's archives for some missing 18th century letters. As he **focused** his attention **on*** the text, he said, he could hardly believe what he was reading. As he **read on**, he realised the importance of what he'd found.

**EDUCATION EXPERT EXPRESSES CAUTION ON HOME SCHOOLING**

Sheila Garrett stated that home schooling was often **frowned on*** by politicians, and she herself had some doubts as to its effectiveness. However, to **spring** a new piece of legislation **on** parents successfully educating their children at home was not right, she said. The education secretary insists that he will **press on** with plans to introduce a new law penalising parents who practise home schooling.

**Children's prank turns to tragedy**
A 13-year-old girl who stole a car and took it for a joyride admits that friends **led** her **on**. The prank resulted in the serious injury of a 25-year-old mother of two.

The verbs marked with * on this page are all transitive and can have *upon* instead of *on* in more formal contexts. When you come across other phrasal verbs with *on*, note whether *upon* is also possible.

# Exercises

**14.1** **In the following sentences, mark each phrasal verb according to whether it has predominantly a dramatic feeling (write D), a negative feeling (N), a feeling of boredom (B), or a feeling of irritation (I).**

1 Professor Taylor was droning on about the Ancient Greeks in his lecture this morning.
2 The success of the peace talks hinges upon both sides maintaining the present truce.
3 Uncle Eric goes on and on about his broken chair. I've told him a hundred times I'll mend it.
4 Dwelling on the past all the time is no way to live your life. Think of your future.
5 If you ask Beatrice about beekeeping she'll ramble on for hours.
6 I wish you wouldn't keep on about money. Let's just enjoy life.
7 The championship now rides on Saturday's crucial game against Real Madrid.

**14.2** **Choose the correct word to complete these sentences. Sometimes there is more than one possible answer.**

1 You can always ...................... on Daniel. He's totally dependable.
a) rely b) count c) hinge d) hang
2 I wish Kelly would stop ...................... on about Dave. It's so tedious!
a) riding b) droning c) going d) harping
3 Do make up your mind soon. So much ...................... on what you decide.
a) hinges b) presses c) rides d) hangs

**14.3** **Correct the mistakes with the phrasal verbs in these sentences. There is one mistake in each sentence.**

1 Try to focus what is really important on and to ignore what is not essential.
2 Now we've had a bit of a rest, it's time to press upon again.
3 I'm hingeing on you to let me know when my talk has gone on for long enough.
4 Your grandmother will always live upon in your memory.
5 This is a quiet neighbourhood where noisy behaviour is counted on.
6 After the first few pages of the book, I decided I couldn't be bothered to ride on.
7 Please stop focusing on about Sheila. Your relationship is over, so just forget her.
8 I am worried about my son's behaviour. He is so easily relied on by his friends.

**14.4** **Complete each sentence with a verb from the opposite page.**

1 Don't try to remember every sentence of the text. Just ...................... on the main points.
2 Hilary is going to ...................... the news on her parents over lunch. I hope they'll be happy for her.
3 Try to look to the future rather than ...................... on the past.
4 We've got a lot of work to finish today so we'd better ...................... on.
5 Julia's not usually naughty herself, but her brothers tend to ...................... her on.
6 In most schools, wearing big, colourful jewellery and dyeing your hair bright colours would be ...................... upon or even forbidden outright.
7 Whether we go for a picnic tomorrow or not will ...................... on the weather.
8 I wish he'd stop ...................... on and on about his ex-wife.

**14.5** **Rewrite these sentences using phrasal verbs from the opposite page.**

1 James is a reliable person.
2 Dad will talk monotonously for hours about European history.
3 Many political reputations are about to be crucially affected by the outcome of next week's election.
4 Josh never stops complaining about the litter in the office car park. It irritates me.
5 While tidying my room, I found an old diary of mine from 1985.

# 15 Out

## A Basic meanings of *out* in phrasal verbs

A very frequent meaning of *out* is the opposite of *in*.

I don't want to leave my job but I suppose they may **kick** me **out**. [(informal) force me to leave]
I've had enough of working for such a difficult organisation and I **want out**. [want to leave]
**Count** me **out**! I'm far too tired to join the skiing trip today. [don't include me]

Another meaning is when something or part of something extends from its surroundings.

The chalet roof **juts out** (over its walls) to help prevent snow from blocking the doors. [sticks out beyond the edge]
The rocky peninsula **juts out** into the bay.

Another meaning is separate.

The boy **picked out** a kitten to take home. [chose one from a large group]
We **spread** our wet clothes **out** on the grass so they could dry in the sunshine.

Another meaning is distribute.

Don't eat all the sweets yourself, Josh. **Share** them **out** among all the children. [give one to each person in the group]

## B Other meanings of *out* in phrasal verbs

| *phrasal verb* | *example* | *definition of phrasal verb* |
|---|---|---|
| **go out** | When we woke up in the morning the campfire still hadn't **gone out**. | (of a fire) stop burning |
| **clean out** sb or **clean** sb **out** | The burglars completely **cleaned** us **out**. | steal or take everything from a person |
| **test out** sth or **test** sth **out** | We need to **test** the product **out** in the market before launching it. | see how it works in a practical situation or find out what other people think of it (the *out* stresses testing something in the environment in which it is intended to be used, not, for example, in a laboratory) |
| **drop out** | The runner **dropped out** halfway through the marathon. | not do something that you were going to do, or stop doing something |
| **lash out** (usually + **at** sth) | Larry **lashed out** at me yesterday for wasting his time. | criticise someone or something in an angry way |
| **yell out** sth or **yell** sth **out** | As I walked past the room I heard someone **yell out**. | suddenly shout something in a loud voice, especially to get someone's attention |
| **draw out** sth or **draw** sth **out** | I wish James wouldn't always **draw** meetings **out** by talking so much. | make something continue for longer than is usual or necessary |
| **sort out** sth or **sort** sth **out** | A management consultant was hired to **sort out** the personnel problems in the company. | solve a problem or restore order to something which has become disordered |

# Exercises

**15.1** **Answer the questions using phrasal verbs with *out*.**

1 Mary gave two apples to each of the four children. What did she do with the apples?
..........................................................................................

2 James took control of the situation and soon everything was okay and back to normal. What did James do? ..........................................................................................

3 Sally looked at all the oranges on the stall and put the best ones in her basket. What did she do with the oranges? ..........................................................................................

4 The manager forced Sam to leave the restaurant because he was behaving badly. What did the manager do? ..........................................................................................

5 The roof extends over the terrace and provides a bit of shade from the midday sun. What does the roof do? ..........................................................................................

**15.2** **The verb in each of these sentences sounds a little formal in the context. Find a phrasal verb from the opposite page to replace the one-word equivalent in each sentence.**

1 I don't have any money so you can <u>exclude</u> me from the shopping trip.
2 I <u>distributed</u> the mints among my friends in the car.
3 We need to <u>resolve</u> this mess about the misprinted tickets pretty soon.
4 He really <u>criticised</u> me when I suggested he'd got it wrong.
5 Look at those big rocks <u>protruding</u> from the sea.
6 <u>Select</u> the good strawberries and leave the rotten ones in the box.

**15.3** **Rewrite the underlined parts of these sentences, using a phrasal verb with *out* that means the opposite of the underlined words.**

1 I opened the door and heard somebody <u>whisper</u> from the staircase below.
2 My position as regards the committee is that I <u>would like to continue as a member</u>.
3 He always <u>shortens</u> the discussion with arguments about political ideology.
4 When we got back to our campsite, the campfire had <u>started burning</u>.
5 <u>Put</u> the leaflets <u>together in one place</u> on the table.
6 The burglars <u>stole absolutely nothing at all from us</u>.

**15.4** **Match the headlines 1–4 with the stories a – d below.**

1 RECORD NUMBERS OF STUDENTS DROP OUT

2 DAVID BLAKE LASHES OUT AT CRITICS

3 **GOVERNMENT TO TEST OUT NEW SPEED CAMERAS**

4 WILSON SAYS COUNT ME OUT OF OLYMPIC TEAM

a) After a trial period of six months a decision will be made as to whether they will be installed throughout the country.
b) He said he did not wish to take part as he had found the pressure too great in the last Games.
c) More than 6,000 withdrew from a range of programmes, almost 1,000 more than last year, according to the minister.
d) He said he was sick of the hypocrisy of people who had never done anything themselves to help the poor.

# 16 Up

## A Basic meanings of *up* in phrasal verbs

You are probably familiar with verbs such as **eat up** and **write up**, which carry a meaning of completion. Here are some more examples:

Come on, children, **finish up** your breakfast. It's time to go.
Well, let's **wrap up** the discussion now and vote. [(informal) finish an activity]

*Up* can also carry the meaning of upward movement or relating to an upper position.

Could you **lift** the table **up** while I put the rug under it?
Tommy, **pick** all your toys **up** from the floor and put them in your toy box.

Another meaning of *up* in phrasal verbs is maintain in an upright position or strengthen, prevent from falling down or failing.

Marian was lying **propped up** on a pillow. [supporting herself in an upright position]
The minister announced new measures to **shore up** the economy. [strengthen or improve an organisation or system that is not working effectively or that is likely to fail]

*Up* can also mean increase or improve.

This sauce is tasteless. I'll add some garlic to **pep** it **up** a bit. [(informal) make something more interesting, lively or energetic]
We **jazzed up** our all-white kitchen by adding red tiles and doorknobs here and there. [(informal) make something more attractive or interesting]

## B Other phrasal verbs with *up*

Read these TV programme previews and note the phrasal verbs with *up*.

**The Man Who Hated Dogs**
**(DDC Tuesday 9pm)**

The hero of this comedy, played by Rickie Farr, finds himself playing daddy to three homeless dogs, but **lands up**[1] in trouble with his girlfriend when the local press publishes a story about him which is **blown up**[2] to make him look like a pitiless animal-hater.

[1] (informal) finally does something, especially without having planned to
[2] made to seem much worse than it is

**History File (ATV Thursday 8.30pm)**

An archaeologist notices some strange, pointed stones **sticking up** from the surface of a lake during a drought. Suspecting they may mark the site of an ancient tomb, she takes infrared photographs from the air. What **shows up**[3] in the images deepens the mystery. After a long investigation she concludes that theories about the ancient Mosa people no longer **stand up**[4].

[3] becomes visible
[4] appear correct when examined

**Chips with everything**
**(HNTV Friday 7.30pm)**

Documentary-maker Blythe Warcross **picks up on**[5] recent rumours in the press that an ultra-rich business tycoon has attempted to **buy up** the world's supply of silicon, **opening up** the terrifying possibility of a world monopoly in computer chips. Warcross tries to **set up** an interview with the mystery tycoon but receives death threats in return.

[5] reacts to something that he has noticed

**Nation on the Move**
**(Globalnews TV Friday 10pm)**

Phrasalia, once a country closed to the rest of the world, has **opened up** since the death of its long-time ruler President Particulos. But will the new-found freedoms ultimately lead to the country **splitting up** into chaotic, rival republics as tensions emerge in its five provinces?

**ERROR WARNING**

We say 'I went into the garden and **picked** some flowers.' Don't say 'picked up some flowers'; **pick up** is used for things which are on or have fallen to the ground.

# Exercises

**16.1** **Complete these sentences using a phrasal verb from A opposite. Put it in the correct form and, if necessary, add a pronoun as object.**

1 Sammy, if you don't ........................... your spinach, you can't have any pudding.
2 We can ........................... the asparagus with a nice oil and vinegar dressing.
3 The Prime Minister appointed three new ministers in an attempt to ........................... his failing administration.
4 You've just dropped some of your letters. Let me ........................... for you.
5 I noticed Tim's bicycle ........................... against a wall outside Joanna's apartment.
6 Your black dress is a little plain – why don't you ........................... a bit with a colourful scarf?
7 I think we should try and ........................... the meeting by 4pm.
8 Can you ........................... that plant pot? I need to put a saucer under it to catch the water.

**16.2** **Complete these dialogues using phrasal verbs from the opposite page so that the second speaker agrees with and repeats more or less what the first speaker says.**

1 Peter: I just don't think his theory is correct when you look at it very carefully.
Ron: No, I agree. It just doesn't ........................... up when you examine it closely.

2 Salima: I think we should ask the students to form small groups.
Hilary: Yes, we should ........................... them up into groups of two or three.

3 Edwin: I think we should try to arrange a meeting with the whole team.
Ian: You're right. We should try to ........................... one up.

4 Nazir: I just knew Patrick's son would get into trouble with the police one day.
Anna: Yes, it was inevitable he'd ........................... up in serious trouble.

5 Terry: She said they'd sold all the tickets for the concert in one go.
Vera: Yes, apparently some mystery person ........................... them all up over the Internet.

6 Sam: Oh look, Paula's freckles are really visible in this photo, aren't they?
Tyler: Yes, they really ........................... up, don't they?

7 Brian: I think the newspapers have greatly exaggerated the story.
Alisha: Yes, they've ........................... it up out of all proportion.

8 Megan: There's a big nail protruding from that floorboard; be careful.
Dave: Yes, I noticed one ........................... up the other day but forgot to mention it.

**16.3** **Which phrasal verb fits into each of these sets of collocations?**

1 to ....................... a photo / a balloon / a story

2 to ....................... a political system / an ailing economy / the foundations of a building

3 to ....................... a business / an interview / a meeting

4 to ....................... unlimited possibilities / an opportunity / a new line of investigation

# 17 Time

## A How time passes

Diana: The sales conference will be **coming around**[1] soon. We'd better start **hurrying** those sales reports **along**[2].
Paul: I can't believe that the conference is **coming up**[3] again already. This last year seems to have **slipped away**[4]!
Diana: I know! There's an awful lot to do **leading up to**[5] the conference, especially as it's going to be held in our branch this year.
Paul: Oh well, at least it **breaks** things **up**[6] and makes life a bit more interesting, I suppose.
Diana: It hasn't been that bad a year, surely. There was all the excitement over the new marketing campaign.
Paul: Oh, that completely **passed** me **by**[7]. It didn't really affect me in my department.
Diana: OK, Paul. Time's **getting on**[8] a bit now. I need to head home. Let's talk about what we need to do tomorrow.

1 (of a regular event) happening at its usual time
2 making someone do something more quickly, making something happen more quickly
3 will be happening soon
4 passed very quickly
5 preparing in the period before an event begins
6 makes a period of time more interesting by being different from what you are doing for the rest of the time
7 went unnoticed
8 (mainly British and Australian informal) it's getting late

## B Spending time

Right, I'm not going to **spin** this **out**[1]. I just have one thing to say. You only have two weeks now till the exams start and you're going to have to **pull your socks up**[2] if you want to pass. We're going to **set apart**[3] the next fortnight just for revision. In other words, we're going to **free up**[4] some time by cancelling all non-exam lessons like sport. All school sports matches will be **held over**[5] until the exams are finished. We felt that would be better than trying to **fit** revision **in**[6] around sport commitments. The sports staff agree that **putting back**[7] these matches won't cause any major problems. We mustn't **set** schedules **back**[8] too much or we won't be able to fit in all the matches before the end of term. So now, put everything else out of your minds and concentrate on your revision. No more **frittering** time **away**[9] – get down to some serious work.

1 make something continue for longer than necessary
2 make an effort to improve, an idiom using a phrasal verb (see Unit 8 for more)
3 use time for one purpose and no other purpose
4 make time or money available for a particular use by not using it another way
5 delayed and arranged for a later date
6 do it between other activities
7 causing something to happen later than it should happen
8 make something happen more slowly, or make something happen later than it should
9 wasting time by using it for unimportant things

**TIP** The following verbs can be used about money as well as time – **free up** and **fritter away**.

# Exercises

## 17.1 Match the beginning of each sentence with its ending.

1 There was a lot of excitement
2 My birthday seems to be
3 The annual meeting will be
4 I'd better go as it's
5 It's getting late – can you start

a) getting on now.
b) hurrying people along?
c) leading up to the final match.
d) coming up some time next month.
e) coming around more quickly every year.

## 17.2 Read these remarks by different people and then answer the questions below.

Noreen: I'm 63 and I've never had an interesting job or done anything exciting.
Jack: I feel I'm wasting a lot of time on useless and unimportant things.
Jenna: I'm trying to improve my performance. I know I've been lazy and inefficient.
Terry: I feel the days are passing very quickly and we need to solve the problem now.
Reeta: I'm cancelling my meetings next week so I can take time off to decorate my flat.

1 Who is trying to free up some time?
2 Who feels that time is slipping away?
3 Who feels life is passing them by?
4 Who is trying to pull their socks up?
5 Who feels they are frittering away their time?

## 17.3 Complete this text with the correct particles.

My staff often spin things ................ (1) much longer than they need to so that they don't get asked to do any more work. As a result they sometimes set the schedules ................ (2) by days or even weeks and then I have to hurry them ................ (3) so that the work gets done on time. And not only do I have to keep an eye on the staff, I also have to find time to fit ................ (4) consultations with management and the unions, and inevitably meetings have to be put ................ (5) because of some unexpected emergency, or important tasks have to be held ................ (6) till the more immediate problems can be sorted out. I try to set ................ (7) at least one hour every day for planning, but it's not easy. I like to take a proper lunch break and get out of the office. I find that breaks the day ................ (8) nicely.

## 17.4 Correct the mistakes with the phrasal verbs in these sentences.

1 You'd get far more done if you didn't fritter out so much time.
2 The children tried to spin their game off so they didn't have to go to bed.
3 Jack might lose his job if he doesn't pull his collar up.
4 We must discuss what we need to do leading up the opening of the new branch.
5 Let's try to make some time apart next month to discuss progress on the project.

## 17.5 Rewrite each sentence, using a phrasal verb from the box in an appropriate form. Make any other necessary changes. You may need to use a dictionary to help you.

| | | | | |
|---|---|---|---|---|
| eke out | drag out | bring forward | space out | creep up on |

1 We've had to reschedule the meeting for this Tuesday as Kerry will be away next week.
2 Ivor always makes any discussion last longer than necessary.
3 I think we should have longer intervals between our meetings.
4 I thought I had ages to prepare for my exams but they have arrived in no time at all.
5 I think we should try to make the printing paper last as long as possible.

# 18 Cause and effect

Many of the phrasal verbs in this unit are usually used in quite formal contexts. Using these phrasal verbs will help you to improve your style when writing formal correspondence, giving presentations and writing reports and essays.

Look at these formal letters to the editor of a newspaper and note the phrasal verbs connected with cause and effect.

Dear Sir/Madam,

Recent events in Herean City **point to**[1] a failure of central government to control spending by local and regional authorities. This failure can be **put down to**[2] a long-standing reluctance to tackle local corruption, which has **resulted in** a situation where certain powerful local politicians feel free to act outside the law. This then **contributes to** a general atmosphere in which all politicians are mistrusted.

Yours sincerely,

G. Johnson (Ms)

1 make it seem likely that something is true
2 thought to be caused by (used for problems and bad experiences)

Dear Sir/Madam,

Jerome Power's explanation for the growth of crime in our cities just does not **add up**[3]. He **attributes** recent rises in crime **to** a decline in leisure facilities for young people and the economic recession. But the problem in fact **stems from**[4] a longer-term neglect of the cities, and dealing with the problem **depends upon**[5] accepting this fact first and foremost. We have been talking about rising crime rates for decades and after the last general election the government set up an inquiry into inner-city crime but as yet nothing seems to have **come out of**[6] this enquiry.

Sincerely,

A. H. Lowe

3 (slightly informal) constitute a reasonable or likely explanation for something
4 is caused by
5 Depend *upon* is more formal than depend *on* (see Unit 14).
6 if something comes out of a process or an event, it is one of the results

Dear Sir/Madam

No one should be surprised that the recent education reforms have **rebounded on**[7] the government. The reforms were **rooted in**[8] a deep-seated elitism, which **accounts for**[9] the fact that inequality has grown rather than diminished, as your report showed (13 November). As always, the effects have **impacted** most **on**[10] poorer families, where the new system has **led to** parents being unable to afford a good education for their children. It all **adds up to**[11] more misery in our schools and fewer opportunities for our young people, especially in the inner cities.

Yours sincerely,

D. Mentedd (Prof.)

7 had a bad effect on the person who did it with the result that they did not achieve what they were trying to achieve (*upon* is also possible but is used less and less frequently with this phrasal verb)
8 based on, or caused by
9 explains the reason for
10 had a noticeable effect on (*upon* is also possible here)
11 results in

**TIP** Always make a note in your notebook if a phrasal verb is formal or informal.

# Exercises

**18.1** **Match the beginning of each sentence with its ending.**

1 Alan's new job will undoubtedly impact
2 How the situation develops will depend
3 Iona's behaviour may well rebound
4 Janet's interest in botany stems
5 His attitude to foreigners is rooted
6 It is impossible to point
7 The new education reform should result
8 Professor Bukowsky attributes the crisis
9 The situation in the country may lead

a) to one clear cause of the crisis.
b) from a childhood spent in the rainforest.
c) in ignorance.
d) in significant social change.
e) to the changes in the country's leadership.
f) on the reaction from the USA.
g) to a civil war.
h) on his family.
i) on her if she is not careful.

**18.2** **Correct the mistakes with the particles in these sentences. There is one mistake in each sentence.**

1 Bill puts the problems down to the government but I attribute them for the general world economic situation.
2 To a large extent, how a person accounts for the problems in their lives seems to depend largely of their own parents' attitudes to difficult situations.
3 I believe the new legislation will contribute to a general improvement in the standard of living but Ben thinks it will result from increased poverty for most people.
4 The desire for reform has come off a general desire to improve the situation but I suspect the proposed changes may rebound on the government.
5 The proposals are rooted in an appropriate awareness of the problems that exist but I do not feel that what is proposed adds up a coherent programme of action.

**18.3** **Rewrite each sentence, replacing the verb with a phrasal verb expression based on the word in brackets.**

1 The school's rituals and traditions have originated from its long history. (ROOT)
2 My father attributes the problem to a decline in moral values. (PUT)
3 How do you think the changes will affect your business? (IMPACT)
4 The economic recession inevitably led to increased unemployment. (RESULT)
5 How would you explain the recent increase in violent crime? (ACCOUNT)
6 Ken's criticism of Anna may have a bad effect on him now that she's his boss! (REBOUND)
7 I do not feel that the writer's analysis of the problem makes sense. (ADD)
8 Some unforeseen problems have resulted from the change in legislation. (COME)

**18.4** **Answer these questions, using full sentences.**

1 What would you put global warming down to?
2 What do you think has led to the current increase in violent crime in most societies?
3 How would you account for the fact that girls tend to do better at school than boys?
4 What would you attribute the success of the MP3 player to?
5 What would you point to as the main cause of social problems today?
6 What would you say your own interest in English stems from?
7 Do you think that mobile phones have resulted in more or less communication between people?
8 What do you think is the main thing that contributes to the difficulty of phrasal verbs?

# 19 Change

## A For better or worse

### MANAGER OF THE MONTH

This month our Manager of the Month is Lewis Keene, who was brought in to **turn around**[1] Phoenix Sportswear when the company was in serious financial difficulty last year. 'The main problem was that the quality of our products was **going down**[2]. I soon realised that we had been **sticking to**[3] a supplier who was no longer able to meet our requirements. It was not going to be enough to just **tinker with**[4] the systems in the organisation. I had to be prepared to **shake** things **up**[5] completely,' said Keene.

As well as changing suppliers, Keene has introduced some drastic changes to the company's structure and processes and, although at first staff were not happy with many of these changes, it is clear that some of them are now beginning to **perk up**[6]. 'I know I've been putting a lot of pressure on staff', says Keene, 'but it is the only way to ensure an effective **turnaround**[7]. I'll **ease up**[8] a bit when we've achieved all our targets. Naturally staff weren't keen on me **messing around with**[9] their routines, but sometimes it was necessary to improve efficiency.'

1 change an unsuccessful business, plan or system so that it becomes successful
2 becoming worse in quality
3 limiting ourselves to doing or using one particular thing and not changing to anything else
4 make small changes to something, trying to improve it, often to repair something
5 make big changes to an organisation in order to improve it
6 become more cheerful or more energetic
7 sudden improvement (especially in a business or the economy of a country)
8 start to treat somebody less severely than before
9 (informal) trying to change or improve something

## B Changing people, things and activities

| *phrasal verb/noun* | *example* | *definition of phrasal verb/noun* |
|---|---|---|
| **turn** (sth/sb) **into** sth/sb | We're planning to **turn** our garage **into** a playroom for the children. Becoming a father has **turned** Tony **into** a completely different, much more responsible, person. | change and become something or someone different, or make something or someone do this |
| **change around/ round** sth or **change** sth **around/round** | When we **changed** the furniture **round** the room felt much bigger. | move objects into different positions, or change the appearance of a room by moving furniture into different positions |
| **change over/ round** | If you start peeling the potatoes, I'll chop some onions and then we can **change over** after ten minutes. | if two people change over, each one starts to do what the other one was doing before, or each one moves to where the other one was standing or sitting before |
| **go back to** sth | My desk was tidy for a day or two but soon **went back to** its usual mess. | return to a particular state |
| **go over to** sth | The school is **going over to** a new rewards system. | change to a new system or new way of doing things |
| **makeover** (n) | The woman looked 20 years younger after her **makeover** on TV. | if someone has a makeover, they have their appearance changed by a specially trained person |

# Exercises

## 19.1 Choose the best word to complete each sentence.

1 Some business people have a great talent for turning *around / over* failing companies.
2 I thought that girl actually looked better **before** her TV *makeover / turnaround*!
3 My little boy was feeling ill this morning but he's *eased / perked* up a lot now.
4 The quality of TV news programmes seems to me to be going *down / back*.
5 It is always difficult when a new boss tries to *stick / shake* things up.
6 My husband is in the garage *tinkering / shaking* with the car.

## 19.2 Complete these horoscopes with the correct verb or particle from the opposite page.

**LEO** *July 23 – August 22*
You need a big change in your life. Be prepared to shake your life ........... (1) completely. Find a good beauty salon and spend some money on a complete ........................... (2); you'll soon be a new person. You are also likely to be particularly clumsy this month, so avoid tinkering ........... (3) those things at home that need repairing – you're more likely to break them than fix them!

**CAPRICORN** *December 22 – January 19*
Someone has been messing ...................... (4) with your life lately and this has been getting you down. Don't worry, you'll soon perk ........... (5). There is a very exciting opportunity just around the corner and you will get the chance to completely turn your life ...................... (6) towards the end of this month. Grab the opportunity.

**ARIES** *March 21 – April 19*
There has been a lot of pressure at work lately from someone above you. However, this person will begin to ........... (7) up a little in the middle of the month and you'll have more time on your hands. This is a good opportunity to do those odd jobs that you have been putting off for a long time. It's a good time to change things ...................... (8) at home, which will make you feel as if you're in fresh, new surroundings. Be brave, throw away those old bits of furniture!

**GEMINI** *May 21 – June 20*
Your quality of life has been ...................... (9) down lately and, despite efforts to start a new phase in your existence, you've just gone ........... (10) to your old, boring ways. Time for a complete ........................... (11)! Unexpected events mid-month will help you make those changes quicker than you think.

## 19.3 Answer these questions using phrasal verbs.

1 Donal: I think we should convert the attic into a spare bedroom.
What does Donal think they should do to the attic? ..................................................................
2 Gavin: You put the wallpaper on. I'll paint, and then we can swap after an hour.
What does Gavin think they should do after an hour? ..................................................................
3 Jessie: I think we should start using the new accounts system in the New Year.
What does Jessie think should happen in the New Year? ..................................................................

## 19.4 Complete each sentence with a phrasal verb from the opposite page.

1 I don't like the layout of this office – let's ...................... the furniture ...................... .
2 Our teacher has been working us very hard but she has promised to ......................
...................... if we all do well in our next test.
3 The government needs to do something drastic about education in this country;
...................... ...................... the system will not be enough.
4 Suzie had made a lot of progress with her exercise programme but then it got busy again at work and she ...................... ...................... to her old habits and stopped going to the gym.
5 When Gary was appointed manager of the company he was determined to ......................
things ...................... as he was convinced that major change was essential.
6 If you get tired of driving, let me know and we can easily ...................... ...................... .

# 20 Memory

In this unit, some phrasal verbs can be grouped by the meaning given by the particle. For example, *up* means uppermost in your mind in **summon up**, **conjure up**, **call up** and **stir up**. *Up* in **store up** memories carries a different meaning in that it means gather or collect. *Back* in **come back**, **flood back** and **flashback** carries a sense of a returning memory. *Behind* and *out* occur with verbs which describe things we don't want to remember (**put** something **behind** somebody, **block** something **out** / **block out** something). Grouping the verbs by the meaning carried by the particle will help you to remember them.

Look at these extracts from the website *Our Stories*, where people talk about their lives.

'When I look at these old photographs, memories come **flooding back**[1]. This one here, of my mother just before she died, **stirs up**[2] sad memories of how she suffered but couldn't afford medication. It **reminds** me **of** how different life was then. But we can't let bad memories **eat away at**[3] us, we should **put** bad experiences **behind**[4] us. I've always tried to live in the present and live for the future.'

1 one suddenly remembers very clearly a lot of things about an experience or period in the past
2 makes one remember events in the past, usually ones that make you feel sad
3 make us unhappy because we think about them too much
4 not think about them any more so that they do not affect our life

'We **store up** so many memories over the years, good ones and bad ones. I **associate** this picture **with** my early childhood. Looking at the photo it suddenly **came back** to me how we used to feed the animals on my uncle's farm. It **summons up**[5] lots of happy memories, and some sad ones, too, like when my favourite old pony died. The happy ones can **stick with**[6] you forever. I still remember one particular picnic we had one summer when I was only about seven. We tend to **block out**[7] sad memories, but sometimes you might get a **flashback**[8] to an unpleasant experience.'

5 makes you remember something or think about something
6 you remember them
7 stop yourself from thinking about something unpleasant because it upsets you
8 an occasion when you suddenly remember something vividly that happened to you in the past

'For me this picture **conjures up**[9] a series of crazy events. I got this diploma, then fell down the steps as I left the stage. As I fell, I grabbed the curtain and all the curtains came down on top of me and the professor! Then all the lights went out! It's amazing how one picture can **call up**[10] an event in such detail. When I look at it, my thoughts always **flash back**[11] immediately to that moment.'

9 makes a picture, image, memory, etc. appear in my mind
10 make one remember or think about a particular memory or idea
11 get a sudden vivid memory of something

# Exercises

## 20.1 Choose the best word to complete each sentence.

1 I was sitting in a train looking out of the window, when my mind suddenly ...................... back to that amazing trip we made to India.
a) put b) flashed c) stirred d) associated

2 Close your eyes and try to ...................... up a picture of a place where you feel at peace.
a) store b) eat c) conjure d) stick

3 Dave has an excellent memory – he can ...................... up precise details of things that happened when he was a small child.
a) come b) flood c) flash d) call

4 Please don't talk about that day – I want to ...................... it all behind me.
a) put b) stir c) block d) summon

5 Roberto should try not to let his regrets for what he has done ...................... away at him.
a) come b) eat c) stick d) flood

## 20.2 Complete this dialogue with phrasal verbs from the opposite page.

Jill: I've just found this old dress at the back of my wardrobe. It ...................... (1) me of that party at Anna's. Do you remember? It must be at least 20 years ago!

Roy: Goodness me! That certainly does ...................... (2) up some memories. I hadn't thought of it for years but it's all ...................... (3) back now! Do you remember all those roses she had everywhere?

Jill: That's right. I always ...................... (4) the smell of roses with Anna.

Roy: We spent all evening dancing together. We had such a lovely evening.

Jill: Actually, I don't know if we did. It's all ...................... (5) back to me now. Don't you remember, as we were leaving the party, Anna's brother came running out accusing you of stealing his wallet? He got really violent and started pushing you.

Roy: Oh yes! That was awful. I'd just completely ...................... (6) the memory out.

Jill: Well, I'm glad you did. If you hadn't ...................... (7) it behind you, then we wouldn't be friends with him now.

Roy: That's right. Anyway, it's the good memories that you want to ...................... (8) with you. Those are the ones to ...................... (9) up for the future.

Jill: Well, we've got plenty of those we can ...................... (10) up when we need them.

## 20.3 Explain the play on words in these titles of newspaper articles.

1 COOK STIRS UP MEMORIES OF 1950s SCHOOL DINNERS

2 MAGICIAN CONJURES UP MEMORIES OF VICTORIAN ENGLAND

3 FILM CALLS UP OLD SOLDIERS' MEMORIES OF CONSCRIPTION

4 HAPPY MEMORIES OF LIFE AT GLUE FACTORY STICK WITH WORKERS

5 MEMORIES OF 1963 BURST PIPES COME FLOODING BACK

## 20.4 Answer these questions, using full sentences.

1 What colour do you associate with your childhood and why?
2 Is there any particular smell that reminds you of your childhood?
3 What music conjures up memories of your youth?
4 Is there any particular memory of your schooldays that you would like to block out?
5 Which makes memories come back to you more powerfully – music or smells?

# 21 Making progress

## A Beginning and ending

| *phrasal verb with collocations* | *example* | *definition of phrasal verb* |
|---|---|---|
| new businesses / political movements / buildings **spring up** | At the turn of the century new left-wing political movements **sprang up**. | suddenly appear or begin to exist |
| new buildings / factories / cafés **sprout up** | Pavement cafés have suddenly **sprouted up** all over the town. | suddenly appear or begin to exist |
| parent/teacher/partner **starts on at** son/pupil/partner | I'd no sooner got home than my parents **started on at** me again about my tattoo. | start complaining to someone about something they have done |
| **open up** opportunities/ possibilities or opportunities/ possibilities **open up** | The new shopping centre will **open up** all sorts of job opportunities. | make possible or become possible |
| **break up** a meeting/party or a meeting/party **breaks up** | I'm sorry to **break up** the party but it's getting very late. | end, people start to leave |
| **finish with** newspaper/ scissors/salt/computer | Can you let me have the newspaper when you've **finished with** it? | no longer need |
| trend/business/price **bottoms out** | The share price fell steadily last year but has now **bottomed out**. | reach a low level and stay there |
| game/match/anger/protest/ conflict **peters out**[1] | The crowd started shouting and protesting but the protests soon **petered out** when they saw the armed police. | gradually become less strong and then stop completely |
| **wind up** a business/interview/ meeting | Jack intends to **wind up** his business soon. | end |

[1] an interesting phrasal verb in that, unusually, *to peter* does not exist as a verb on its own

## B Helping and hindering progress

How's progress with your business?

We couldn't continue when our cheap supply of materials **dried up**[1].

We had some staffing problems but the new HR person has **magicked** them **away**[4].

Things've been **falling apart**[2] since the new manager arrived.

We **got up to** the third stage of our plan but haven't made much progress since.

We can't do anything at the moment because the money's **run out**.

My PA has really improved things recently, so I hope we can **hang on to**[5] her.

We're **pressing on**[3] though we've had lots of problems.

The CEO's **whittling away**[6] the authority of middle managers.

[1] came to an end
[2] not working well
[3] continuing in a determined way
[4] made them disappear, as if by magic
[5] keep
[6] gradually reducing

# Exercises

## 21.1 Answer these questions.

1 Would you be happy or unhappy if the exchange rate between your currency and the US dollar bottomed out?
2 If somebody starts on at you, are they happy with your behaviour or unhappy?
3 Which two verbs from the opposite page could you use to complete this sentence?
Wind farms seem to be ........................... /........................... up all over the countryside these days.
4 *Open up* and *break up* can both be used with or without an object. True or false?
5 If someone whittles away your confidence, do you feel more or less confident?
6 If your anger peters out, does it become more or less strong?

## 21.2 Complete the film blurbs below, using the correct verb or particle from the opposite page.

**In the Net** (PG)
Leaving home and going off to college ................. (1) up new possibilities for Joanne, a shy girl from a small town. However, she soon finds that her life starts falling ................. (2) when she gets involved with a handsome basketball player. Desperate to hang ................. (3) to her new love, she embarks on a dangerous course of action.

**The Polyard Murders** (18)
As the food, drink and conversation dry ................. (4), a social gathering at a large house in the town of Polyard ................. (5) up around midnight and everyone heads home. However, two couples vanish on the way home and a murder hunt begins. Four more murders take place but the killer's luck finally runs ................. (6) when a new, young detective from the city takes over the case.

## 21.3 Rewrite these sentences to make them sound less formal, using phrasal verbs instead of the underlined words.

1 When you <u>no longer need</u> the scissors, could you pass them to me?
2 They <u>terminated</u> the business in 2004 after a year of low sales.
3 Okay, so who's <u>made</u> the bottle opener <u>vanish</u>? It was here a minute ago!
4 We've had some setbacks but we'll <u>continue undeterred</u>.
5 I only <u>reached</u> page 12 of the book before I got bored and stopped reading it.

## 21.4 Explain the play on words with the phrasal verbs in these sentences.

1 Mr Bellamy decided to wind up his clock-making business after 35 years.
2 Three new greengrocers' shops have sprouted up in the town centre recently.
3 Even though the dry cleaner's was not getting much business, the owners decided to press on.
4 A new trampoline factory has sprung up on the outskirts of the town.
5 The *Speedyheels* training shoe company has run out of money.

# 22 Conflict and violence

## A Particles in phrasal verbs connected with conflict and violence

Some of the phrasal verbs in this unit have the particle *up* (**smash up**, **flare up**) where *up* suggests extreme or complete. In **come at** and **fly at** *at* indicates the direction of the violent action. *Off* suggests remove in **bump off** [(informal), kill] and **fight off**, and *out* suggests completely in **wipe out** [completely destroy]. Thinking about the meaning the particle adds will help you learn the verbs in groups and remember them better.

## B Talking about conflict and violence

Nick: Why couldn't you phone for help?
Carole: Vandals had **smashed up** the phone box and pulled the wires out.

Fatima: What happened to you? Are you hurt?
Alex: A man **pushed** me **over** and tried to steal my bag. He **came at** me from behind.
Fatima: Oh, that's dreadful! Did he take your bag?
Alex: No, I managed to **fight** him **off**, then some people came and he ran off.

Dorota: What did the boss say when you all complained?
Juan: Well, he just **flew at**[1] me and said I was irresponsible, then he **rounded on**[2] the others and ordered them to get back to work. I've never seen him **flare up**[3] like that before, you know, he just **flew into**[4] a rage as soon as I opened my mouth.
Dorota: So relations are not good now?
Juan: No. It's the biggest **bust-up**[5] we've ever had with him. But we're not going to let him **push** us **around**[6].

1 suddenly spoke to me very angrily
2 suddenly turned and attacked them or shouted at them angrily
3 suddenly become very angry
4 if someone flies into a particular state (e.g. rage, panic), they are suddenly in that state
5 (informal) an angry argument
6 tell someone what to do in a rude or threatening way

Ana: I hear your neighbours have been fighting one another!
Ben: Yes, Joss said Arthur had stolen some plants from his garden, so he **set** his dog **on**[7] him. Arthur kicked the dog, then punched Joss and almost **knocked** him **out**. The police had to come and **break** it **up**!

7 attack someone, or make a person or animal attack someone

Jan: What happened at the end of the film?
Katya: Well, they caught the man who'd been **bumping** everyone **off**, of course.

## C Metaphorical uses of phrasal verbs to suggest conflict or violence

The verbs in this group are particularly typical of newspaper language because they have metaphorical meanings, which is good for word play.

The government promised to **wipe out** poverty. [make it disappear completely]

The Minister is **fighting off** calls for her resignation.

The police are determined to **stamp on** football hooliganism. [use forceful methods to get rid of something that you disapprove of]

Some newspapers are trying to **drag** the Prime Minister **into** the scandal. [talk about or bring someone or something into a difficult or unpleasant situation, especially when that person or thing is not seen as being connected with the situation]

He published an article in a national newspaper as a way of **striking back at** his critics. [attacking someone who has attacked you (the literal meaning of striking is hitting)]

# Exercises

## 22.1 Complete these sentences by adding one word to the end of each one.

1 I couldn't get anything from the vending machine because some hooligans had smashed it ................ .
2 When Diana told her father she had scratched his car, he flew into a ................ .
3 He's terribly bossy, so make sure you don't let yourself be pushed ................ .
4 Tom hit the man so hard that he knocked him ................ .
5 Don't interfere in the fight yourself – wait for the police to come and break it ................ .
6 Maggie did her best, but she didn't manage to fight her attacker ................ .
7 If someone criticises you unfairly, it is better to ignore them than to strike ................ .
8 My neighbour went to jail for trying to bump his boss ................ .

## 22.2 Correct the six mistakes with phrasal verbs in this paragraph.

There was a terrible bust-off at work today. The departmental manager came into the office in a terrible temper. He flew on his PA and when people tried to calm him down, he rounded at them. I don't know what had got into him. He pushes everyone over a lot but he's not normally quite so aggressive. I tried not to get dragged onto it, but when it seemed as if he might actually hit someone, then I felt it was time to do what I could to break things out.

## 22.3 Do the phrasal verbs in these sentences need an object? If so, add an appropriate object in an appropriate place.

1 When I tried to enter the house, the dog flew at.
2 Jack can seem quite happy one moment and then the next he'll flare up.
3 They threatened to bump off if he told anyone about the robbery.
4 Because she had learned some judo as a child, Tina found it much easier to fight off.
5 I was completely taken by surprise when someone suddenly came at from behind.
6 After only ten seconds in the ring, Henry's opponent had knocked out.

## 22.4 Rewrite these sentences using the word in brackets.

1 Paul tried to involve me in the argument but I managed to stay out of it. (DRAG)
2 The old man thought the boys were trying to break into his house, so he told his dog to attack them. (SET)
3 The aim of the organisation is to completely abolish cruelty to children. (WIPE)
4 Although he is small, James is strong and he quickly managed to hit his attacker so hard that he became unconscious. (KNOCK)
5 Uncle Walter can lose his temper very quickly if you say the wrong thing. (FLARE)
6 The witness saw the thief attack the woman just as she was opening her car door. (COME)
7 The government is determined to get rid of smoking in public places. (STAMP)
8 The robbers came running out of the bank, knocking down an old lady who was in their path. (PUSH)
9 Older people often find it harder to get rid of colds and other infections than younger people do. (FIGHT)

**FOLLOW UP**

Find a story in a newspaper dealing with conflict or violence in some way. Note down any phrasal verbs that it contains in their context.

# 23 Sound

## A Loud or unpleasant sounds

Hi Mick,

Thanks for your email.

I've more or less settled in to my new cottage. It's lovely – except for the neighbours. They are just so noisy! I can hear their TV **blasting out**[1] at all hours of the day and night and one of them plays the trumpet – he's **belting out**[2] jazz most evenings. At least he plays well, so that noise doesn't **grate on**[3] me as much as it might! Much worse is the fact that one of them has a very loud voice and is also very bad-tempered. When he's angry he **bangs** things **down**[4] and his voice **booms out**[5] and sometimes the arguments even **drown out**[6] my own music. I've asked them nicely if they could **keep** the noise **down** a bit but they have ignored me. And I thought I was moving to a quiet village where the only loud noise would be church bells **pealing out**[7] on a Sunday morning!

Hope all goes well with you.

Cheers,

Pat

[1] producing a lot of noise, especially loud music
[2] (informal) playing a musical instrument or singing very loudly
[3] (of sound or behaviour) annoy
[4] puts down with force because he is angry
[5] makes a very loud noise
[6] prevent from being heard
[7] ringing loudly (of bells)

## B Sounds starting and finishing

Hi Pat,

Interesting to hear about your new flat. I'm attaching an ad for some ear-plugs which claim to help you **shut** anything **out**[1]!

I moved into a new flat a month or so ago, too. It's next to the football stadium. I can't see the matches but I can follow what's going on from the sounds I hear. A cheer **goes up**[2] whenever the home team shoots. But the sound quickly **dies down**[3] if the ball doesn't go in. Every time there's a match I find myself **listening out for**[4] the cheers. When I told my girlfriend that I wanted to stay at home to listen to the sounds of a football match she **burst out**[5] laughing, thinking I was joking, and started talking about how we could decorate the flat. When another cheer went up from the stadium, though, her voice **trailed off**[6] and she rushed to the window in excitement. Then she stayed in the flat with me and spent all afternoon at the window watching spectators going in and out of the stadium.

Cheers,

Mick

[1] prevent a sound from being heard (can also be used about preventing a sight from being seen)
[2] if a shout (e.g. cheer, cry, groan) goes up, a lot of people make that noise at the same time
[3] becomes less loud or strong and then stops
[4] making an effort to hear a noise which you are expecting
[5] (of a sound) suddenly started (collocates with *laughing*, *crying*, *with a comment/remark*)
[6] gradually became quieter and then stopped

# Exercises

**23.1** **Put these phrasal verbs into two groups, a 'noisy' group (making noise) and a 'not noisy' group (reducing noise).**

belt out    boom out    die down    trail off    keep down    blast out

| *making noise* | *reducing noise* |
|---|---|
| | |

**23.2** **Complete these sentences with phrasal verbs from 23.1. Use each verb only once.**

1 She was telling us about how angry Simon had made her, but her voice ...................... off when he entered the room.
2 As we entered the club, the singer was ...................... out his latest song.
3 Rock music was ...................... out from an open window as I passed the house.
4 Children, please ...................... the noise down – Grandpa's having a rest.
5 Major Frogshort's voice ...................... out across the square as he issued orders to his men.
6 At 6 pm the noise of the machines ...................... down and the workers went home.

**23.3** **Choose the correct particle to complete these sentences.**

1 Suddenly a cheer went ........... as the President appeared on the balcony.
a) out b) up c) on
2 I'll listen ........... for your car and come down to the street so you don't have to park.
a) with b) to c) out
3 Jean was so angry she banged the phone ........... .
a) down b) on c) away
4 These ear defenders shut ........... 90% of external noise.
a) down b) away c) out
5 When she heard how the story ended she burst ........... laughing.
a) into b) out c) in
6 I love to hear the bells pealing ........... at New Year.
a) out b) on c) off
7 The noise of a plane passing overhead drowned ........... the radio and I missed the news.
a) down b) off c) out
8 She has such an awful voice; it just grates ........... me every time she sings.
a) to b) at c) on

**23.4** **Answer these questions. Use a dictionary if necessary.**

A–Z

1 If someone's voice drones on, are you likely to enjoy listening to them or not?
2 If birds are chirping away and if a person is chattering away, *away* suggests a continuing sound. True or false?
3 What particle would be best here?
The cheers of the crowd built ........... to a roar as the runners approached the finish line.
4 What particle would be best here?
The noise of the train died ................ in the distance as it headed for the coast.
5 What phrasal verb with *ring* can be used for all of these things?
church bells    a cry    a shot    a shout    applause
6 What phrasal verb with *come* would fit in this sentence?
Suddenly an announcement ................ ................ the public address system warning everyone to evacuate the building.

# 24 Supporting and opposing people or views

## A

In these television interviews, Members of Parliament (MPs) are defending their positions.

Interviewer: Recently you seem to have **come out against**[1] those in your party who want stronger anti-terrorist laws. Why?

MP: I haven't changed my position at all, and I **stick by** what I've always said. Those who **side with**[2] the terrorists or support them in any way must be opposed. But we need a mature debate about the causes of terrorism.

[1] stated publicly that you opposed an issue (opposite: **come out in favour of**)
[2] support a person or group in an argument

Interviewer: You said you were determined to introduce higher fuel charges, but after the opposition from the trucking companies you seem to have **caved in**[3]. Why?

MP: We are a listening party and we always **defer to**[4] expert opinion. We were advised that higher charges would have a negative economic effect in the long term, so we have decided to **go with**[5] that advice.

[3] agreed to something that you were against before, because of persuasion or threats
[4] (formal) accept someone else's opinion because they know more or are more important
[5] accept a plan or an idea

Interviewer: You seem to be **leaning** increasingly **towards**[6] more conservative policies, even though you are a member of the Liberal Party. Is there any truth in the rumour that you are about to **cross over**[7] to the Conservative Party?

MP: No. The values I **stand for**[8] are liberal values, but I see no point in **siding against**[9] the Conservative Party on those issues where I agree with them.

[6] support or begin to support a particular set of ideas or a particular political party
[7] start to support a different, often opposing, person or group
[8] support
[9] oppose a person or group in an argument

## B

Note the phrasal verbs for supporting and opposing people or views in these newspaper extracts.

17-year-old boy claims he was **egged on**[1] by his friends to steal cars.

[1] encouraged to do something, often something that is wrong, stupid, or dangerous

**Cheered on**[2] by her supporters, Jenny Hinds beat the world record.

[2] received encouraging shouts

Mrs Gilmore, who celebrated her 104th birthday, when asked what her secret was, said she **swears by**[3] a glass of hot milk with a little sugar every night before bed.

[3] believes that something is very effective and that it will always work well

Mr West said the club would **not hear of**[4] letting children attend the concert.

[4] not allow something, or not allow someone to do something (always in the negative)

The peace campaign was **buoyed up**[5] recently by a donation of €500,000.

[5] supported and made more successful

He was someone who always **stuck up for**[6] the rights of the poor and the homeless.

[6] (informal) defended or fought for something important

# Exercises

**24.1 Look at A opposite. Complete these statements from a political manifesto.**

This party................ for equality for all.

We do not hesitate to ................ out strongly against any case of injustice.

We ................ by our principles at all times and never ................ in to threats or pressure from the opposition.

We ................ with the underdog and do not ................ to those who are wealthy and powerful.

**24.2 Look at B opposite. Put the words in the correct order to make sentences.**

1 runners / The / cheered / line / on / the / were / as / they / spectators / for / the / by / finishing / headed
2 rely / sister / Tim / You / to / on / stick / little / can / his / for / up
3 grandfather / by / My / garlic / a / of / raw / himself / as / way / from / colds / protecting / swears / catching
4 bungee / My / have / mother / would / tried / we / never / hadn't / her / jumping / on / egged / if
5 all-night / to / wanted / to / go / mother / party / an / it / her / wouldn't / but / of / She / hear
6 of / discovery / the / years / British / gas / the / North / The / up / buoyed / in / economy / Sea / some / for

**24.3 Which word from the opposite page could fit into all the sentences in each set? Note any new meanings of the word which you come across.**

1 If a politician doesn't ................ by what he has said, he will lose the voters' trust.
Don't forget to ................ a stamp on each of your postcards.
It is not always easy to ................ up for what you believe in if others are attacking you.

2 I cannot believe that you would ................ with the government on the issue of the war.
Peter was warned not to ................ against the Minister if he wanted to have a successful career in politics.
You will find a lot of interesting phrasal verbs on the left-hand ................ of the page.

3 Please come and ................ me on in the tennis match.
Danny is a bit miserable so we really should go round and try to ................ her up.
A ................ went up as the Prince entered the Stadium.

4 Harry Carr's investment should help to ................ up the company.
We always try to ................ each other up before giving important presentations in front of large audiences.
You must try to sail the yacht round that red ................ .

**24.4 Are these sentences correct? If not, correct them.**

1 My preferred course of action would be to get with what Ivan has recommended.
2 He began his political life as a Conservative but crossed across to the Labour Party when he realised that he would be more likely to get a seat in Parliament that way.
3 Many people start to lean more towards right-wing ideas as they become middle-aged.
4 Either side with the Prime Minister or against him – don't abstain from voting.
5 I shall have to defer on your superior knowledge of the situation.
6 My mother promises by a daily spoonful of honey to keep healthy all year long.
7 Josh is not usually naughty himself but he is quick to egg others off.
8 The headteacher said she would not hear of pupils coming to school with dyed hair.

# 25 Understanding and having ideas

## A Understanding

As a maths teacher I find it interesting to see how children cope with my subject. Some **pick up** every new topic very quickly while others take rather longer to **catch on**[1]. Some have to **grapple with**[2] the topic for a long time but eventually understand it very well. Some find it **goes in** better if they are presented with the whole picture right from the beginning, whereas others like me to **break** a topic **down** into small bite-sized chunks. Then they gradually **piece** it all **together** for themselves. Although some find it harder than others to **keep up**[3] with what I tell them, everyone usually **cottons on**[4] in the end.

[1] (informal) understand
[2] try hard to deal with
[3] be able to understand something that is happening or changing fast
[4] (informal) begins to understand

## B Having ideas

| *phrasal verb* | *example* | *definition of phrasal verb* |
|---|---|---|
| **occur to** sb | It suddenly **occurred to** me that he hadn't told me his name. | come into your mind |
| **hit on** (an idea) | We weren't sure how to celebrate our anniversary until James **hit on** the idea of spending the weekend in Paris. | have a good idea (especially one that solves a problem) |
| **rough out** | The novelist said he always **roughs out** several plots before he decides which one to use. | write or draw the outline of an idea without going into details |
| **reflect on/ upon** | We all need to take some time to **reflect on** what has happened. | (slightly formal) think very hard about something |
| **think up** sth or **think** sth **up** | Can you help me **think up** an idea for my presentation? | create an idea or plan using your imagination and intelligence |
| **play with** (an idea) | The headteacher **played with** the idea of introducing compulsory lessons in good manners. | consider an idea but usually do not do it |
| **leap out at** | I couldn't solve the crossword clue last night but this morning the answer **leapt out at** me. | be immediately obvious |

## C Discussing ideas

I have some great colleagues. Whenever I have a problem at work, I **talk** it **through**[1] with my supervisor. She always **comes at**[2] problems from a slightly different angle and **thrashing** an issue **out**[3] with her helps me to see the problem more clearly and to find a solution. Then there is my marketing team. I am very proud of them. In our regular meetings to discuss new promotional activities, we **bounce** our ideas **off**[4] each other until we find something that we all like. We find that **batting** our ideas **around**[5] like this is really productive and results in great campaigns.

[1] discuss something in order to understand it better
[2] approaches
[3] discussing something in order to find a solution
[4] (informal) tell someone about an idea to find out what they think of it
[5] (slightly informal) discussing different ways of dealing with an issue

# Exercises

## 25.1 Complete this conversation using verbs from the box.

reflect break rough cotton thrash hit grapple occur piece bounce talk

Student: I've been ........................... (1) with this idea you talked about in your lecture, that written language is becoming more like spoken language these days, but I'm finding it difficult. I've been trying to ........................... (2) out some chapters for my dissertation and I like this topic, but I think I need to ........................... (3) it through with you first.

Lecturer: Well, let me ........................... (4) a few ideas off you, see if they make sense. When you write emails to your friends, how formal are they?

Student: Pretty informal usually.

Lecturer: Let's just ........................... (5) on that for a moment. What makes them informal?

Student: I suppose it's grammar for one thing. I use contractions like 'I'm' or 'it's' instead of 'I am' or 'it is'. And slang words and so on.

Lecturer: Yes, and hasn't it ........................... (6) to you that what you're doing is sort of talking to people rather than writing to them?

Student: Ah. I see. I think I've ........................... (7) on now. Things like email and text messages and chat rooms and so on are changing the way we write, is that it?

Lecturer: Exactly. Go away and think about it a bit more and I'm sure you'll ........................... (8) on a few more ideas. Look at a few newspapers and magazines. Try and ........................... (9) the topic down into different themes, like grammar and vocabulary.

Student: OK, thanks. I'll probably be able to ........................... (10) it all together now.

Lecturer: Yes, and come back if you need more help and we can ........................... (11) it out together and try and clarify it more. Okay? Bye.

## 25.2 Choose the correct particle to complete these sentences.

1 I've been trying to think *about / up / over* a plan for a surprise birthday party for Ben but I haven't hit *on / out / up* the right idea yet.
2 I thought about the problem for ages then the solution just leapt *over / away / out* at me.
3 Some of the trainees are very good at picking *on / over / up* new techniques, while others take a long time to catch *on / across / in*.
4 It's hard to keep up *to / with / for* all the reading for my literature course.
5 We formed a committee to bat a few ideas *over / up / around* for the college open day.
6 For a while we played *with / on / at* the idea of making all the courses compulsory but we dropped it because it would be so unpopular.
7 I think we should try and come *into / on / at* the problem from a different angle.
8 I tried to explain it to him, but new information takes a long time to go *on / in / off* sometimes!

## 25.3 Find phrasal verbs from the opposite page which seem to treat ideas as if they are:

1 balls that can be played with
2 parts of a puzzle
3 things that you need physical strength to deal with

*Bob stared at the crossword for ages then the answer suddenly leapt out at him.*

# 26 Arranging things

## A

A group of students are organising things for a college open day. Note how they use phrasal verbs to talk about arranging things.

Ben: We need something to **prop up**[1] the camcorder. Maybe we could use that big box?
Anne: Or we could rest it on the bookcase. That could **double up as**[2] a camera support.

1 make something stay in a particular position by putting something underneath or against it
2 also be used as

Tim: Let's **gather up** all those brochures and **stack** them **up** in one pile over here.
Kim: Okay, then I'll have to **see about**[3] an extra table; we've got too much stuff.

3 deal with something, or arrange for something to be done

Raul: We need to **space out** the tables a bit; they're too close together at the moment.
Liz: Yes, and we should **line** them **up** a bit better too so that it all looks neat.
Paul: Why don't we **separate off**[4] all the student work displays and put them all together in the other room?
Jake: Yes, okay. I'll **round up**[5] some more helpers; it's going to be quite a big job.
Paul: Yes, and then **separate out**[6] the first-year students' work, the second-year students' work and the third- and fourth-year students' work and make a special display of it. That would be nice.
Jake: Okay, but how will I **know** the first-year stuff **from** the rest?
Paul: The name and the year are on the back of each piece of work.

4 remove something from a large group of things
5 find and gather together a group of people or animals
6 divide a group of people or things into smaller groups

Kelly: Hey everyone, if you could **pile up** all your rubbish in the corner there, I'll get someone to take it all away at once.
Paul: Okay but I think we should **sift through**[7] everything before we throw it away in case we're throwing away things we should keep.

7 examine a large collection of something, especially papers, usually in order to discover something or to decide what is important

## B Other verbs connected with organising and arranging things

We **hoarded away** dozens of bottles of water as we knew there would be a shortage in the hot weather. [put a supply of something in a safe place so that you can use it in the future]

I've been trying to **fix up** a meeting with our local MP so we can get to know her better. [(informal) arrange]

If you have teenage children, you spend a lot of time **picking up after** them. [(informal) put things back in the right place after someone has untidily left them in the wrong place]

He **folded up** the scarf, wrapped it in gold wrapping paper and **did** it **up** with a red bow, ready to give to Peter on his birthday. [fasten or tie something]

The headteacher **geared** his speech more **towards** the parents than the pupils. [designed something so that it was suitable for a particular purpose, situation, or group of people]

Norton College **ranks among** the best in the country. [has a particular position in a list arranged in order of quality]

# Exercises

## 26.1 Answer these questions about the verbs in A.

1 What other things can someone round up, apart from people?
2 What might you prop your head up with if you're reading on the sofa?
3 Which other verb in A is close in meaning to *stack up*?
4 If you sift through papers, what are you doing?
5 Does the particle *up* seem to have any similar meanings in the verbs in A?

## 26.2 Choose the correct phrasal verb to complete these sentences.

1 We had to *stick up* / *stock up* / *stack up* the chairs after the meeting and lock the hall.
2 Could you *round in* / *round up* / *round off* some people to help move the furniture?
3 Let's *separate off* / *separate away* / *separate out* the blue forms, the green forms and the white forms so that they don't all get mixed up together.

## 26.3 Complete the gaps in the texts with a particle from B opposite.

My nine-year-old son is so untidy. I'm tired of picking ............ (1) ............ (2) him and of trying to get him to fold his clothes ............ (3) and put them neatly into drawers. The trouble is, his drawers are full of other things – toys and games, stones and pieces of wood that he has hoarded ............ (4) for some reason or another.

I've just done a presentation of our company's products with a major firm we'd like to do business with. It's ranked ............ (5) the biggest in the country, so we could make a lot of money if they agree to let us supply them with our boxes. I geared my presentation ............ (6) the quality of our boxes and at the end of it I presented their team with one of our boxes done ............ (7) in specially-designed paper in their company colours and filled with information about our company. I think they may be interested. They've certainly agreed to fix ............ (8) another meeting.

## 26.4 Answer these questions using a phrasal verb based on the verb in brackets in your answer.

1 What would you do if you wanted to discuss a business idea face-to-face with your bank manager? (FIX)
2 If students are taking an important written exam, what are schools usually required to do with the desks where they sit to write their exams? (SPACE)
3 If one leg of a table is shorter than the others, how might you use a book? (PROP)
4 If you recycle your rubbish, why might you need several different containers? (SEPARATE)
5 For school photographs, how does the photographer typically arrange the pupils? (LINE)
6 If you are a student living in one room and you often have friends and family to stay with you, why might it be useful to have a large sofa? (DOUBLE)
7 If you have a lot of papers on the floor and you want to tidy your room, what do you do with the papers? (GATHER)
8 If you are going to meet a pen friend who you've never met before at a crowded railway station, why might you each agree to wear a red carnation? (KNOW)
9 You are arranging a party and want to ask an artistic friend to deal with decorating the room where the party is to be held. What could you say to your friend? (SEE)
10 You have a pile of papers that you think it may be all right to throw away, but what is it a good idea to do with them first? (SIFT)

# 27 Talking about size and number

## A Increasing and totalling

| *phrasal verb* | *example* | *definition of phrasal verb* |
|---|---|---|
| **build up** (sth) / **build** (sth) **up** | Jane has been doing a lot of long-distance running to try to **build up** her stamina. | increase in amount, size or strength, or make something increase |
| **bump up** sth / **bump** sth **up** | Hotels in this town always **bump** their prices **up** when the film festival is on. | (informal) increase the size or amount of something, e.g. price, by a large amount |
| **round up** sth / **round** sth **up**[1] | The taxi fare came to £9.25 but we **rounded** it **up** and gave the driver £10. | increase a number to the nearest whole number |
| **push up** sth / **push** sth **up** | The TV series about Clarice Cliff's pottery **pushed up** the value of her work. | increase the amount, number or value of something |
| **put on** sth / **put** sth **on** | Harry's **put on** six kilos since he stopped playing football. | if a person or animal puts on weight, they become heavier |
| **amount to** sth | When we added living costs to the fees, the cost of the course **amounted to** £14,000. | become a particular amount |
| **add up** | Bringing up children is an expensive business. Clothes, shoes, food, toys, – it all **adds up**! | (informal) increase and become a large number or amount |

1 (opposite: **round down** sth / **round** sth **down** = reduce to nearest whole number)

## B Decreasing

Ice cream sales are high in summer but **tail off** as winter approaches. [decrease in amount]

Since they employed a new chef, the quality of the food has really **fallen off**. [become smaller or lower]

We'll never be able to get on a bus now. Let's wait till the football crowds **thin out** a bit. [become fewer in number]

Laura was so keen to get rid of her old car that I was able to get her to **knock** the price **down** a bit. [(informal) reduce]

I'm afraid we have no choice but to **slim** the business **down** and some redundancies will be announced next week. [make it smaller in size, often by employing fewer people]

## C Staying the same

This year 16-year-old girls have again done much better than boys in their school exams. However, the differences in grades between the sexes now seem to be **levelling off**[1] by the time pupils reach 18. At 18, boys' results now **average out at** 66% per exam, whereas the equivalent figure for girls is 67%. Ten years ago there was concern at the rapidly rising rate of academic success among girls in comparison with boys, but this rate has clearly now **flattened out**[2]. It is believed that greater use of technology in the classroom might have helped to **balance** things **out**[3], reviving boys' interest in their school work.

1 becoming more similar (can also be **level out**)
2 stopped increasing or decreasing and begun to stay at the same level
3 make things equal

# Exercises

**27.1** **Correct the mistakes with the phrasal verbs in these sentences.**

1 The total cost of our holiday amounted at nearly £500.
2 The bill came to £22.20 each, so we rounded it over to £25 to include a tip.
3 Helena has pushed on a lot of weight recently.
4 It will take Joe some time to build on his strength again after such a long illness.
5 The college hoped that the advert would push off enrolments for its new course.
6 The new fertiliser claims to dump up agricultural yields considerably.

**27.2** **Match the statements 1–6 with the illustrations a–f.**

a

b

c

d

e
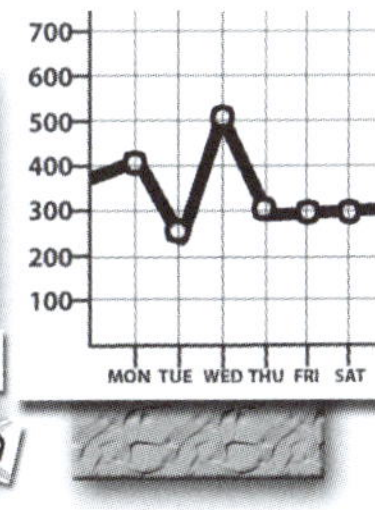


f
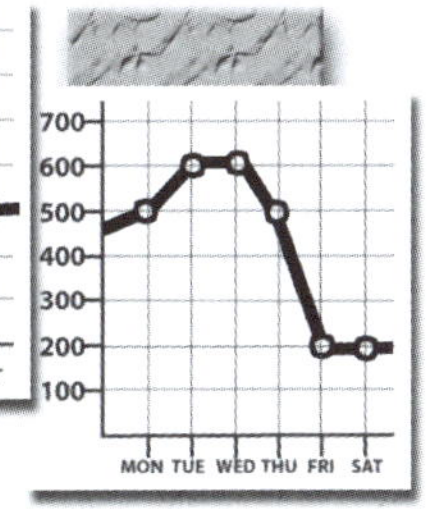


1 Sales levelled out at £300.
2 The prices averaged out at £300.
3 The price was rounded down.
4 They knocked the price down.
5 Sales tailed off later in the week.
6 The price was bumped up.

**27.3** **Answer the questions.**

1 The new manager has decided to slim the business down.
What does the new manager intend to do?
2 We picnicked in the forest in a place where the trees were beginning to thin out.
Why might this have been a good place for a picnic?
3 The graph showing hits on our website begins to flatten out in May.
How many hits did the website get in June?
4 Interest in politics seems to be falling off now, particularly among young people.
Are young people more or less interested in politics than they used to be?
5 Jim's lack of interest in housework is balanced out by his love of gardening.
How does the speaker probably feel about Jim and what he does at home?

**27.4** **Complete this email with phrasal verbs from the opposite page.**

Dear Gordon,

Sorry I haven't been in touch for a while. I'm not finding it so easy running my own business. We've had to ...................... ...................... (1) our prices because of strong competition, so our profits are beginning to ...................... ...................... (2). They still ...................... ...................... (3) a pretty sizeable sum but, even so, it's a bit worrying to see them ...................... ...................... (4). I'm planning to close one of our factories and hope that by ...................... ...................... (5) the business in this way I may be able to ...................... ...................... (6) our profits again. All the worry has made me ...................... ...................... (7) a lot of weight too because I tend to eat snacks to make me feel better. And as you know, it all ...................... ...................... ! (8)

Suzie

# 28 Talking about success and failure

## A

The chief executive of a company is making a speech to the staff at a dinner. Note the phrasal verbs connected with success and failure.

This year has been an eventful one. We've been able to **capitalise on**[1] the publicity we got in the new year with the launch of our new lines, and we've **come out** stronger than ever, despite strong competition. We've **succeeded in** reversing the downward trend we were suffering last year. What's more, we've managed to **win back** customers from the competition. We had been **losing out to**[2] international players but now we can **pride** ourselves **on**[3] being able to offer better quality products at lower prices. In the middle of the year we faced a hostile takeover bid from *Diotecnics*. We fought hard against it and finally **won through**[4], as I knew we would. That bid **fell through**[5] and we are now stronger than ever. So I want to thank you all.

1 use a situation in order to achieve something good for yourself
2 being less successful than
3 be proud of
4 succeeded after trying hard to achieve something
5 failed to happen

## B

Two students are talking on the phone about studying for exams.

Harry: I don't think I'll **get through**[1] the end-of-term exam this time.
Liz: Oh, really? Why?
Harry: Well, I've been really busy with the drama club, that's the problem. I wish I could be one of those people who **sail through**[2] exams and still manage to **pack in**[3] a huge amount in their spare time.
Liz: Yes, me too. But never mind, you did your presentation the other day and you managed to **carry** that **off**[4] quite well.
Harry: I managed to fool everyone, you mean! I **got by**[5] only because I found some useful stuff on the Internet the night before.
Liz: Well, that's okay. That's what the Internet's for. As long as you didn't just copy it!

1 pass
2 easily pass
3 (informal) manage to do a lot of activities in a period of time
4 succeed in doing or achieving something difficult
5 (informal) had just enough or knew just enough of something to deal with a difficult situation

## C Other verbs connected with succeeding and failing

I couldn't really afford the time to go to a lecture on bees but my curiosity **won out** and I went. [(informal) was stronger than other, competing emotions]

The general lack of enthusiasm **doomed** the plan **to** failure. [made it sure to fail]

The support of my friends and family helped to **pull** me **through** a very difficult time. [succeed in dealing with a difficult period of your life, or to help someone else to do this]

You have to learn to **rise above** negative criticism if you want to succeed. [not allow something bad that is happening or being done to you to upset you or to affect your behaviour]

Did you see the match on Saturday? We've **fallen behind** Liverpool by three points now. [failed to score as many points as another team or player in a competition]

# Exercises

**28.1** **Rewrite each sentence using a phrasal verb based on the word in brackets in an appropriate form.**

1 Some people were going to buy our flat but at the last moment the sale failed to happen. (FALL)
2 Steve is very proud of his organisational skills. (PRIDE)
3 The company was able to take advantage of the unusually wet weather by promoting its inexpensive umbrellas. (CAPITALISE)
4 The England team lost the trophy in 2004 but regained it the following year. (WIN)
5 It's been a difficult year for us but we have emerged from it with renewed vigour. (COME)
6 Leila managed to pass her driving test at her first attempt. (SUCCEED)
7 Darren was beaten by his brother in the finals of the tennis tournament. (LOSE)
8 They had a long battle in court to prove their innocence but finally they succeeded. (WIN)

**28.2** **Complete the text below using the correct verbs.**

Richard was very pessimistic about my plans to ride my bike from the very north of France to the south. He was convinced the project was ...................... (1) to failure despite all my attempts to persuade him that I would be able to ...................... (2) it off. He said I would never be able to ...................... (3) in so many miles in the short period of time I had at my disposal. I knew I'd be unlikely to ...................... (4) through the trip without any problems but I made a great effort to ...................... (5) above all his negative comments. I am so glad I did! It wasn't an easy ride, and my French isn't great, but I managed to ...................... (6) by using gestures and a phrasebook. My determination ...................... (7) me through and in the end I ...................... (8) in reaching my destination just one day later than planned. I'm glad to say Richard was there to congratulate me.

**28.3** **Say whether the people in these sentences (a) succeeded in doing something, (b) succeeded in doing something but only in the face of difficulty, or (c) failed to do something.**

1 He was so nervous when he stood up to sing but I think he carried it off rather well.
2 She sailed through the interview and was offered the job immediately.
3 I lost out in the job interview to another woman who had more experience than me.
4 I'd hoped to go to Peru in March but the trip fell through.
5 We packed in such a lot on our trip to Korea – we saw all the main cities and sights.
6 The college authorities ignored our protests at first but we won through in the end.

**28.4** **Correct the ten mistakes with phrasal verbs in this paragraph.**

Oliver has always wanted to become an engineer but it was quite difficult for him to get a place at college. He didn't get in at his first attempt, losing off to applicants with better exam grades. However, at his second try he succeeded to win a place. He then sailed over all his first-year exams, but failed some of his exams in the second year, as he started spending a lot of time on the rugby pitch, playing for the college first team, rather than in the library. Then, his team fell back in the college league after three games, so he wasn't too happy and he did even less work, and as a result he failed three exams. However, he's always prided himself for being able to revise very efficiently when he's really under pressure, and in the third year he did enough to pull himself across. His friends were amazed that he managed to carry it out, as they were sure he could not have packed up enough study in such a short time to get by the exams. But Oliver knew that he had only just got over and he resolved to organise his life much better after leaving college.

# 29 Discussing problems

## A Describing problems

Rosie: How's life with you, Jean? Is everything going OK?

Jean: Not really. They're threatening to make some redundancies at my husband's work, so that's **hanging over**[1] us. All because senior management **botched up**[2] and lost the company millions of pounds last year! My daughter's relationship with her boyfriend of five years has **broken down**[3] because pressures they were both having at work began to **spill over**[4] into their private lives and they just couldn't cope. Then, my son, the journalist, was in Phrasalia and got **caught up in**[5] the revolution there – he **ran into**[6] difficulties when he was trying to leave and we don't know when he'll get home. He even **landed in**[7] prison for a few days.

Rosie: Oh dear! And how are you **bearing up**[8]?

Jean: Oh, it's hard, but I'm OK. But how about you, what's going on in your life?

Rosie: It's quite stressful, too, as we've just learnt Bob's sister is **riddled with**[9] cancer ...

1 making us worry about what is going to happen
2 (informal) spoiled something by doing it badly
3 failed
4 have an unpleasant effect on another situation
5 involved in an activity or situation which prevented him from moving
6 began to experience
7 found himself in a difficult situation or unpleasant place
8 dealing with a sad or difficult situation
9 full of something unpleasant or bad

## B Dealing with problems

### COPING WITH PROBLEMS

We must all **resign** ourselves **to**[1] the fact that we will encounter problems throughout our lives. We cannot **safeguard against**[2] all unpleasant events. Nor can we **walk away**[3] from every difficult situation that comes along. We have to find ways of **living with**[4] the bad situations that we inevitably face from time to time and find ways of **ironing out**[5] difficulties. We should not be too proud to **fall back on**[6] our parents for advice – we may be surprised at how helpful they can be. If the problem is a disagreement, then we may be able to **smooth** things **over**[7]. Explaining how we feel will sometimes be all that is needed to **clear up**[8] a misunderstanding. If we have behaved badly, then we should apologise and find a way to **make up for**[9] our actions. The important thing is not to **resort to**[10] behaviour that we know is wrong even if it seems to offer a temporary solution. Don't just **grasp at**[11] the first chance of an easy way out – it may not be the right thing to do.

1 accept that something we do not want to happen will happen
2 do things to stop something unpleasant happening
3 stop being involved in a situation that is difficult to deal with
4 accepting a difficult situation and continuing with our life while it exists
5 doing something to resolve a problem
6 use something when other things have failed, or when there are no other choices
7 make a disagreement or problem seem less serious or easier to deal with, especially by talking to the people involved in it
8 give or find an explanation for, or deal with, a problem or disagreement
9 do something good so that the bad thing seems less important and does not cause a problem any more
10 do something that you do not really want to because you cannot find any other way of achieving something
11 quickly use or accept an opportunity to do or have something, especially because you are unhappy with the present situation

# Exercises

**29.1** **Complete these emails between Liz and Sharon using phrasal verbs from the opposite page.**

Hi Sharon,

Life's never easy, is it? I've had a big misunderstanding with my colleague Peter and I want to ....................... (1) it up but I'm not sure how. It's been ....................... (2) over me for a week now, and I don't want relations to ....................... (3) down between me and him as I have to meet with him once a week. He thinks I told people he took time off when he wasn't really sick and as a result he ....................... (4) in trouble with the boss. All I had said was I was glad to hear it wasn't anything serious. What should I do? Advice greatly appreciated!

Liz

Dear Liz,

Well, you're right not to try to ....................... (5) away from the situation. It's bound to ....................... (6) over into your professional dealings with him. It sounds like you've got ....................... (7) up in some malicious office gossip. Invite him out to lunch, explain, and apologise for causing him any problems. That should ....................... (8) things over a bit. Tell him what a wonderful colleague he is. At moments like this you have to ....................... (9) to flattery! It's usually the only way to ....................... (10) up for saying or doing something you wish you hadn't. Most people can't resist being flattered!

Hope that helps.

Love,

Sharon

**29.2** **Rewrite the underlined parts of these sentences, using a phrasal verb from the opposite page. Make any other necessary changes.**

1 When the doctors examined the dead man, they found his body was <u>full of</u> disease.
2 I just <u>quickly accepted</u> the first opportunity to get out of my boring job and do something more exciting. I wasn't prepared to just <u>continue to accept</u> it; I had to make a change.
3 I <u>was forced to use</u> my knowledge of map reading from my days as a boy scout to help us find a way out of the valley.
4 I'm sorry, I've <u>done things the wrong way</u> and caused a lot of problems for everyone.
5 A healthy diet and plenty of exercise is the best way to <u>protect yourself from</u> heart disease.
6 Her life is difficult. Her husband died. Now she just has to <u>be brave and determined</u> and try to carry on as best she can.
7 I'm afraid we just have to <u>reluctantly accept</u> the fact that we are going to have to sell the house.
8 She tried very hard to <u>resolve</u> the misunderstandings between the two groups.

**FOLLOW UP**

Look at the problem page of any English language magazine or newspaper and see how many phrasal verbs are used to talk about problems. Make a note of any you find, especially any not practised in this unit. There are also many problem pages in English on the Internet. Try doing a search for 'problem page'.

# 30 Deciding and influencing

## A

Horoscopes are often about making decisions and influencing people and events.

**LEO** *July 23 – August 22*
Time to **decide on** that interesting offer you had last week. You've **mulled** it **over**[1] but now you need to say yes or no. Just be careful not to **tie** yourself **down**[2] to something you may regret later.

1 thought carefully about something for a long time
2 stop yourself from being free to do what you want to do

**SCORPIO** *October 23 – November 21*
For a long time you've been **flirting with**[3] the idea of doing something completely different with your life. The opportunity will come this week but you'll have to **size up**[4] the situation very carefully before you say yes or no.

3 considering or being interested in something but not very seriously
4 carefully examine a situation or person in order to make a judgement

**CAPRICORN** December 22 – January 19
Changes are being **pushed through**[5] at work which may result in somebody **doing** you **out of**[6] a promotion you deserve. You find yourself in a difficult position with a colleague you are fond of, as your boss tries to **play** you **off against**[7] each other. Be patient. Later in the month another senior person will **single** you **out**[8] for praise for something you did recently.

5 made officially accepted
6 (informal) stopping you from getting or keeping something, in a dishonest or unfair way
7 encourage you to compete against or argue with another, hoping to get some advantage from this situation
8 choose one person or thing from a large group usually in order to criticise or praise them

**PISCES** *February 19 – March 20*
You have a disagreement with a good friend about some plans you've made together. You try your best, but it's impossible to **reason with** some people. Don't let them **play on**[9] your good nature, if it's important to you, don't give in. You'll **work** things **out**[10] in the end.

9 use your fears or weaknesses in order to make you do what they want, often in a way that is unfair
10 think carefully about how you are going to do something and make a plan or decision

## B

In these dialogues the second speaker uses a phrasal verb to paraphrase what the first speaker says.

Dennis: I might say no to the Berlin trip and go to Moscow instead, but I'm not sure.
Kim: So you're **tending towards** the Moscow trip? I thought you might.

Lucy: I think I now agree with you that we should postpone the new product launch.
Jeff: Ah-ha! So you've finally **come round** to my way of thinking.

Peter: That's it. I've decided. I'm going to take the job in Madrid.
Father: Good! I'm glad you've **arrived at** a decision at last. You won't regret it.

Dan: So who's going to have the extra ticket? I've got a coin, if you like.
Mick: OK, let's **toss for**[1] it. 'Heads' – you get it, 'tails' – I get it.

1 throw a coin into the air to see which side lands facing upwards. For British coins, 'heads' means the side with the Queen's head on it; 'tails' is the other side.

Sylvia: We need to encourage people to join the campaign and work with us.
Lenny: Yes, we need to **drum up** more support.

**TIP**
**Do** sb **out of** sth is not the only informal phrasal verb with *do*. We also find it in **do in** sb [kill], **do out** sth [decorate], **do yourself up** [make yourself look more attractive] and **do without** [manage without something]. Where verbs form groups like this, record them together.

# Exercises

## 30.1 Find phrasal verbs in A that match these definitions.

1 play with an idea, consider it but not very deeply ..................................................
2 try to discuss something rationally with someone ..................................................
3 consider something carefully over a period of time ..................................................
4 make up your mind about something ..................................................
5 unfairly deprive someone of something ..................................................
6 evaluate someone or something ..................................................
7 restrict or limit someone ..................................................
8 select one person from a large group ..................................................

## 30.2 Answer these questions about the verbs in B.

1 What do you need if you and a friend agree to make a decision by tossing for it?
2 If someone is tending towards something, have they made a definite decision?
3 What is a *drum* and why do you think it is used metaphorically in collocations like *drum up support* or *drum up business*?
4 If someone comes round to a decision, how quickly did they arrive at that decision?

## 30.3 Complete these sentences with a phrasal verb from the opposite page.

1 If we talk about the problems between us properly, I'm sure we'll be able to ...................... things ...................... .
2 I thought it was very unfair of Mr King to ...................... you ...................... for criticism in front of everyone else like that.
3 Although the redevelopment plans are unpopular, the government is determined to ...................... them ...................... .
4 Clara is very keen that her daughters should not ...................... themselves ...................... by getting married too young.
5 I hope it won't take you too long to ...................... ...................... a decision.
6 If we don't manage to ...................... ...................... some more business soon, we may have to close down.
7 Sometimes children seem to be able to sense a new teacher's weakness and they ...................... ...................... it to their own advantage.
8 If you can't agree on which film to go and see, we'll have to ...................... ...................... it.
9 You don't need to made a decision immediately – take time to ...................... it ...................... .
10 Joe is only two, but he is already very good at ...................... his father ...................... ...................... his mother.

## 30.4 Correct the mistakes in these sentences. If there are no mistakes, put a tick at the end of the sentence.

1 Everyone is trying to dissuade me from taking the job but I'm tending for accepting it.
2 You'll need to take time to shape up the situation before you decide what to do.
3 Wicked Uncle Fred succeeded in making his brother out of his rightful inheritance.
4 Sally is flirting with the idea of going to live in Australia but I don't think she'll do it.
5 It took Lily ages to get her father to go round to the idea of her training as a bus driver.
6 The careers teacher helps pupils in their final year decide on a career.
7 The advert plays off people's desire to appear young and attractive.
8 I don't want to do the washing-up either. Get a coin and we'll throw about it.

# 31 Exclamations and warnings

The exclamations on this page are all informal. Be careful with the ones marked * as you risk insulting the person you are speaking to.

## A Encouraging others

[1] a command used in musical contexts, meaning 'Start playing/singing!'

## B Expressing impatience

| *expression* | *possible context* | *you say this in order to ...* |
|---|---|---|
| **Roll on (Friday)!** | You are in the middle of a very busy week at work. | show that you are looking forward to a time or event |
| **Dream on!** | A not very musical friend is telling you about their plans to become a famous rock star. | tell someone that what they hope for is not possible and will not happen |
| **Grow up!*** | A middle-aged colleague sticks his tongue out at a fellow worker. | tell an adult to stop acting like a child |
| **Hang about!** | A friend is telling you about a problem when you suddenly think of something that might solve their problem. | tell someone to stop doing or saying something, to wait a minute |
| **Knock it off!***<br>**Cut it out!*** | People are arguing noisily next to you when you are trying to concentrate on your work. | tell someone to stop doing something which is annoying you |
| **Go on!** | A friend has just told you that he's been invited to appear in a Hollywood film. | tell someone that you do not believe what they just said (Note: spoken with a falling intonation) |
| **Come on!**<br>**Come off it!** | A friend is claiming he plays better chess than you – and you pride yourself on your play. | tell someone you don't believe them or disagree or are angry with them |
| **Wake up!** | You are telling someone how to do something but they are clearly daydreaming. | tell someone not paying attention to listen to what you say |
| **Pipe down!*** | Three or four small children are all telling you something at the same time. | tell people, usually children, to stop talking so loudly |
| **Shut up!*** | Your two brothers are arguing when you are trying to concentrate. | tell someone to stop talking |

# Exercises

**31.1** **Using exclamations from the opposite page, what could you say to a friend who ...**

1 was about to start a race in the hope of breaking a record?
2 was acting in a childish way which was annoying you very much?
3 told you a very surprising bit of news?
4 told you he/she had just seen a flying saucer? (give two possible answers)
5 was in a long-distance race and who was looking very tired and about to give up? (give two possible answers)
6 was daydreaming and had not listened to something important you just said?
7 was continually kicking your chair in a very irritating manner? (give two possible answers)
8 said he/she intended to be an astronaut?

**31.2** **Complete these sentences with a verb from the opposite page.**

1 ................ on the end of term! I'm sick of studying.
2 Hey, you kids, ................ down, will you! I'm trying to have a conversation with your granddad and I can't hear myself speak.
3 Oh, ................ about! I've just found her number; we don't need to ring directory enquiries after all.
4 ................ up, everyone! Your glasses are still half-full. We have to leave now if we're to catch the film!
5 Tim: Can I print something out on your printer?
Mona: Of course, go ................ ! You don't need to ask!
6 (Older brother to younger brother) ................ up Tom, will you! I'm trying to listen to this CD.
7 (Emma is standing at the side of the pool)
Emma: Mum, watch me dive in!
Mum: Okay, ................ on then, but be careful, darling!
8 Come on, ................ up, children! It's wrong to waste food.
9 (Singer to guitarist) Okay, ................ it away! One, two, three!

**31.3** **Which exclamations from the list would fit these situations? Use a dictionary if necessary.**

Get off! Watch out! Come along! Listen up! Calm down! Go easy on it!

1 A child is dawdling behind the rest of the family walking to the bus stop. What might the parents say?
2 Someone is starting to lose their temper. What might you say?
3 A child is pulling at the clothing of another child, who is getting annoyed. What might the second child say?
4 Someone is about to cross a busy road without looking. What might you say?
5 Someone is using too much force to try to open your expensive camera. What might you say?
6 A group of children are about to board a train for a school trip; the teacher wants to get their attention to give them important information. What might the teacher say?

# 32 Work

Read these statements by different people talking about their jobs.

The boss

I'll be retiring next year. I already find that I can **farm out**[1] tasks I used to do myself. I'm slowly **easing off**[2] now so that I can **step aside**[3] next year knowing I've left everything in good hands.

1 give work to other people instead of doing it yourself
2 starting to work less or do things with less energy
3 leave a job or position, especially so that someone else can do it

The union representative

We never like to **call** people **out**[4] on strike, but when we do, we have to be determined to **see** it **through**[5] to the end. We have to keep talking constructively and try not to get **bogged down**[6] in lengthy negotiations which only prolong the strike.

4 order workers to strike
5 continue doing a job until it is finished, especially when it is difficult
6 (informal) become so involved in the details of something that you cannot achieve anything

The assembly-line worker

My job is monotonous. I just **slog away**[7] day after day. People like me **get passed over**[8] for promotion, so we're not motivated. I often feel like **packing** this job **in**[9] and finding something else. One day I'll just **hand in** my notice and go.

7 (informal) keep working very hard, usually for a long time
8 are not given a higher position because it is given to someone else
9 (informal) stopping doing something, especially a job

The secretary

In this job you just have to **fling** yourself **into**[10] your work and **beaver away**[11] to get things done each day. I spend a lot of time **running round** helping other people. It's not a bad job, and some days I can **get off**[12] early if the boss isn't around.

10 start to spend a lot of your time and energy doing something
11 (informal) work hard at something for a long time, especially something you are writing
12 leave the place where you work, usually at the end of the day

The scientist

I decided to **go in for** research, as I wanted to do something exciting. I don't think I'm **cut out for**[13] teaching. University was fun, but now I've got to **knuckle down**[14] and build my career.

13 have the right qualities for something, especially a job
14 start to work or study hard, especially if you have not been working very hard before (see also **buckle down**, Unit 33)

The office worker

Well, in this job you just **plug away**[15] and hope the day will pass quickly. If I have to write a report, I do what I can to **cobble** something **together**[16] but I don't ever feel that I achieve anything worthwhile. Most people in my position just **coast along**[17] and dream of the summer holidays.

15 (informal) work hard at something for a long time
16 make something quickly and not very carefully
17 do only the things that you have to do without trying to go faster or be more successful

# Exercises

## 32.1 Answer these questions about the phrasal verbs in this unit.

1 Which verb focuses on working with enthusiasm?
2 Which three verbs focus on stopping work?
3 Which two verbs focus on working without using too much energy?
4 Which four verbs focus on working hard?
5 Which verb is based on an animal metaphor?
6 Which two verbs are based on metaphors connected with the land?

## 32.2 Rewrite the underlined parts of these sentences, using the word in brackets in an appropriate form. Make any other necessary changes.

1 Louise always <u>approaches</u> her work <u>with great enthusiasm</u>. (FLING)
2 I really think that it is time you <u>applied yourself much more seriously</u> to your studies. (KNUCKLE)
3 As a research scientist, you just have to keep <u>working hard</u> at your experiments <u>over a long period of time</u> and eventually you'll get results. (PLUG)
4 If this morning's meeting goes smoothly, I should be able to <u>leave work</u> by 1 pm. (GET)
5 The meeting was going well until we got <u>really involved with</u> the details of the sales conference party. (BOG)
6 I'm not sure exactly what I'm going to say in my speech but I'm sure I'll be able to <u>get something ready</u> by tomorrow morning. (COBBLE)
7 There comes a time when it is best for an older manager to <u>withdraw</u> and let a younger person take over. (STEP)
8 I always say that if you start a job, you should <u>make sure you finish it</u>. (SEE)

## 32.3 Correct the six mistakes with particles in this paragraph.

I'd hate a job where I could just coast about without needing to think about what I was doing. I'd far rather keep busy and really don't mind how much I have to slog off each day. I'd soon pack off any job that didn't keep me working hard. I fling myself onto everything I do. Even when I was at school, I used to beaver up at my homework as soon as I got home from school. My brothers certainly never used to knuckle into work in the way I did.

## 32.4 Complete these sentences using verbs from the box and the correct particles. Put the verbs in the correct form and make any other necessary changes.

| | | | | | | | |
|---|---|---|---|---|---|---|---|
| call | cut | ease | farm | go | hand | pass | run |

1 I can't stand the sight of blood, so I'm not really ............................................... nursing.
2 If you hate your job so much, why don't you just ............................................... your notice?
3 When several workers were unfairly dismissed, the trade union official decided it was time to ............................................... on strike.
4 As a PA I spend most of my time ............................................... after my boss.
5 We've had a very busy few months at work but things are beginning to ............................................... now.
6 Liam is very good at his job, so I can't understand why he always gets ............................................... while less able people get promoted.
7 Our company has started doing a lot of outsourcing, which means that we ............................................... jobs that we previously used to do ourselves.
8 Ever since she was a little girl she has wanted to ............................................... medicine.

# 33 Study

## A Going through college

Sam and Ben are twin brothers. They have a very rich grandfather who offered to **put** them **through**[1] university. Sam **sailed through**[2] his exams at school and easily **got into**[3] a good university. Ben wanted to go to the same university, but it was harder for him to **get in**. However, in his last few months at school, he **buckled down**[4] to his studies and managed to **get through**[5] all the necessary exams. Both brothers wanted to **major in**[6] law. Sam had worked in a law firm in several summer holidays and this experience was able to **count towards**[7] his degree. Ben spent his holidays playing sport. Sam continued to study hard and soon **left** most of the other students in his group **behind**[8]. At the end of six months the professor **creamed off**[9] the best students and **moved** them **up** to the next class. Sam was in this group but Ben was not. The professor felt he was more interested in rugby than law and this **counted against**[10] him. He was **marked down**[11] for careless mistakes in a number of his essays and by the end of the year he had **fallen behind**[12] the rest of his year. His tutor says he'll be lucky if he even **scrapes through**[13] his exams. His grandfather has arranged to come and visit him and Ben is feeling a little nervous.

1 pay for them to study at university
2 easily passed
3 succeeded in getting a place (at a school, college, or organisation)
4 started working hard
5 succeed (in an examination or competition)
6 (US, Aus) study something as their main subject at university
7 be part of what was needed in order to complete something
8 made much faster progress than others
9 separated the cleverest or most skilful people from a group and treated them differently
10 contributed to his bad marks
11 given a lower mark
12 failed to remain level with a group of people that was moving forwards
13 (informal) passes but only just

## B In the library

Let me try to describe this scene in a university library. A girl with long hair is **poring over**[1] a map. Next to her a boy is **skimming through**[2] some books, looking for some information on wind energy for his thesis. At the same table is a girl with short hair, who has **buried** herself **in**[3] a journal. Next to her a boy is **checking off**[4] names on a list – he's **crossed off**[5] one of them. There is a busy and studious atmosphere in this library and I hope this has **come across**[6] in my description.

1 studying carefully
2 reading quickly without studying the details
3 given all her attention to
4 writing something next to each item on a list in order to make sure that everything or everyone on it is correct, present, or has been dealt with
5 removed a word (e.g. name) from a list by drawing a line through it
6 been expressed clearly enough for the reader to understand it

# Exercises

## 33.1 Match each sentence on the left with a sentence which follows logically on the right.

1 He took three weeks off in the middle of term.
2 He didn't read the book thoroughly.
3 He searched the manuscript carefully.
4 He decided he had wasted far too much time.
5 He was very successful at college.
6 He didn't keep to the set topic for his essay.

a) He buckled down to his studies.
b) He got through all the exams.
c) He was marked down.
d) He just skimmed through it.
e) He fell behind with his work.
f) He pored over it for hours.

## 33.2 Complete these sentences using the correct particles.

1 It cost Rick and Nina a huge amount of money to put three children ...................... college.
2 Vlad sailed ...................... all his exams at school but found things much harder at university and only scraped ...................... his final accountancy exams.
3 I'm afraid you'll have to cross my name ...................... the list for the trip next Saturday.
4 The college basketball team always seems to cream ...................... the best athletes and other sports suffer as a result.
5 She was so brilliant, she left all the other students ...................... .
6 The end-of-semester marks in each year all count ...................... your final degree.
7 I like Professor Watson's lectures; they're so clear. His ideas don't come ...................... nearly as well in his books.
8 He was on the borderline between pass and fail, but his poor attendance on the course counted ...................... him and they failed him in the end.

## 33.3 Rewrite each sentence using a phrasal verb based on the word in brackets.

1 As each person arrived she asked their name and put a tick on her list. (CHECK)
2 She picked up her favourite novel and became completely absorbed in it. (BURY)
3 He decided to take economics as the main subject for his degree. (MAJOR)
4 His tutor transferred him to a higher class. (MOVE)
5 What sort of grades do you need to be given a university place in your country? (GET)
6 I applied to Oxford University but I wasn't accepted. (GET)

## 33.4 Make suitable questions which could come before these answers. Use a dictionary if necessary.

1 I'd like to go on to university.
2 I just wanted to take up a new subject; that's why I gave it up.
3 No, she dropped out at the end of the first year.
4 I can't – I'm snowed under. I've got two essays to do for tomorrow.

## 33.5 Answer these questions about your own experience of study.

1 At school did you usually sail through or scrape through your exams?
2 How soon before an exam do/did you usually buckle down to work?
3 Do you think a teacher has ever marked down your work unfairly?
4 What other things apart from exam results can count towards getting into a good university in your country?

# 34 Writing essays

This unit contains phrasal verbs which are all suitable for use in formal essays.

## A

Read Sally's notes for an essay she is going to write on the subject of 'Globalisation'. Her notes contain useful phrasal verbs for essay-writing.

Plan:

**Devote** a paragraph each **to** opposing arguments

Mention how globalisation often **deprives** workers **of** their rights

But also mention how poorer countries can **profit from** global markets

**Relate** globalisation **to** other changes (mobility, Internet, etc.)

**Refer to** recent international gatherings (G8 etc.)

**Cater for** non-technical readers as well as specialists

What best **sums up**[1] the present situation – give examples/quotes

Things to remember!

**Aim at** being neutral

**Base** opinions **on** sound evidence

Don't let irrelevant details **detract from**[2] the main argument

[1] represents the most typical qualities of something (Note that this is the only verb on this page where the particle can come either before or after the object.)

[2] make something seem less good than it really is or than it was thought to be

## B

Look at these extracts from essays where phrasal verbs have been used successfully, helping to create a good written style.

Furthermore, it is a quiet village and basically **consists of** families with very young children.

Democracy is **founded on** the ideal of equality for all citizens. [(always passive) based on a particular idea or belief]

The people have many difficulties to **contend with:** poor soil, inadequate roads and lack of investment. [have to deal with a difficult or unpleasant situation]

Government economic policies have **resulted in** an improved standard of living in the region.

We need to find ways to **improve upon** the current system of distribution of goods. [do something in a better way or with better results than when it was done before]

Efforts to **interest** young people **in** the political process often fail. We need to **invest** more thought **in** finding ways of involving young people in politics.

Many people **object to** their leaders treating them as if they were not capable of running their own lives. (Note the -ing form of the verb after **object to**)

The university has always **insisted upon** a high standard of teaching and research.

**TIP** With the verbs **base on**, **found on**, **improve on** and **insist on**, the particle *upon* can be used in place of *on* and is a good choice in a formal essay.

# Exercises

**34.1** **Look at A. Complete this paragraph with the correct particles.**

In this essay I intend to discuss the advantages and disadvantages of the information revolution. I shall relate technological change ............ (1) other changes in society, referring extensively ............ (2) the literature in the field. I shall consider how some people, particularly those in wealthier countries, have profited enormously ............ (3) the information revolution. However, I shall also devote considerable attention ............ (4) the way in which some people in poorer societies suffer by being deprived ............ (5) access to the information which others enjoy. I shall then present the mobile phone as the device which seems to sum ............ (6) the essence of the information revolution, basing my opinions ............ (7) the evidence I have presented and aiming always ............ (8) objectivity.

**34.2** **Complete these sentences using the correct particle and an appropriate ending.**

1 The research team consists ................................................ .
2 Immigrants to the UK have to contend ................................................ .
3 The headteacher would like to interest more pupils ................................................ .
4 The examinations board insists ................................................ .
5 It is essential that society should invest ................................................ .
6 The change in the law resulted ................................................ .
7 The government is keen to improve ................................................ .
8 The writer's philosophy is founded ................................................ .
9 Some critics have objected ................................................ .

**34.3** **Find the only example sentence on the opposite page where the particle could be in a different place. Rewrite that example sentence, putting the particle in the alternative position.**

**34.4** **Rewrite each sentence so that it keeps the same meaning, using a word from the box. Use each word only once.**

| | | | | | | | | | |
|---|---|---|---|---|---|---|---|---|---|
| aimed | cater | consists | deprived | detract | devoted | objected | refers | resulted | sum |

1 The teaching materials will bear historians as well as economists in mind.
2 The recent problems in the company are bound to make its reputation less favourable.
3 The policy of clearing the hillsides of trees appears to have led to an increased danger of flooding.
4 There are three players from France, one from Sweden and two from Russia in the football team.
5 Many people did not like being moved from their houses to high-rise flats.
6 Having your freedom taken away from you is a very difficult punishment to endure.
7 In her article, the writer frequently quotes a research study carried out in Canada in 2005.
8 The book has been written for undergraduate students who have little previous knowledge of the subject.
9 For me, this song captures the atmosphere in rural England in the 1960s.
10 Much of the book deals with the writer's experiences in the United States.

**FOLLOW UP**

Choose a subject that you specialise in or are particularly interested in and write a paragraph relating to that subject. Use as many of the phrasal verbs from this unit as you can in your paragraph.

# 35 Business

## A Structuring a business

### Business News in Brief

Howard Green of M and Q is moving to Paris to **head up**[1] the company's new French operations. Green will also be **looking after**[2] M and Q's interests in Francophone Africa.

There are growing rumours, as yet unconfirmed, that Scottish Mobiles is planning to **buy out**[3] its rival Celtic Telecom.

20-year-old pop star Shandy is reported to have **set** her parents **up**[4] with the restaurant business they have always dreamed of.

Property company Savages has announced plans to **hive off**[5] its residential department in order to focus on commercial business.

1 be in charge of (or, simply, head)
2 responsible for
3 buy a company (or part of a company) so that you own all of it
4 given them the money they need to start a business
5 separate one part of the company from the rest

## B Doing business

Here are some useful business collocations or common word combinations using phrasal verbs.

| *phrasal verb* | *collocating words* | *definition of phrasal verb* |
|---|---|---|
| **aim** sth **at** sb | a product/programme/magazine at women / young people / students | intend something to influence someone, or be noticed or bought by someone |
| **break into** sth | a new market / work in the media / Hollywood | become involved in a type of business or activity that is difficult to become involved in |
| **bring in** sb/sth or **bring** sb/sth **in** | customers / clients / new business | attract people, encouraging them to buy products or services |
| **bring out** sth or **bring** sth **out** | a new product / a book | produce something to sell to the public |
| **deal in** sth | art/arms/drugs | buy and sell particular goods as a business |
| **firm up** sth or **firm** sth **up** | arrangements/prices/details | make something more definite or precise or less likely to change |
| **sign up** sb or **sign** sb **up** | a new employee / a model / a film star / a basketball player | get someone to sign a document stating they will work for you |
| **turn out** sth or **turn** sth **out** | cars/films/computers | make or produce something for sale |
| **turn over** sth or **turn** sth **over** | $6 million / £100,000 | generate a specific amount of money in a particular period of time |

**TIP** When you come across a new phrasal verb in a business context – or indeed in any context – it can be useful to note it down with two or three collocating nouns.

# Exercises

**35.1 Complete this radio interview using words from the box. Use each verb in the correct form only once, unless otherwise indicated.**

aim  deal  firm  set  hive  break  head  turn (use twice)  look  bring (use twice)  buy

Interviewer: Welcome to our weekly spot 'The two-minute interview'. My guest this week is Gordon Flockheart, chairman and CEO of the Kiros group. Gordon Flockheart, you've ...................... (1) up several major companies during your long career, most recently the Kiros empire, which ...................... (2) over more than £500 million last year. What's the secret of your success?

Flockheart: Well, first and foremost, I owe a huge debt of gratitude to my grandfather, who ...................... (3) me up in business at the young age of 24. Since then I have been very fortunate in getting the right people to ...................... (4) after my interests. Secondly, we ...................... (5) in high-value, luxury personal goods and we've succeeded in ...................... (6) into markets where other companies thought they had a monopoly. We've ...................... (7) out new products at the right time and at the right price, and we've ...................... (8) them at the higher end of the market.

Interviewer: There are rumours that you would like to ...................... (9) out one of your main rivals, *Lasaque*. Any truth in that?

Flockheart: We are in negotiations with *Lasaque*, there's no secret about that, but nothing has been ...................... (10) up yet. The markets will just have to wait and see.

Interviewer: There have also been rumours that you are considering ...................... (11) off your clothing range and focusing on accessories and electronics. Is that true?

Flockheart: No, it's just a silly rumour! We're actually ...................... (12) out more clothing items than ever and have ...................... (13) in a lot of new customers thanks to our latest range of menswear.

Interviewer: There we must leave it. Gordon Flockheart, thank you.

**35.2 Complete each of the sentences below with an object from the box. Put it in the correct place or places in the sentence.**

10,000 pairs of shoes  a new sports car  modern art  the US  arrangements
the new department  a young Brazilian footballer  the lower end of the market

1 Our business has had lots of success in Europe but now we'd like to break into.
2 Have you heard? Hilary has been asked to head up.
3 Arsenal has signed up.
4 Her father made his fortune by dealing in.
5 Get your people to call my people to firm up.
6 The new factory is already turning out a week.
7 The Alpha model is aimed at.
8 The company is planning to bring out soon.

**35.3 Many phrasal verbs can have different meanings in other contexts. Write two sentences illustrating two different ways in which each of these phrasal verbs can be used. Use a dictionary if necessary.**

set up  break into  bring in  bring out  turn out

# 36 Money

## A Coping with money

Hi Jess,

How are you coping financially this term? My parents had to **bail** me **out**[1] last week cos I couldn't pay my fees; I'd **run through**[2] a huge amount of money without realising it. But they **coughed up**[3] without a protest. I guess I'll have to **work off**[4] the debt in the holidays. Expensive being a student, isn't it?

Freda

1 help a person or organisation to get out of difficulty by giving them money
2 spent a lot very quickly
3 (informal) provided money, often unwillingly
4 reduce the size of a debt by earning money to pay for it

I can't believe my mobile phone bill. It **gobbles up**[5] a large part of my salary every month. And I've had so many other bills, I've had to **break into**[6] my savings and use money I'd **put by**[7] for the holidays.

5 (informal) uses a lot of something, especially money
6 start to use an amount of money that you have been saving
7 saved in order to use it later

Hi Dave,

Just back from my trip to South America, which was fantastic, but it **set** me **back**[8] €5,000 and **cleaned** me **out**[9] completely. I was just wondering if you could lend me a couple of hundred euros? I'll **square up**[10] with you when I get my next pay cheque.

Robert

8 (informal) cost a particular amount of money, usually a large amount
9 (informal) you used all the money you had on it
10 (informal) pay somebody the money that you owe them

I **came into**[11] some money recently. My great aunt died and left me a tidy sum and I got a big bonus at work last month, too, so the money's been **rolling in!**[12] I'm seriously considering buying a flat and **renting** it **out**.

11 got money from someone who died
12 (informal) arriving in large amounts

## B Financial services

If you are unable to pay everything in the same month, we'll arrange for your payments to be **carried forward** to the next month.

What are the best ways of **ploughing back**[1] profits into a small business? Call us for advice.

1 putting money that you have earned into a business in order to make the business bigger or better

If your aim is to **put aside**[2] money regularly, our monthly savings plan enables you to **pay** a regular sum **into** your bank account each month.

2 save money for a particular purpose

# Exercises

## 36.1 Answer these questions about the verbs on the opposite page.

1 Which five verbs in A suggest that a large amount of money is being spent or received?
2 Which three verbs suggest that someone is putting money into a bank account or saving it in some other way?
3 Which two verbs in A suggest that someone is paying back a debt in some way?
4 Which verbs are more informal ways of saying:
   a) settle a debt
   b) give someone money to help them
   c) make someone spend all their money
   d) use a lot of money rapidly
5 Which verb relates to earning money from property?

## 36.2 Complete these sentences using phrasal verbs from the opposite page.

1 My father told me not to rely on him to ...................... me out if I got into debt.
2 I couldn't pay everything this month but I've been allowed to carry the remainder ...................... to next month.
3 The burglars took everything I had; they totally ...................... me out.
4 Have you managed to ...................... any money by for the holidays?
5 My car is terribly expensive – it seems to gobble ...................... all the money I earn.
6 If you can lend me £20, I'll ...................... up with you when I get paid.
7 Buying property and then ...................... it out is supposed to be a very good investment.
8 Every birthday, Grandpa gives me some money to ...................... into my savings account.
9 For the first couple of years, we ploughed our profits ...................... into the business.

## 36.3 Match the beginning of each sentence with its ending, completing each sentence with the correct particle.

| | |
|---|---|
| 1 It is going to take me ages to work | a) ................ more than I had anticipated. |
| 2 For the first few years we ploughed | b) ................ some money on your gran's death. |
| 3 Do try to put a little bit of money | c) ................ my student debts. |
| 4 I'm grateful to my dad for coughing | d) ................ my savings for as long as I can. |
| 5 You will certainly come | e) ................ enormous sums of money. |
| 6 Buying a car unfortunately set me | f) ................ enough money for me to buy a car. |
| 7 I want to put off breaking | g) ................ all our profits into the business. |
| 8 Chris started gambling and he ran | h) ................ each month for a rainy day. |

## 36.4 Here are some more phrasal verbs relating to money. Work out from the context what they mean and rewrite the sentences replacing the underlined verbs with a word or phrase that means the same.

1 I never had much money when I was a student but I managed to <u>scrape by</u> somehow.
2 If everyone <u>chips in</u>, then we should be able to afford a nice leaving present for Juliet.
3 Harold's been <u>raking in</u> money ever since he had that brilliant idea for a website.
4 At the bakery it was Amanda's job to <u>cash up</u> at the end of every day.
5 Adrian <u>staked</u> a ridiculous amount <u>on</u> a horse race and, needless to say, he lost it all.

## 36.5 Answer these questions.

1 How much did your last holiday set you back?
2 What kind of things do people usually put money aside for?
3 What, apart from a flat, might gobble up your money?
4 What do you think it is worth breaking into savings for?
5 Who would you ask to bail you out if you had financial problems?

# 37 At home

## A Moving house

Hi Ralph,

I'm just **settling in**[1] to the new house now and beginning to enjoy it. There were so many things that needed doing in the first few days. I had to **chuck away**[2] some old bits of furniture that belonged to the previous owner, **put up**[3] my bookshelves in the study, **smarten up**[4] the living room with a coat of white paint, **wash down** the kitchen walls and units, **put away** all the kitchen things that were still in boxes, **mop up**[5] a pool of oil in the garage, **stop up**[6] a suspicious-looking hole that could have been a mouse hole (aargh!) and **put** all the empty boxes **out**[7] in the rubbish. I thought I'd never finish! As I'm writing this I'**ve got** the TV **on** and there's one of those home-improvement programmes on. Oh no, I can't take any more!

Once I've got the place **straightened up**[8], I'll invite you over for a meal.

Love,

Kirsten

1 becoming relaxed and happy in new surroundings
2 (informal) get rid of something that is not needed any more (also **chuck out**)
3 fasten a piece of furniture (e.g. shelves, cupboard) to a wall
4 make a place (or a person) look tidier
5 use a cloth to remove a liquid that has been dropped or that has spread
6 fill a hole so that nothing can pass through it
7 (common collocation: put the rubbish out)
8 made tidy

## B At home

**Draw/Pull up** a chair and come and sit next to me. I want to show you something. [move a piece of furniture (especially a chair) near to something or someone]

The last person to leave has to **lock up**. [lock all the doors and windows of a building when you leave it]

We were sorry to **part with** our old sofa, but our son needed one for his flat. [give something away, usually when you do not want to]

**Pull/push** the door **to**, will you? It's cold in here. [only used of doors and windows: close or almost close a door or window by pulling it towards you / pushing it]

Here, let me **plump up** this cushion, then you can rest your head on it and relax. [make something (e.g. cushion, pillow) rounder and softer, especially by shaking it]

We'll have to move those bags and shoes; they're just **cluttering up** the hallway. [fill something in an untidy or badly organised way]

We've had the bedroom **done out** in pale green. It's a nice relaxing colour. [decorated]

This morning I forgot to **clear away** the breakfast things before leaving the house. [remove in order to make a place tidy]

I'm fed up with having to **clean up after** / **clear up after** my flatmates. [remove dirt someone has made / make the place tidy by putting things back where they belong]

**TIP** Associating a set of phrasal verbs with a place or a situation (e.g. your house or flat) will help you remember them better.

# Exercises

**37.1** **Look at the pictures and complete the descriptions below with verbs from the opposite page.**

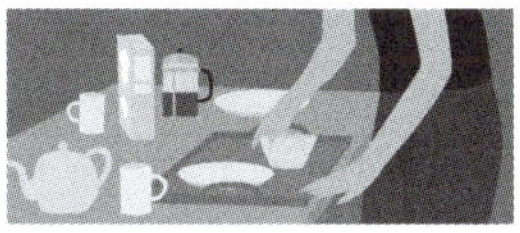

1 She's .......................................... the breakfast things.

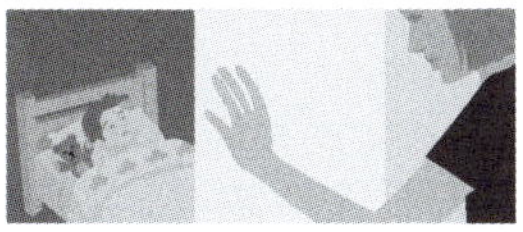

2 She's ........................ the door ........... .

3 She's .......................................... a hole.

4 She's .......................................... the pillows.

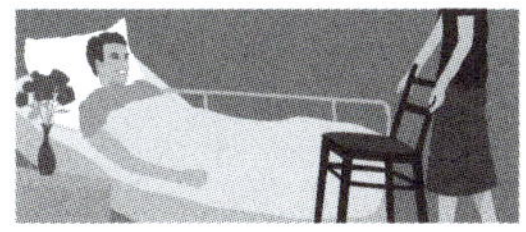

5 She's .......................................... a chair.

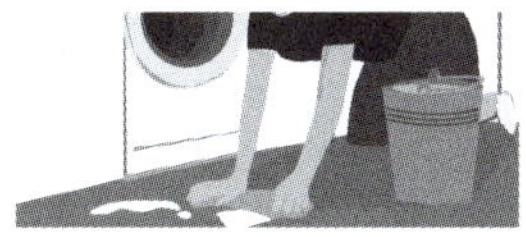

6 She's .......................................... some spilt milk.

**37.2** **Answer the questions using one of the verbs from A opposite.**

1 What do you do with the cups and plates after you have washed them up?
2 What do you do if a child has put greasy fingerprints all over your walls?
3 What do you do if someone spills some juice on your kitchen floor?
4 What should you do with your old newspapers? (give two possible answers)
5 What might you do if you want to display your favourite ornaments in your room?
6 What would you do if you noticed a small hole in the wall?

**37.3** **Match the phrasal verbs on the left with their definitions on the right.**

| | |
|---|---|
| 1 settle in | a) move something nearer |
| 2 do out | b) discard |
| 3 pull to | c) improve the appearance of something |
| 4 chuck away | d) close |
| 5 stop up | e) feel at home |
| 6 clutter up | f) fill |
| 7 draw up | g) decorate |
| 8 smarten up | h) make a mess somewhere |

**37.4** **Complete these sentences in an appropriate way. Use one of the phrasal verbs from the opposite page and any other words that you need.**

1 I didn't hear you come in because I'd .......................................................... rather loud.
2 My husband tends to make a mess when he's cooking and leaves me to .................................. .............................. him.
3 When you go to bed, please don't forget to .......................................................... .
4 The bookcase was too big for our new flat, so we had to .......................................................... .
5 Anita is untidy. There are always lots of things .......................................................... her room.
6 Our hall hasn't been decorated for years – it's time we .......................................................... .
7 Living in a student hostel was odd for Ali at first but he soon .......................................................... .
8 If I lay the table, you can .......................................................... after the meal.
9 You'll make the room look nicer if you .......................................................... on the sofa.
10 It took me all day to .......................................................... those wild, crazy kids and get the place .......................................................... again. (Use two phrasal verbs.)

# 38 Clothing and appearance

## A Actions connected with clothing and appearance

**roll up** one's sleeves

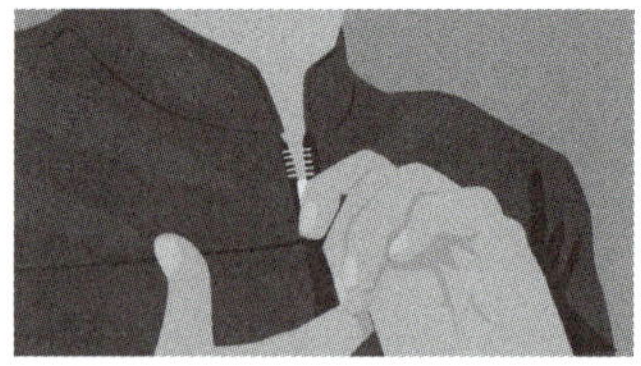

**zip up** a jacket

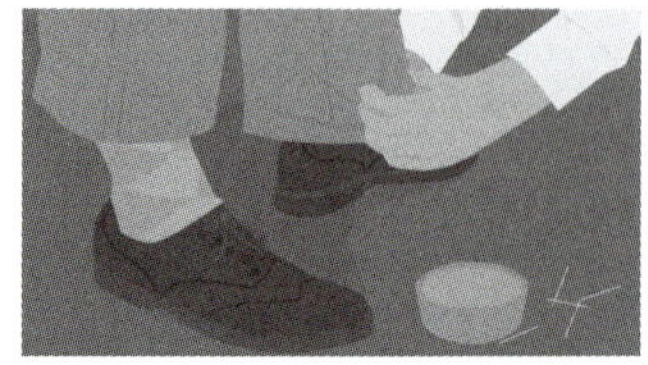

The trousers are too short, so **let** them **down**.

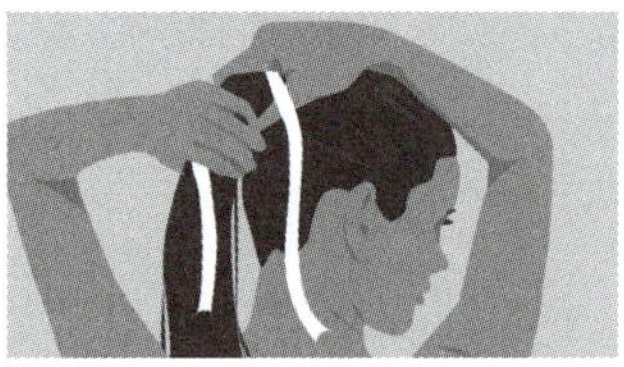

**tie back** your hair

The trousers are too long, so **take** them **up**.

The children love **dressing up**.

## B Dressing for a party

Edwina is telling Fran about a party she went to.

Edwina: Some of the girls had really **dolled** themselves **up**[1], and some of them were in such strange **getups**[2] it looked as if they thought it was a fancy-dress party!

Fran: (*laughs*) What did you wear?

Edwina: Well, to tell you the truth, it wasn't easy. I wanted to wear my little black dress but I had trouble **getting into**[3] it. I think I've put on a bit of weight. I'll have to get my mum to **let** it **out**[4], or else lose some weight! When I'd finally squeezed into it, I looked so awful in the mirror I just took it off again, **pulled on**[5] a boring old sweater and got out my old navy suit.

Fran: Oh, I like that suit.

Edwina: Well, so do I, but the jacket was all creased and I didn't have time to iron it, so I just **smoothed** it **down**[6] with my hands and hoped for the best. I was so late by this time, I didn't realise till I got to the party that I **had** the wrong shoes **on**. I must have looked as if I was wearing **cast-offs**[7]! But it didn't really matter because when the music started, we all **flung** our shoes **off**[8] to dance anyway.

Fran: (*laughs*) No, you always look nice whatever you're wearing.

Edwina: Oh, you're so sweet!

1 (informal) tried to make themselves more attractive than usual by putting on special clothes and make-up
2 (informal) usually refers to some special kind of clothing, e.g. for sports or fancy dress
3 be thin enough to be able to put your clothes on
4 make a piece of clothing wider by removing the sewing from the side edges and then sewing closer to the edge of the material
5 put on clothes quickly
6 press with your hands in order to make something flat
7 clothes which have been given to somebody else because the first owner cannot use them any more
8 removed very quickly

**TIP** Remembering a story and the verbs used to describe the events is a good way of learning a series of verbs at the same time.

# Exercises

## 38.1 Answer these questions.

1 What other item of clothing can you roll up apart from your sleeves?
2 What are you probably going to do if you roll up your sleeves?
3 What else can you zip up apart from a jacket?
4 Do you know the opposite of zip up? (Clue: it is not a phrasal verb.)
5 Can you think of anything else you might tie back apart from hair? (Clue: don't think of clothing – think of something that might hang down or grow too much.)
6 What other things apart from trousers can be let down or taken up?
7 What do you think you are doing to trousers if you (a) let them out or (b) take them in?
8 What sort of clothes do people put on when they dress up, for example as a famous person, or as someone from another historical age?

## 38.2 Choose the correct word to complete these sentences.

1 I had no time to think about what I looked like, so I ................ on my old jeans.
a) dolled b) pulled c) let d) rolled
2 Come on – time to ................ up your sleeves and get down to work.
a) pull b) zip c) roll d) tie
3 Fiona stood up, ................ down her skirt and began to address the audience.
a) smoothed b) got c) tied d) dolled
4 To my embarrassment I suddenly realised that I ................ my T-shirt on backwards.
a) took b) had c) got d) let
5 I ate so much on holiday that I had difficulty ................ into my suit today.
a) pulling b) dressing c) getting d) zipping
6 Do we need to ................ up for the party tomorrow?
a) doll b) fling c) tie d) dress
7 I was so tired that I just ................ off my clothes and fell into bed.
a) rolled b) got c) flung d) let
8 When I was a child I always hated wearing my older brother's ................-offs.
a) let b) cast c) get d) zip

## 38.3 Complete these sentences with the correct phrasal verb expression from the opposite page.

1 We were surprised when we arrived at the party because the host was wearing a kind of Superman ...................................... with a mask, cape and blue bodysuit.
2 My daughter's only 13 but she already wants to get ...................................... in make-up and high-heeled shoes.
3 Now that I'm pregnant I can't ...................................... any of my clothes.
4 Those trousers look a little tight around the waist. Shall I ...................................... a bit for you?
5 (Father to little child) You'd better ........... your jacket ..........., darling, it's cold outside.

## 38.4 Answer these questions.

1 Who do children often get cast-offs from?
2 Have you ever gone out with the wrong shoes on?
3 Have you ever had difficulty getting into something you haven't worn for a long time?
4 Do you think a lot about what to put on or do you just pull on the first thing you find?
5 If your jeans needed to be taken up, would you do it yourself or get it done for you?
6 Have you ever had to dress up in fancy dress for a party? If so, who or what did you dress up as?

# 39 Relationships

## A Getting to know someone

Tamara: You and Lee have been **going out together**[1] for ages now, haven't you?
Isabelle: Yes, we have. Longer than I'd ever have imagined when we first met.
Tamara: Why, didn't you like him much at first?
Isabelle: No, I **warmed to**[2] him at once – it was just the odd way we met.
Tamara: Oh, how was that? At a club or at work?
Isabelle: No, we got stuck together in a lift that broke down. That's what **brought us together**[3]! We were the only people there and we were there for nearly an hour, so we soon **struck up**[4] a conversation. We discovered we'd got a mutual friend – Jenny Gordon. You know her, don't you?
Tamara: I **know of**[5] her. I've **heard of**[6] her because my brother used to talk about her a lot, but I've never actually met her. She went to work in Australia, didn't she?
Isabelle: That's right. Lee had just **heard from** her, so he told me all her news and then we got on to all sorts of other things. Anyway, I thought he was really nice.
Tamara: So, you **flirted with**[7] him, no doubt!
Isabelle: Just a little, perhaps. Anyway, by the time they'd repaired the lift he'd asked me to **go out with** him. And that was six months ago!

1 having a romantic relationship
2 started to like
3 caused us to be friendly with each other
4 started (collocates with *conversation*, *friendship*)
5 have heard of her but don't know her personally
6 know a little about her because of being told about her
7 talked and behaved in a way which shows someone that you are sexually attracted to them

## B Relationship problems

### Ask the readers

**Let our readers help with your relationship problems. Here are this week's letters. We'll publish some of your answers next week.**

I really like a boy in my English class. I'd love to ask him to **come out** with me, but should I wait for him to make the first move? – Anna, London

I am worried about my partner. He got **mixed up with** some untrustworthy people when he started a new job six months ago. Should I say anything to him? – Bea, Dundee

I have been happily married for ten years. However, lately, my husband has been getting more and more distant with me. I now suspect he may be **cheating on**[1] me. What should I do? – Melanie, Belfast

A few weeks ago I told my daughter-in-law that she **fusses** too much **over**[2] her children. I didn't mean to upset her, just to help. But it has caused a major **bust-up**[3] in our relationship and it's **come between**[4] me and my son as well. How can I **patch** things **up**[5]? – Carla, Glasgow

My best friend is always **sucking up to**[6] our lecturer. I think she's trying to **butter** him **up**[7] so she gets better grades. It's annoying and unfair. Should I say anything? – Di, Cardiff

1 (informal) having a sexual relationship with someone else
2 pays too much attention to
3 (informal) break (in a relationship)
4 spoilt the relationship
5 improve the situation
6 (informal) trying to make the lecturer like her by doing and saying things that will please him
7 (informal) be very nice to someone so they will do what you want

# Exercises

**39.1** **Rewrite the underlined part of each sentence, using a phrasal verb from A opposite. Make any other necessary changes.**

1 Cindy: Do you know the novelist Jenny Parker?
Alex: No, but I <u>know a bit about her from what one or two people have told me</u>.

2 Robert: I was surprised to hear Nick and Kirsten have got engaged.
Anna: I wasn't. They've been <u>having a romantic relationship</u> for two years.

3 Max: Did you see Tim talking to that American girl at the party?
Will: Yeah, he was <u>chatting to her and behaving in a way which showed he was attracted to her</u> all evening.

4 Jane: Did you have any success getting to know that dark-haired guy?
Fiona: No. I tried to <u>start</u> a conversation with him, but he wasn't very friendly.

5 Derek: You seem to like the new boss, anyway.
Freda: Yes, I <u>started to like him</u> straight away in fact. He's very nice.

6 Sara: Did you and Liam first meet at the tennis club?
Diane: Yes, you could say it was tennis that <u>caused us to be friendly with each other</u>.

**39.2** **Correct the mistakes with the particles in these sentences.**

1 I've never met Carol Goff, but I know with her because Charles works with her.
2 I had an email last month from Tony, but I haven't heard to him since then.
3 I think Joe is cheating to me. Somebody saw him out with another woman.
4 Mrs Looney fusses ever so much on her two sons, even though they're adults.
5 Irena spent all evening flirting to her friend's brother.
6 I'm afraid my son is getting mixed up of some bad company at university.
7 Marek struck off a conversation with the person sitting next to him and the flight passed quickly.
8 Rosa told me about your bust-out with Tony.

**39.3** **Answer these questions.**

1 Janice and Roger are trying to patch things up. Are things good or bad between them at the moment?
2 If you warm to somebody, do you feel (a) anger towards them, (b) in love with them (c) a liking for them?
3 If a discussion about money comes between two people, what does it do to them?
4 If you suck up to your teacher, do you (a) say things to annoy him/her (b) say things to please him/her (c) respect him/her?
5 If you want someone to do something for you, what could you do to encourage them?
6 If you have a bust-up with someone, do you have (a) a big party to celebrate something (b) a match or competition to see who's best (c) an argument causing a break in your relationship?
7 If someone says 'Mary got mixed up with some guy from London', do they think Mary was in a good relationship or an undesirable one?
8 Which is correct in this sentence, *go* or *come*, or both?
I really like Josh; I wish I had the courage to ask him to ........... out with me.

**FOLLOW UP**

Women's magazines are full of articles about relationships. Find an example of one. Make a note of any phrasal verbs that you find in the article you choose and write them down in their context.

# 40 Character and personal qualities

## A Talking about negative qualities

Dina: What do you make of Natasha's new boyfriend? He's **getting on**[1] a bit, isn't he?!
Becky: Yes. He must be at least ten years older than her. I must say I didn't like him very much. His eyes were **boring into**[2] me and it made me rather nervous.
Dina: I'm glad you felt like that too. He really scared me.
Becky: Scared you? You need to **toughen up**[3] a bit! You shouldn't let anyone scare you. It's not just his eyes, though, is it? He's so **outspoken**[4]! In fact, he's rude.
Dina: He swore at me the other day. I didn't answer back though. I wouldn't **descend to**[5] his level. And how about the way he speaks about his sister?
Becky: No wonder she's a bit odd. Having a brother like that would **screw** anyone **up**[6]!
Dina: I'm amazed Natasha's so keen on him. I **had** her **down as**[7] a sensible person.
Becky: You know, sometimes I think she's like a teenager who needs to **grow out of**[8] her immature ways. I mean, she's 21, not 13!

1 (informal, always continuous) becoming old
2 looking very hard at
3 become stronger and more able to deal with problems (also transitive: **toughen** sb **up**)
4 having a tendency to express opinions even though they may offend people
5 behave so badly
6 (informal) make someone feel confused and unhappy about their life
7 (informal) thought that they were a particular type of person (especially when they are not in fact like that)
8 stop doing something as you get older

## B Talking about positive qualities

Look at this speech by a company manager at a party for a colleague who is retiring.

Jack is leaving us today and I want to wish him a happy retirement. Having worked closely with him, I can personally **vouch for**[1] his unswerving loyalty to the company over the last 21 years and his extraordinary skills as a personnel manager. Right from the beginning, his ability to handle people **shone through**[2]. He **prided** himself **on**[3] the good relations he enjoyed with junior staff; he knew that good relationships mean everything in the workplace. It was always such a pleasure to see how his face would **light up**[4] whenever he managed to solve a tricky personnel issue; for him, resolving a difficult situation was its own reward. Jack was also excellent at **drawing out**[5] younger, less experienced members of staff and he showed that rare talent for **bringing out**[6] the best in all his colleagues. I'm sure everyone would agree that he always **came across**[7] as calm, professional and committed to his staff. His departure will be a great loss to the company, and I wish him

1 say that you know someone and that you can promise that they have a good character or good skills
2 became apparent
3 took pride in
4 look very happy
5 helping people to feel more confident
6 making qualities more noticeable
7 appeared to be

**TIP** Note how the meaning of a phrasal verb can sometimes vary depending on whether it is used with an object or not. For example, **come across** (see above), when it is used with an object means 'find or meet something/somebody by chance': *I **came across** an old friend I hadn't seen for years at a party the other night.* Make a note of any verbs whose meanings change in this way.

# Exercises

**40.1** **Look at these pages from Joanna's private diary, where she writes about people she knows and works with. Complete the text, using phrasal verbs or adjectives from A opposite.**

| | |
|---|---|
| **MON 17**<br><br>The affair with John seems to have ...................... (1) Rita up quite badly, she seems so unhappy and confused. She'll have to ...................... (2) up if she's to cope with life and all the horrible things that can happen when you're in love. Poor girl. | **WED 19**<br><br>Funny, I ...................... (5) Lisa down as a fairly ...................... (6) person but she's actually the complete opposite, quite shy and quiet when you get to know her better. The good thing is, she seems to have ...................... (7) out of her girlish infatuation with that stupid man Henry at last. I guess she's more mature now she's turned 30! |
| **TUE 18**<br><br>Spent the evening with Yasmin and her new partner. I don't know how old Simon is, but he's definitely ...................... (3) on a bit and his hair's going grey.<br><br>Bad day at the office today – some documents got lost. The boss suspected me and Jane. His eyes just ...................... (4) into us in a very accusing way and he questioned us for a long time. | **THU 20**<br><br>Hilary and I almost had a serious row last night. She insulted me a couple of times and I felt furious, but I refuse to ...................... (8) to her level, even though it would be easy enough! |

**40.2** **Complete these annual appraisal summaries, written by a personnel manager, with the correct particles.**

1 Tyra sometimes comes ...................... as a little aggressive, but in general she has good relations with her colleagues and seems to bring ...................... the best in the staff she manages.
2 Jane has had to overcome a great deal due to her physical disability, but her determination and will to succeed always shine ...................... , despite the difficulties.
3 Luke prides himself ...................... his ability to cope with huge amounts of stress and to meet deadlines. He has always met deadlines, though I can't personally vouch ...................... his ability to deal with a major crisis.
4 It's always so nice to see how Donald's face lights ...................... whenever he is praised for his achievements, and he has had some notable successes in the last 12 months. Let's hope it continues that way.
5 Tina is very good at drawing ...................... the shyer and less confident members of staff. She seems like an excellent candidate for promotion in the next round.

**FOLLOW UP** Try and find some job advertisements in English. Job descriptions often refer to personal qualities needed for the job. Note any phrasal verbs you find.

# 41 Feelings

## A

Horoscopes often contain verbs connected with feelings. Here are some Chinese ones.

**Tiger** * * * * * * * * * * * * * * * * * * * * *
Some days it's hard to **summon up**[1] the energy to get out of bed in the morning. Perhaps you've finally **gone off**[2] your job, or maybe there's someone at work you **don't care for**[3]. But persist, keep going and things will change for the better before the week is out.

**Rabbit** * * * * * * * * * * * * * * * * * * * * *
Someone **has got** something **against**[4] you. You're not sure what it is, but you sense they're trying to **turn** other people **against**[5] you too. But you shouldn't **work** yourself **into**[6] a state about it. Stay calm and confront the person who's causing the problem; it's the only way to resolve the situation.

**Dragon** * * * * * * * * * * * * * * * * * * * *
You feel a bit low, but you have to **snap out of**[7] it. Why not enjoy some special treat you've been promising yourself for ages? You'll soon **perk up**[8]. Secretly you're **hankering after**[9] a change in your career, but now is not the right time.

**Snake** * * * * * * * * * * * * * * * * * * * * *
You are usually **brimming with**[10] enthusiasm for everything; however, this week things could get difficult. Don't **give in to**[11] negative impulses and keep smiling; things will get better.

1 find (used about someone trying hard to find a quality that is needed)
2 (UK, Aus) stopped liking
3 don't like
4 dislikes for some reason
5 make others dislike
6 make yourself feel very upset
7 (informal) force yourself to stop feeling sad and upset
8 become happier or more energetic
9 wanting very much
10 showing a lot of a good emotion
11 if you give in to an emotion, you stop trying not to feel it and you allow your actions to be controlled by that emotion

## B

Note how the second speaker uses a phrasal verb to paraphrase the first.

Erica: Tessa was very angry. She was almost crying.
Julian: Yes, it was obvious she was **choking back**[1] her anger and **fighting back**[2] the tears.

1 forcing herself not to show her feelings
2 trying hard not to show an emotion

Will: Karl looked so surprised when he reveived his leaving gift, didn't he?
Paula: Yes, I think he was **bowled over** by everyone's generosity.

Zara: Vanessa suddenly started talking uncontrollably about her emotions.
Luke: Yes, she let it all **spill out**, didn't she?

Elaine: You didn't look physically and mentally able to tolerate such a long meeting.
Rose: No, I wasn't **feeling up to** it. I'd had a cold and was feeling tired and weak.

Aisha: I really feel sorry for Geoff with all the illness he's had lately.
Natalie: Yes, poor man. My sympathies **go out to** him.

Rob: I think the news shocked Joanna and really upset her.
Sheila: Yes, it obviously **shook** her **up** a lot.

Fran: As I stood at the War Memorial, I suddenly felt very sad.
Lena: Yes, a feeling of sadness **came over** everyone, I think.

Emma: We should stay calm and not do or say anything stupid.
Jack: Yes, we mustn't let our emotions **run away with** us.

# Exercises

## 41.1 Complete these sentences with a verb from A.

1 When you came for the job interview, you were .......................... with self-confidence.
2 I just couldn't .......................... up the courage to tell my boss I wanted a pay rise.
3 Please try to .......................... up and look a bit more cheerful before our visitors arrive.
4 Jo has a nervous disposition but usually manages not to .......................... in to her fears.
5 She's .......................... after a major career change so she might go back to university.
6 Try not to .......................... yourself into a state about everything; calm down.
7 I've really .......................... off football recently. I used to love it, but now it just bores me.
8 Stop being so bad-tempered. Just .......................... out of it!

## 41.2 Which verb in B matches each definition?

1 force yourself not to show some feeling ..............................
2 begin to affect ..............................
3 surprise or please a lot ..............................
4 make someone feel shocked or upset ..............................
5 encourage us to do foolish things ..............................
6 feel physically and mentally strong enough to do something ..............................

## 41.3 Which phrasal verb from the opposite page fits each set of collocations?

1 to .............................. anger / tears / disappointment

2 to be .............................. by someone's charm / beauty / generosity

3 to .............................. an easy life / (a) change / a fast car

4 to .............................. excitement / enthusiasm / self-confidence

## 41.4 Read the remarks about different people and then answer the questions below.

Anna doesn't care for her boss.
Bert was quite bowled over by the news.
Dolly ought to perk up a bit.
Emma is brimming with anticipation.
Geoff can't snap out of his bad mood.
Hannah tried her best to choke back her tears.
Olga is turning people against the boss.
Aaron has something against his teacher.

| | |
|---|---|
| 1 Who is feeling down? | |
| 2 Who is finding it hard to change how he feels? | |
| 3 Who is feeling dislike? | |
| 4 Who is making people dislike someone? | |
| 5 Who wanted to cry? | |
| 6 Who dislikes someone for a reason that is not apparent? | |
| 7 Who was very surprised about something? | |
| 8 Who is really looking forward to something? | |

## 41.5 Rewrite each sentence using the word in brackets.

1 Gina let her feelings become very obvious. (SPILL)
2 Grandma doesn't think she could manage a long flight. (FEEL)
3 We must not allow our feelings to make us do something we'll regret. (RUN)
4 You mustn't let those feelings of insecurity take over. (GIVE)
5 Everyone suddenly felt very tired. (CAME)
6 We extend our sympathies to all the victims of the disaster. (GO)

# 42 Social life

## A Social and emotional commitments

Hi Howard,

What did you **get up to**[1] at the weekend, anything exciting? We had quite a nice weekend here. It was my mum's birthday, so my sister and I **treated** her **to**[2] a night out. We **took** her **out** for dinner on Saturday, then we **went on to** a jazz club because she's a great jazz fan.

Zenab

[1] (informal) do
[2] paid for her to do something pleasant

Hi Zenab,

Glad to hear you had a nice weekend. I did too. I was **passing by** an old friend's place on Sunday, so I **called in on**[3] him. Luckily he was at home. We didn't do anything special, just **hung out**[4] and chatted.

Howard

[3] visited for a short time, usually on your way to somewhere else
[4] spent time together not doing anything special

Hi Jane,

I've had another big **letdown**[5] in my love life. The day after we had that terrible row last week, Kenneth **dropped by**[6] and offered to take me out for a meal. I thought that would be a chance for us to forget it, you know, and **move on**[7]. I should have refused, but I said yes, then he **blew** me **out**[8] again. He phoned afterwards and said sorry and now he's all romantic again and suggesting we meet. I should say no, and I know what you're going to say – it's your fault, **deal with** it.

Alex

[5] disappointment
[6] made a short visit to someone, usually without arranging it
[7] go forward in one's life and not look back to the past
[8] (informal) disappointed someone by not doing something that had been arranged

## B Other aspects of social life

We're having a little **get-together** at our place on Saturday night. Would you like to come? [informal social gathering]

Shall I call Anne on her mobile and see if we can **hook up with** her and Teresa and go clubbing? [(informal) meet someone for a particular purpose]

It's six o'clock. I'd better **shoot off** or I'll be late for dinner. [(informal) leave]

I think that restaurant's really **gone off** lately. [become worse in quality or standard]

Wow, that was a fantastic meal. I'll need a couple of days to **sleep** it **off** now, though! [sleep until you feel better, especially after too much alcohol or food]

Loads of people **rolled up** to see Bill's band at Zino's last night. [arrived in large numbers] They had to **turn** people **away** as there wasn't enough room. [refuse to allow them to enter]

I'm really **getting into** snowboarding. It's amazing. [becoming involved in an activity]

Let's invite Dan too. We mustn't forget him just because he's **moved away** from the village.

# Exercises

**42.1** **Complete the phrasal verbs or phrasal expressions in the second speaker's answers.**

1 Mark: Do you still find it difficult being separated from your wife?
Rob: Well, I've just got to ...................... with it and ...................... on. It's no good living in the past.

2 Ramesh: Was the concert as good as you expected?
Steve: No, it was a big ...................... . Very poor. A complete disappointment.

3 Louise: Did you have a nice date with Sheila last night?
Ron: No. She ...................... me out. I waited for her for over an hour and then I went home.

4 Gerard: Can't you stay for dinner? We've got loads of food.
Kerry: No, I'd better ...................... off now; I've got a report to do for tomorrow morning.

5 Freda: Jim, how nice to see you! I wasn't expecting a visit!
Jim: Well, I was just ...................... by so I thought I'd come and say hello.

6 David: How was Harry's birthday celebration?
Rachel: Well, we all ...................... up expecting a big party, but there were only a few members of his family there.

**42.2** **Answer these questions.**

1 If someone says a particular hotel has gone off, what do they mean?
2 If someone says they've been getting seriously into bird-watching, what do they mean?
3 If someone asks you what you got up to over the summer, what do they want to know?
4 If someone said they were having a family get-together, what would be happening?
5 If someone says to you, 'Let's just hang out', what do they want to do?
6 If someone said they wanted to take you out, is it likely they want to (a) kill you (b) go out with you and pay for you (c) go with you to show you the way out of a building?

**42.3** **Read these remarks by different people and then answer the questions below.**

Hilary: Chris dropped by the other day.
Dana: It would be nice to hook up with Jake and Liam.
Shirley: Mum and Dad treated me to a fabulous weekend in Paris.
Ed: I'll need a week to sleep off that dinner!
Tina: I got turned away from that disco once.
Ralph: I moved away from Hobblethorpe because I needed a change.
Louise: It'd be nice to call in on Jody when we're in town.
Li: After the meal we went on to a really great club.

| | |
|---|---|
| 1 Who had far too much of something? | |
| 2 Who was not allowed to enter somewhere? | |
| 3 Who wants to visit someone? | |
| 4 Who went to live in a different place? | |
| 5 Who was visited by someone? | |
| 6 Who was already out somewhere and then went somewhere else? | |
| 7 Who wants to meet someone? | |
| 8 Who had a nice time and didn't have to pay? | |

# 43 Health and symptoms

## A Talking about how you are

Mrs Smith: How are you these days? Have you managed to **throw off**[1] that cold you had when we last met?

Mr Jones: Well, yes, it **cleared up** after a couple of days, but I'd no sooner **got over** that than I **picked up** another one. It's horrible. My nose is completely **bunged-up**[2]. And I keep **breaking out in**[3] a sweat.

Mrs Smith: Well, I hope you don't **pass** it **on** to me. I'm feeling bad enough as it is. My arthritis has **flared up**[4] again. And you know I fell and cut my hand a week ago? It's only just started to **heal over**[5] and the swelling hasn't **gone down**[6] yet.

Mr Jones: I think we should both go to the doctor's again, don't you?

1 (informal) get rid of a slight illness
2 (informal) blocked
3 (of sweat, spots, rash) suddenly appears on the skin
4 (of illness) returned
5 become covered by new skin
6 returned to its normal size

## B Feeling tired

There are a lot of phrasal verbs in English relating to the idea of sleep and feeling tired. For example, **drop off** and **nod off** are both informal and both mean fall asleep, but **nod off** is used particularly about situations when you did not intend to fall asleep.

Here are some more phrasal verbs relating to being very tired.

| *phrasal verb* | *phrasal adjective/noun* | *example* | *definition of phrasal verb* |
|---|---|---|---|
| **wear out** sb or **wear** sb **out**<br>**tire out** sb or **tire** sb **out**<br>**do in** sb or **do** sb **in** (informal) | **worn out**<br>**tired out**<br>**done in** (informal)<br>**wiped out** (informal) | Going round the shops all day has **worn/tired** me **out** / **done** me **in**.<br>What a day I've had! I am **worn out** / **tired out** / **done in** / **wiped out!** | make someone very tired |
| **burn out** | **burnt-out** (noun = **burnout**) | Don't work too hard – or you'll **burn out** before you're 30! | become so ill or tired that you can't work creatively, because of overwork |
| | **washed out** | What's the matter with Kay? She looks **washed out**. | tired, pale and ill |

## C At the doctor's

Don't worry. There's a lot of it **going around**[1]. I'll **put** you **on** some tablets to help you sleep. They should **knock** you **out**[2]. Keep taking them for at least a fortnight – you shouldn't **come off** them until I say so. This particular bug **takes** a lot **out of**[3] you, so when you begin to feel better, make sure you eat lots of fruit and vegetables to **build** yourself **up**[4].

1 a lot of people are complaining of this
2 make you sleep heavily
3 makes you feel very weak
4 make yourself stronger

# Exercises

## 43.1 Rewrite the underlined parts of these sentences, using a phrasal verb or phrasal expression from the opposite page. Make any other necessary changes.

1 Doctor: So, how can I help you today?
Patient: I think I've <u>caught</u> a chest infection. I'm coughing and wheezing a lot.

2 Doctor: When did you first notice the problem?
Patient: Well, <u>a rash suddenly appeared</u> on my neck about a week ago.

3 Doctor: And what's troubling you, Mrs James?
Patient: Well, I had an ear infection about a month ago. It seemed to <u>disappear</u> when I took the antibiotics you gave me but now it's <u>returned</u> again.

4 Doctor: Mr Kelly, hello, how are things?
Patient: Well, okay, but my nose is <u>blocked</u> all the time. Can you give me something for it?

5 Doctor: Miss Peters, what can I do for you?
Patient: Well, I sprained my ankle a week ago and the swelling just hasn't <u>diminished</u> and it's still painful.

6 Doctor: Right, Mr Troy, what's troubling you?
Patient: Well, Doctor, I just seem to feel absolutely <u>exhausted</u> all the time. I simply have no energy to do anything.

## 43.2 Read the remarks about different people and then answer the questions below.

Janice: I just can't seem to throw off this cold.
Kenji: I hope Janice doesn't pass on her cold to me.
Grace: I'm getting over the flu now.
Rajiv: My scar is healing over nicely now.
Natasha: This bronchitis is taking a lot out of me.
Ray: I know I look really washed out.
Harry: I feel totally burnt out.
Dan: I keep nodding off and missing parts of the TV show.

| | |
|---|---|
| 1 Who is feeling weak because of an illness? | |
| 2 Who is ill but getting better? | |
| 3 Who is feeling sleepy? | |
| 4 Who is finding it difficult to get better? | |
| 5 Who is completely exhausted from overwork? | |
| 6 Who is pale, ill and tired? | |
| 7 Whose skin is looking better? | |
| 8 Who is keen not to catch someone else's illness? | |

## 43.3 Match the beginning of each sentence with its ending.

1 The doctor put me
2 I've come
3 The tablet knocked me
4 I found it difficult to
5 There's a lot of flu going
6 I'm quite weak, so I need to build
7 I feel worn

a) out and I slept deeply.
b) out from all that work.
c) off the antibiotics.
d) myself up a bit.
e) on a course of antibiotics.
f) drop off last night.
g) around right now.

**FOLLOW UP** Find a magazine article on a health issue and make a note of any phrasal verbs that are used in it.

# 44 The body

## A Phrasal verbs referring to actions or positions of the body

It was very cold and we **huddled up** in front of the campfire to keep warm.

Mervin **stuck** his head **out** of the window to see what was happening in the street below.

During the dance we had to **spread** our arms **out** and go round in a circle.

She **stretched out** her hand to try to reach the fruit on the other side of the fence.

The cat **curled up** on the sofa and went to sleep.

Molly **bent down** to pick up the little dog.

## B More phrasal verbs connected with the body

| *phrasal verb* | *example* | *definition of phrasal verb* |
|---|---|---|
| **screw up** sth or **screw** sth **up** | She **screwed up** her face in disgust when she heard what had happened. | make your eyes narrower, or twist your face into a different shape, often in order to show an emotion |
| **loosen up**<br>**warm up** | We always do exercises to **loosen up** / **warm up** before playing tennis. | prepare your muscles for a physical activity by stretching and doing simple exercises |
| **swing around/ round** | I **swung round** when I heard my name and saw Lee running towards me. | suddenly turn around so that you can see someone or something behind you |
| **tense up** | 'Relax! Don't **tense up** and you'll float!' said the swimming instructor. | if you tense up, your muscles stiffen because you are not relaxed |
| **thaw out** | 'Oooh! It was freezing outside! Turn the heater on! I need to **thaw out**.' | (slightly informal, metaphorical) become warmer after getting very cold |
| **waste away** | Poor old Mrs Jones is just **wasting away**. She's been so ill, poor woman. | gradually get thinner and weaker, usually because of illness |
| **pick** yourself **up** | (Parent to child who has just fallen) 'Come on, darling, **pick** yourself **up**! There! Don't cry.' | stand up again after you have fallen |
| **double up** | When she told me, it was so funny I just **doubled up** laughing. | suddenly bend your body forwards because you are laughing a lot or in a lot of pain |
| **turn around/ round** (sb/sth) or **turn** (sb/sth) **around/round** | (to somebody who is trying on a skirt) '**Turn around**, let me see it from behind.'<br>He **turned** the car **around** and drove back home. | turn so that you are facing the opposite direction, or make someone or something do this |

# Exercises

**44.1** **Look at A. Match the beginning of each sentence with its ending.**

| | |
|---|---|
| 1 If you all huddle up together | a) the horse will take the carrot from your hand. |
| 2 If you stretch out your arm | b) you'll be able to see our car. |
| 3 Spread out your arms | c) and go to sleep if you like. |
| 4 Now bend down | d) you'll feel a bit warmer. |
| 5 If you stick your head out of the window | e) and move them in circles. |
| 6 You can curl up in the armchair | f) and touch your toes. |

**44.2** **Answer these questions using one of the phrasal verbs from B.**

1 What do you normally need to do before starting on an exercise routine?
2 If you suddenly go from a dark place into very bright sunlight, what do you do?
3 If you have been outside for a long time on a very cold day, what may it take you some time to do when you go indoors again?
4 What do you have to do if you fall over?
5 What do you do if you hear a sudden noise behind you?
6 What happens to your muscles if you are feeling very anxious?
7 What happens if someone doesn't eat enough over a long period of time?
8 If you suddenly have an excruciating pain, what may you do?

**44.3** **Correct the six particle mistakes in this paragraph.**

I'm rather worried about my neighbour. I saw her the other day in the garden and she was doubled out in pain. She also looks as if she is wasting off. I asked her about it and she said she was just trying to lose some weight, but she clearly didn't like my talking about it and I could sense her tensing in. I think she's probably been doing far too much exercise. She spends hours outside bending away to touch the ground or spreading off her arms and swinging them in circles. I can see that she's screwing in her face in pain and I long to tell her to relax a bit.

**44.4** **Rewrite each sentence using the verb in brackets in an appropriate form.**

1 You must be freezing – do come inside and get warm. (THAW)
2 Look at me – now face in the opposite direction. (TURN)
3 The little girl was lying in a little ball on her bed with her thumb in her mouth. (CURL)
4 When the teacher turned his back, the boy put his tongue out at him. (STICK)
5 If you don't eat more, you'll get far too skinny. (WASTE)
6 The stand-up comic was so good that we spent the evening in fits of laughter. (DOUBLE)

**44.5** **Explain the play on words in these sentences.**

1 The twins doubled up laughing.
2 The carpenter screwed his face up as the job was very difficult.
3 The grammar teacher tensed up when Maria said 'writed' instead of 'wrote'.
4 The taxi driver picked himself up after he tripped over the suitcase.

# 45 How people speak

## A

In these dialogues, the second speaker uses a phrasal verb in their response.

Parent: Go and study! You haven't done anything this week! Did you hear me? I said study!
Child: Okay, okay! Don't **go on at**[1] me! I'll do it later.

[1] criticise someone continuously

Jim: Can you explain to me what we have to do at the meeting?
Paul: Okay, I'll just **run through**[2] the main points.

[2] explain or read something to someone quickly

Russ: How long do you need for your presentation? You can have two hours.
Jane: Two hours sounds far too long! I don't think I'd want to listen to someone **holding forth**[3] for that long. It'd bore everyone stupid.

[3] talk about a particular subject for a long time, often in a way that other people find boring

Archie: How do you think we should present our case to the committee?
Iris: I think we should emphasise the good things and perhaps just **gloss over**[4] the difficult bits.

[4] avoid discussing something, or discuss something without talking about the details in order to make it seem unimportant

Morris: How can we distract Richard while I bring in his present?
Ruth: Well, I'll **engage** him **in**[5] conversation and you can leave the room discreetly.

[5] try to start a conversation with him

## B

Look at these sentences with more phrasal verbs connected with speaking.

Mr Holroyd **reeled off** a list of names. [(informal) said a long list of things quickly and without stopping]

The detectives tried to **wring** the truth **out of** the suspect. [force or persuade someone to give you money or information]

The reporters **bombarded** the minister **with** questions. [directed a lot of something at one person]

Somebody raised their hand to **put** a question **to** the speaker.

I didn't really have a conversation with her. She just **talked at** me for an hour. [talked to someone without listening to them or allowing them to speak]

Without thinking, he **blurted out** the name of the hotel where the star was staying. [said something suddenly and without thinking, especially because you are excited or nervous]

I'll introduce the plan in general and then you can **expand on** it.

In the middle of my welcome speech I just **dried up**. [stopped speaking, especially because you suddenly forget what to say next]

The teacher kept asking him questions but he was nervous and he just **clammed up**. [(informal) became silent or refused to speak, usually because of shyness or fear]

I'd like to get a flat of my own but I'll have to **sound** my parents **out** first. [talk to someone to discover what they think about an idea or plan]

We were talking about the Olympics and that **led into** a discussion about drugs.

Are you going to tell the truth or do I have to **drag** it **out of** you? [make someone tell you something that they do not want to tell you]

# Exercises

**45.1** **Rewrite the underlined part of each sentence, using one of the phrasal verbs in A.**

1 It's so boring listening to Uncle Bill <u>lecturing us</u> about the morals of young people today.
2 I'll try to <u>get into a conversation with your father</u> so he won't notice you leaving.
3 I wish my parents would stop <u>criticising</u> me all the time.
4 OK, before everyone starts working, I'd like to quickly <u>remind you of</u> the instructions.
5 The personnel manager <u>said very little about</u> salary progression during our interview.

**45.2** **Read the sentences and then answer the questions.**

1 After Sue got back from the party, her flatmates bombarded her with questions.
Did Sue's flatmates ask her a lot of questions or a few questions?
2 Towards the end of the play one of the main actors suddenly dried up.
Would the actor have been pleased with his performance or not?
3 Nathan reeled off the names of all 50 states of the USA.
Did Nathan have to pause and think of the name of each state?
4 Jackie clammed up as soon as Brian came in the room.
Did Jackie speak more or less after Brian arrived?
5 The detective eventually managed to wring her attacker's name out of the girl.
How easy was it for the detective to get the girl to tell her the truth?
6 Matt decided to sound out the editor before he started to write the article.
What do you think Matt talked to the editor about?
7 Terry has a dreadful habit of talking at people.
Why is this habit of Terry's dreadful?
8 Frances glossed over the accident when she was telling her parents about her trip.
What did Frances tell her parents about the accident?

**45.3** **Complete these sentences, using a phrasal verb from the opposite page.**

1 Now, who'd like to ............................ the first question to our guest speaker?
2 In this essay I shall first outline three key issues. I shall then expand ............................ each of these in turn.
3 Our discussion of modern education soon ............................ into an argument about whether schools are better now than they used to be.
4 I'd love to join your expedition to the North Pole but I should ............................ my wife out first.
5 My son doesn't tell us much about school. We have to drag things ............................ of him.
6 The children were so interested in the topic that they ............................ their teacher with questions.
7 Veronica just ............................ up whenever I tried to get her to talk about her work.
8 During the press conference, she was nervous, and unintentionally ............................ out the name of the secret agent.

**45.4** **Here are some more phrasal verbs connected with ways of speaking. Can you work out what they mean and rewrite the sentences replacing the underlined verbs with your own words?**

1 Jim was so rude – he <u>cut in on</u> the conversation I was having with Susan about her new job and started to ask her questions about her son.
2 I don't know how you'll manage to <u>explain away</u> the scratch on your father's car.
3 I wish he'd stop <u>wittering on</u> about the weather – it's so boring.

**FOLLOW UP**
Look up the verbs from 45.4 in a good dictionary. Write down some more examples of how they are used.

# 46 How people move

## A Coming and going

The little boy **stole away** while his parents were sleeping. [left quietly without anyone knowing]

I'm sorry! I only **crept up on** you for a joke. I didn't mean to frighten you. [approached someone so quietly they did not know you were there till the last moment]

My landlord told us that if we didn't **clear out** by the end of the week, he'd contact his lawyer. [(informal) leave]

I'm terribly sorry for **walking in on** you in the shower! [going into a room and seeing what someone is doing when they do not want to be seen]

## B Moving with other people

| *phrasal verb* | *example* | *definition of phrasal verb* |
|---|---|---|
| **drop back** | George started out in the lead in the race but soon **dropped back** to fifth place. | move to a position nearer the back |
| **hang back** | The others rushed forward to see the tiger but I **hung back**. | not move forwards with other people, usually because you are shy or afraid |
| **pile into / out of** | The schoolchildren **piled into / out of** the bus. | (informal) enter/leave a place or vehicle quickly and not in an organised way |
| **squash up** | If you **squash up**, there'll be room for Tim on the sofa too. | (informal) move closer together in order to make space for someone else |
| **gain on** sb/sth | The helicopter could see that the police car was **gaining on** the robbers' car. | get nearer to someone or something that you are chasing (*upon* also possible) |

## C A long walk

We're having a great holiday. Yesterday we went for a long walk in the hills. It was longer than it needed to be because Tony misread the map and we walked quite a long way but then came to a big cliff and had to **double back**[1]. We saw lots of wildlife. In the early evening we **stumbled on**[2] some deer. At first they were startled and **drew back**[3] from us, but we stood still and they soon relaxed and went back to their grazing. We **stood** well **back** so as not to frighten them and watched them for some time. Then we realised that it was getting late and we'd better **push on**[4]. Anyway, we were **bowling along**[5] and making good progress but it was getting dark and I **tripped over**[6] a fallen branch. I thought I might have sprained my ankle but we managed to get home and it's fine today.

Seb

Mr. Yan
22 rue
Paris
FRANC

1 go back in the direction we'd come from
2 found/met by chance (*upon* also possible)
3 moved away because they were surprised or afraid
4 continue on our walk
5 (informal) moving quickly and energetically
6 fell because I accidentally hit my foot against something while walking

# Exercises

**46.1 Complete these sentences using the correct particles.**

1 I accidentally walked ................ ................ Kevin and Elaine the other day at the office and they were kissing each other!
2 They stole ................ in the middle of the night; nobody knew they had left.
3 I looked in the rear-view mirror and saw that the mysterious motorcyclist was gaining ................ me.
4 We all piled ................ the car but we had to squash................ as it was only small and there were five of us.
5 Oh! I didn't realise you were there! You shouldn't creep ................ ................ me like that!

**46.2 Complete these sentences with a verb from the opposite page.**

1 We all ...................... into the taxi and headed off to a club to end our perfect night out.
2 Old Mrs Gifford ...................... over the edge of the carpet and fell and hurt her ankle.
3 I don't think we have time to stop for lunch; we'd better ...................... on if we want to get there before it gets dark.
4 The fire chief told everyone to ...................... well back as there was the risk of an explosion.
5 His father, furious, told him to ...................... out of the house because he never wanted to see him again.
6 When I was putting some books in the attic, I ...................... on an old picture I hadn't noticed before.
7 Crossing the valley, we were ...................... along at a steady rate but then the car suddenly broke down as we went up a hill.
8 I suddenly realised I'd left my wallet in the café where we'd stopped for breakfast, so we had to ...................... back.

**46.3 Explain the play on words in these sentences. Use a dictionary if necessary.**

1 When he had finished his painting, the artist drew back to see his work from a distance.
2 When their bus broke down, the cricket team bowled along the road to make their match on time.
3 Squash up, kids, and when you're all sitting down, I'll give you some juice.
4 The twins set off in one direction but then doubled back to try to lose their pursuers.
5 The robbers stole away as soon as they heard the police car outside the bank.

**46.4 Complete the chart with four verbs which can be used with *back* to match the meanings in brackets. Then make four sentences, each using one of the verbs.**

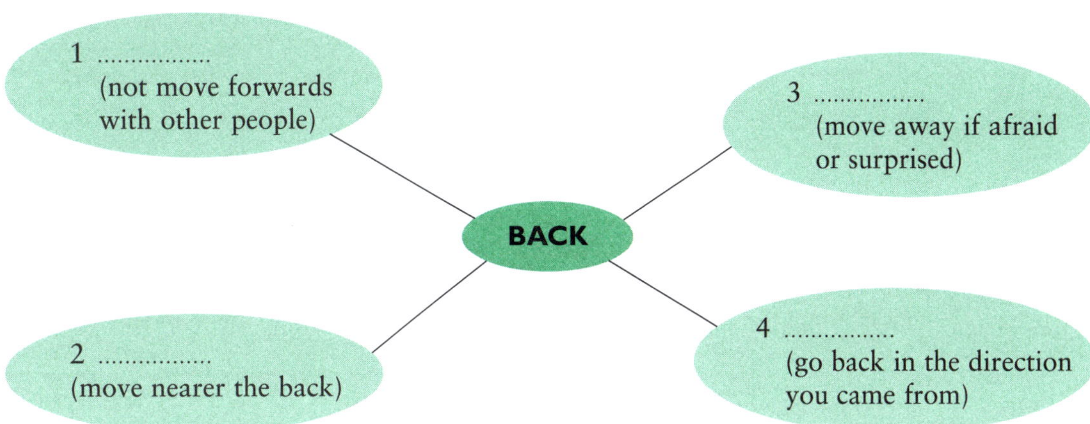

# 47 Nature

## A Animals and plants

Elephants **feed on** plants. By **pulling down** trees to eat leaves, **breaking off** branches and **pulling out** roots, they create clearings in which new vegetation can grow to provide nutrition in the future. However, their destructive habits have meant that a number of plants are in danger of **dying out**[1].

The cherry laurel requires consistently moist soil; do not allow it to **dry out**. In favourable areas it is very invasive; if you **cut** the tree **down**, it will still **send out** limbs from the root and **offshoots**[2] from the bottom of the stem. Very hard to **dig up**. The cherry laurel has small flowers which **come out** in late spring.

The South African secretary bird **preys on**[3] insects, snakes, tortoises and rats. Small prey are **picked up** in the bill and swallowed. Larger prey are first stamped to death and then eaten. The secretary bird also stamps its feet on the ground to **flush out**[4] prey.

1 becoming more and more rare and eventually disappearing completely
2 plants which have developed from a larger plant
3 catches for food
4 force an animal to come out of its hiding place

## B Water and sky

| *phrasal verb* | *example* | *definition of phrasal verb* |
|---|---|---|
| **dry up** | The river is in flood now – it's hard to believe it completely **dried up** six months ago. | disappear (used about water) |
| **freeze over** | In the far north, the sea **freezes over** for several months each year. | become covered with ice |
| **go out** / **come in** | When the tide **goes out**, we can look for shellfish. But we'll have to be careful as the tide **comes in** quickly here. | move further away from the beach / nearer the beach |
| **come out** | It is spectacular here at night when the stars **come out**. | appear in the sky (used of the sun, moon or stars) |
| **go in** | Let's go indoors now – the sun has **gone in** and it's getting chilly. | become hidden by a cloud |
| **overcast** | I don't want to go to the beach today as it is so **overcast**. | grey, covered in cloud (used about the sky) |
| **wash away** | An old car abandoned on the beach was **washed away** by the unusually high tide. | carry away by water |
| **eat away at** | The sea is **eating away at** the cliff and houses close to the edge are at risk. | gradually destroy by taking little bits at a time |

# Exercises

**47.1** **Complete these commentaries from television nature documentaries with the correct phrasal verbs. You are given the first letter each time.**

Here in this cold landscape of cliffs and stony beaches, these birds f................ ................ (1) the many fish which are found offshore. Seals also p................ ................ (2) the abundant fish stocks. It is hard to imagine that if global warming increases, these wonderful creatures may d................ ................ (3) and never be seen again at this latitude. Sea levels will rise and e................ ................ ................ (4) the cliffs and rocky shores, w................ ................ (5) their natural habitats forever. And, paradoxically, as the temperature and sea levels rise, some of the inland lakes may d................ ................ (6) altogether, leaving an arid landscape.

These elegant creatures p................ ................ (7) the higher branches of trees and eat the succulent leaves. In the course of their feeding, they often b................ the branches ................ (8) causing damage to the trees, and even more so by p................ ................ (9) the youngest saplings altogether. Fortunately, nature always revives, and the destroyed and damaged trees s................ ................ (10) new o................ (11) so that, in time, the forest renews itself. Only humans are the real enemy, c................ ................ (12) the trees and d................ ................ (13) the most precious plants to collect specimens, denuding the forest forever, and all for commercial gain.

**47.2** **Answer these questions using phrasal verbs or phrasal adjectives from the opposite page.**

1 What would happen to a pond if the temperature dropped to –10°C?
2 What might happen to a shallow lake if the weather is very hot and there is no rain for a long time?
3 What adjective can describe the sky when it is grey and covered in cloud?
4 Why is the sea not always at the same place on a beach?
5 If the police suspect that bank robbers are hiding in a forest, what might dogs help them to do?

**47.3** **Rewrite these sentences using phrasal verbs or phrasal adjectives from the opposite page.**

1 As night fell, the stars appeared.
2 The sun became hidden by a cloud and the temperature fell suddenly.
3 Cats (both large and small) lift their young with their teeth to move them around.
4 It was lovely and sunny this morning but now the sky is grey.
5 Many wild animals and plants are on the verge of becoming extinct.

**47.4** **Complete the encyclopaedia entry, using phrasal verbs from the box in the correct form. Use a dictionary if necessary.**

| watch over | take over | move in | bring up | fend for | chase out |
|---|---|---|---|---|---|

In many places, grey squirrels have ...................... ...................... (1) and ...................... the native red squirrels ...................... (2). They have then ...................... ...................... (3) their territory. Many animals ...................... ...................... (4) their young in a similar way to human parents, ...................... ...................... (5) them till they are mature; others leave their young to ...................... ...................... (6) themselves shortly after birth.

# 48 Weather

## A Rain and snow

| *phrasal verb* | *example* | *definition of phrasal verb* |
|---|---|---|
| **beat down** | Lying in bed I could hear the rain **beating down**. | come down in large amounts with force |
| **pelt down** | The rain was **pelting down** by the time we got to the top of the mountain. | (informal) fall very heavily |
| **come on** | As soon as we had left the shelter of the forest, the rain **came on**. | start |
| **hold off** | Fortunately the snow **held off** until we had got safely home. | not start, although you expect it to |
| **freeze up** | It was a very hard winter last year and many people had problems with pipes **freezing up**. | become blocked with ice and stop working |

## B Sun and clouds

If the sun **breaks through** (the clouds), it starts to appear from behind the clouds.

If the sun **beats down**, it shines very strongly and makes the air hot.

If some kind of bad weather such as clouds or fog **rolls in**, it appears in a large amount.

If cloud or smoke **blots out** the sun, it covers it and prevents it from being seen.

If windows or glasses **fog/mist/steam up**, they become covered with small drops of water and you can't see through them.

## C Metaphors

I suspected there would be trouble at the office as soon as the new boss **breezed in**[1] on his first day. He was very competent and he'd **breezed through**[2] the job interview apparently, but he had no patience at all for anyone less able and he had a very sharp tongue. I noticed that as soon as he spoke to anyone, their face **clouded over**[3]. He asked the office junior to explain some contradictory figures in such an aggressive manner that she **froze up**[4] and couldn't say a word. I could see her eyes **misting over**[5]. By the end of that first day, his PA had **stormed out**[6], saying she would never return. The rest of us got together in the evening and decided that we had no choice but to try to **freeze** him **out**[7]. We agreed only to speak to him if we absolutely had to.

1 walked in quickly and confidently (breeze = light wind)
2 (slightly informal) succeeded very easily
3 suddenly looked unhappy
4 became so afraid she couldn't do or say anything
5 filling with tears
6 left in an angry way
7 make him feel that he is not welcome by being unfriendly

# Exercises

**48.1** **Complete the text below, using the correct particles from A opposite.**

The weather forecast said that there would be rain later on but we were all hoping that it would hold ................ (1) until Julia's birthday barbecue was over. When we first arrived, the sun was beating ................ (2) and some people were too hot. But then grey clouds appeared and the rain came ................ (3). At first it was quite light but then it began to pelt ................ (4). We had to cook indoors but Julia wasn't too disappointed.

**48.2** **Mark these sentences with a ☺ if you are happy in this situation or a ☹ if you are not happy in this situation. Explain your answers.**

1 Your pipes at home freeze up while you are on a skiing holiday.
2 You receive a letter that makes your face cloud over.
3 You are walking by the sea when fog rolls in.
4 You can hear the rain beating down outside as you sit by a big log fire.
5 You are on a long country walk and the rain holds off.
6 You have to give a speech at a friend's wedding and you freeze up.
7 You breeze through an important exam.
8 You storm out of a meeting.
9 A group of friends start to freeze you out.
10 You are sitting on the beach and the sun is beating down.

**48.3** **Write a sentence about each picture, using a phrasal verb from the opposite page.**

1 

2 

3 

4 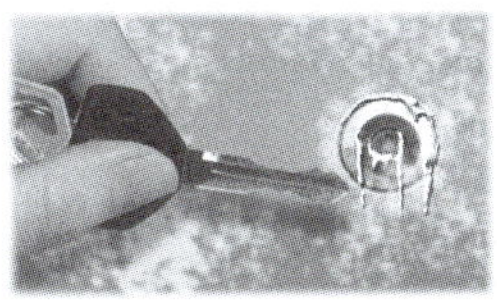

5 

6 

1 ..........................................................................
..........................................................................
2 ..........................................................................
..........................................................................
3 ..........................................................................
..........................................................................
4 ..........................................................................
..........................................................................
5 ..........................................................................
..........................................................................
6 ..........................................................................
..........................................................................

**48.4** **Complete these sentences, using a phrasal verb from the opposite page in an appropriate form. Add any other words that are needed.**

1 Jack arrived an hour late but he didn't seem worried; he just ...................................... .
2 It was such a sad film. When the hero died I could feel my eyes ...................................... .
3 Whenever I go from a cold street into a heated shop my glasses ...................................... .
4 I can see a little bit of blue sky. I think the sun is trying to ...................................... .
5 We're going to an open air concert tonight. I hope the rain ...................................... .
6 I think the weather's changing for the worse. Look at those clouds ...................................... .
7 Don't worry about your driving test. I'm sure you'll ...................................... .
8 I always get really nervous before oral exams. I'm afraid I'll ...................................... .

# 49 Places

## A Tourist brochures

The unspoilt little market town of Steeple Bunting stretches out along the winding River Tare. The town is **steeped in**[1] history and great care has been taken to ensure that modern buildings **blend in**[2] well and do not **encroach on**[3] the 16th-century centre. A particularly well-preserved building from that period is Elderflower Cottage, a delightful half-timbered house **set back**[4] from the High Street. The beauty of this white-walled cottage is **set off**[5] by the colourful flower gardens which surround it and visitors must also not miss the walled herb garden which **opens off** the rose garden. There are many other must-see sights in Steeple Bunting and the town is **dotted with**[6] pleasant cafés where you can relax if you just want to sit and **soak up**[7] the atmosphere. The town is **bursting with**[8] tourists at the weekend and visitors who prefer to avoid crowds are advised to come during the week.

1 has a lot of (collocates strongly with *history*, also with *tradition*)
2 look similar, do not seem very different
3 advance beyond proper limits
4 a little distance from
5 made to look even more attractive
6 has many, all over the place
7 enjoy an experience
8 very full with (only used in continuous form)

## B Improving houses and towns

### KINGSMILL RENOVATIONS TO BEGIN NEXT WEEK

The **run-down**[1] Kingsmill area near the city's football ground is at last about to be **done up**[2]. Signs have **gone up**[3] around the area indicating that work will start next Monday. The first stage of work will affect the buildings which **back onto** the football ground and Stadium Road will be **closed off** from Monday morning while the area is **reduced to** rubble[4]. Drivers wishing to access the stadium car park will need to approach it by Grant Lane, which **branches off** Rampart Street just after the petrol station.

Local resident Hilda James (74) told us, 'I'll be glad to see the back of the **boarded-up**[5] windows in the area. It's very dangerous – a ceiling **fell in** once when my grandsons were playing in one of the abandoned buildings.'

Local architects Taylor and Summers have been employed to design the reconstruction and readers can visit their office to examine the plans showing how the area will be **laid out**[6] and to see a large-scale **mock-up**[7]. Richard Taylor commented, 'The renovations will inevitably be expensive but we hope that the costs will to some extent be **offset**[8] by the use of reclaimed sandstone, slate and even rubble.'

1 shabby, in disrepair
2 repaired, improved
3 been fixed
4 made into a pile of bricks and stones (a strong collocation but note also: Sally was **reduced** to tears = Sally started crying)
5 covered with pieces of wood
6 arranged, structured
7 model showing how something will look when it is built
8 compensated for

**TIP** If you notice a phrasal verb in a text, it may be useful to copy out the whole sentence. This can help you to be able to use it as well as understand it.

# Exercises

## 49.1 Complete these two emails, using phrasal verbs or adjectives from the opposite page.

Hi Rosanne,

Here I am in my new flat. It's in an old house ................................ (1) back from the road in a big garden, on the top of a hill. The town ................................ (2) out below us. It's an old town, ................................ (3) in history, but ................................ (4) with all the excitement of a big modern city. Sometimes I just stroll through the streets ................................ (5) up the atmosphere. From the back of the house we look up into the hills, which are ................................ (6) with little white houses. The road that runs past our house branches ................................ (7) down to the river, so it's a nice place to go for a walk. I hope you can come and see me.

All the best,

Pedro

Hi Pedro,

Now you've left university you can live in luxury, but I'm still a poor student. June and I have moved into our accommodation for this year. It's in a rather ................................ (8) part of town which was rich and prosperous years ago, but now there are lots of ................................ (9) shops and cheap restaurants. We're in a house that backs ................................ (10) an old factory whose roof has fallen ................................ (11) and next to that was another building which has been completely ................................ (12) to rubble and the area is all closed ................................ (13). So it couldn't be more different from your view! The flat itself is OK. There's a living room and a small kitchen which opens ................................ (14) it, then two bedrooms and the bathroom. We've talked to the landlord and he's going to let us do it ................................ (15) and he'll pay for the paint and stuff. It may not be the Mediterranean, but it's home.

Love,

Rosanne

## 49.2 Correct the mistakes with the phrasal verbs in these sentences.

1 New housing developments are encroaching against the countryside on the edge of town.
2 Those climbing red roses really set that old white cottage out, don't they?
3 The architects made a large-scale mock-on of the new shopping centre.
4 The plain lines of the marble walls are upset by the ornate windows; together they produce a harmonious building.
5 This plan shows how the area will be lied out when it is redeveloped.
6 Signs have gone out round the area to be demolished warning the public to keep away.
7 The 1960s buildings do not blend on very well with the older houses around them.
8 The whole area is steeped with history.

## 49.3 Answer these questions.

1 Can you name a modern building that blends in well with older surroundings?
2 What is the nearest place to you that is sometimes bursting with tourists?
3 To what extent do you think that the place you live in is steeped in tradition?
4 What does your own home back onto?

**FOLLOW UP**

Look at tourist brochures or websites written in English for any city or town you are interested in. Note any phrasal verbs you find.

# 50 Transport

## A Driving

Read about Barry's nightmare car journey and note the phrasal verbs.

The whole journey was a complete nightmare. I'd only been going five minutes on the motorway when somebody **cut in**[1] on me and I had to brake really quickly to avoid an accident, but that was only the start of it. A bit further on I **pulled out**[2] to overtake a big lorry but as I did, my engine just died. I tried revving the engine and after a couple of seconds it started again, but I had to **change down**[3] and get back into the slow lane and go very slowly indeed. Because I was so slow, I was **flagged down**[4] by a police officer who checked the car and told me that one of my tyres was worn. He said it wasn't illegal and let me continue but warned me to get it changed. The car started again without any problems, so I set off again, **picked up**[5] speed, and after a couple of miles, guess what, the worn tyre **blew out**[6]! The police were right. So I changed the tyre, which was another half hour wasted. Then I **picked up** a student who was hitch-hiking – I felt sorry for him. After a while we **branched off**[7] the motorway and I left him where he wanted to be and went to a nearby café for a cup of tea. When I came out, someone had **blocked** me **in**[8]. Then to cap it all, I realised the student had stolen my camera from the back seat!

1 suddenly drove in front of me, not leaving enough space between the two vehicles
2 drove onto a road or onto a part of the road where the traffic is moving faster
3 put a vehicle into a lower gear, usually in order to go slower
4 made to stop by waving at the driver
5 started to go faster
6 suddenly burst
7 turned onto a smaller road
8 put a car or other vehicle so close to another vehicle that it cannot drive away

## B Other phrasal verbs connected with transport

Five planes were **stacked up** over the airport waiting for permission to land. [flying over an airport at different heights waiting to be told they can land]

Two young men had **stowed away** on the ferry, hoping to enter the country illegally. Police said they had already arrested more than 20 **stowaways** at the port this year. [hidden on a ship, aircraft, or other vehicle, in order to travel secretly or without paying; person who does this]

There's a popular TV programme where celebrities pretend they have been **cast away** on a desert island and have to survive. [left on an island with no other people after swimming from a ship that is sinking]

She was **knocked over** by a cyclist and broke her arm. [hit by a vehicle and injured or killed]

A police car **pulled** us **over** to the side of the road and two police officers searched the car.

The traffic lights were very slow to change and all around me impatient drivers were **revving up**. [make a car's engine work faster while the car is not moving]

# Exercises

**50.1** **Look at A. Choose the correct word to complete these sentences.**

1 The train started slowly but soon *revved* / *picked* / *pulled* up speed.
2 I hate drivers who *cut* / *block* / *flag* in on you when you're driving on a motorway.
3 You *pull* / *blow* / *change* down when you want to reduce your speed.
4 I wish my neighbour wouldn't *rev* / *blow* / *change* up outside my window early in the morning.
5 Take care when you *blow* / *change* / *pull* out to overtake.

**50.2** **Look at these pictures and then complete the sentences about them below, using phrasal verbs from the opposite page.**

1

3

5

2

4

6

1 The police officer is ..........
2 The driver is ..........
3 The aeroplanes are ..........
4 The tyre has ..........
5 The car is ..........
6 The car has been ..........

**50.3** **Put the words in the correct order to make sentences.**

1 down / The / flagged / on / a / police / ten / found / lorry / board / stowaways / and
2 bedroom / car / was / a / I / woken / revving / by / window / up / outside / my
3 car / on / caused / cutting / an / by / nearly / accident / in / us / That
4 very / blew / motorway / out / when / I / was / frightened / the / tyre / my / on

**50.4** **Complete these sentences, using a phrasal verb from the opposite page.**

1 The boy managed to .......... .......... on a plane to Australia and was only discovered when he arrived in Sydney.
2 The old man was .......... .......... by a car that was speeding away from a burglary.
3 I couldn't get out of the car park – someone had .......... me .......... .
4 A police officer .......... Kerry .......... and fined her for driving too fast.
5 *Robinson Crusoe* is about someone who was .......... .......... on a desert island.
6 Take that little road that .......... .......... the main road just after the railway bridge.
7 I'm taking my car to work tomorrow so I can .......... you .......... on the way.
8 I hate it when your plane has to spend ages .......... .......... waiting to land.

**FOLLOW UP**

People often talk about journeys they have made. Write sentences about your journey to work or school or about any other interesting journeys you have made using some of the phrasal verbs on this page – together with any other phrasal verbs connected with travel that you know.

# 51 The news

## A How journalists get the news

Some news comes from press releases that are **put out** by companies or organisations. However, journalists also **pick up**[1] stories from their contacts. Occasionally a story **gets out**[2] when a politician or film star **confides in**[3] someone who is not discreet. Sometimes a rumour starts and journalists **sound out**[4] people in the know to check its truth. It may sometimes be difficult for them to **root out**[5] the information they want but journalists get very good at **worming** stories **out of**[6] people who don't want to talk to them. Sometimes they may **stake out**[7] their potential subject's house until they get the story they want. In fact, the ability to **ferret out**[8] a story may be as important for a journalist as the ability to **write** it **up** well.

1 learn by chance
2 becomes known (of something secret)
3 tells something private or secret to someone
4 get an opinion from
5 search for and find something that is difficult to find
6 getting information from someone who does not want to give it
7 watch continuously
8 find out something after searching for it

## B Political news

**PENSIONS PROTEST**

A major protest took place yesterday after news **leaked out**[1] about the government's plans to raise the retirement age. Workers of all ages **walked out** from factories and offices to **join in** public demonstrations. Police attempts to **head off** the main protest march failed but fortunately all the demonstrations **passed off** without any major incidents. The government has denied that it is planning to use force to **put down** any future protests.

1 became known

**BROOKES JOINS INFLUENTIAL COMMITTEE**

Tim Brookes, the MP for Hamley, has been voted on to the Environmental Committee. Brookes has been an MP since his party first **got in** in 1997 and he claims that his main ambition has always been to **get onto** this important committee. There were a number of powerful contenders for the place which became free when Dan Herzog retired but Brookes succeeded in **whipping up** considerable support and won the coveted place. Brookes' critics say that he has a tendency to **dumb down** complex issues but he argues that anything that gets people talking about the environment is worthwhile.

## C The police and the army in the news

| *sentences from newspapers* | *meaning of phrasal verb* |
|---|---|
| If there are not enough voluntary troops, the government will have to **call** people **up**. | order people to join the armed forces |
| The new general **joined up** when he was 21. | joined the army |
| The enemy continues to **hold out** in the south. | defend itself against attack |
| The army is to be **sent in** to help earthquake victims. | (of people with special skills) sent to an area |
| Troops are expected to **pull out** before May. | move out of an area |
| Two planes were **shot down** last night. | destroyed by enemy fire |
| The kidnapper **gave** himself **up** last night. | allowed the police to catch him |
| The police will **move in** if the situation escalates. | go to a place to deal with a difficult situation |

# Exercises

**51.1** **An experienced journalist is talking to a new young reporter. Complete his advice below using phrasal verbs from A. You are given the first letter of each phrasal verb.**

A lot of your time will be spent trying to r................ ................ (1) information, and that can be boring – going to libraries, surfing the Internet, reading press releases p................ ................ (2) by government departments, that sort of thing. It's also important to hang out with other journalists and see what you can p................ ................ (3) from them. You might discover a story that has l................ ................ (4). The secret with celebrities is to get them to c................ ................ (5) you. If they just think you're trying to w................ private information ................ ................ (6) them to create a scandal, they won't give you anything. And they hate it when journalists s................ ................ (7) their homes. With politicians, it's best to s................ them ................ (8) about various topics to find out what they want to talk about; don't be aggressive, that won't get you anywhere. Just like the celebrities, if they think you're trying to f................ ................ (9) a story that's going to g................ ................ (10) and cause them embarrassment, they'll keep quiet and you'll get nothing. And take your time w................ your stories ................ (11). Don't rush it.

**51.2** **Match each headline 1–7 with an extract from the article a–g.**

1 **OIL PROTEST PASSES OFF PEACEFULLY**
2 **UN TROOPS TO PULL OUT OF PHRASALIA**
3 **ARMY MOVES IN TO QUELL DISTURBANCES IN NORTHERN PROVINCE**
4 **RESERVISTS CALLED UP AS SITUATION WORSENS**
5 **PAINTSHOP WORKERS WALK OUT AT AUTO PLANT**
6 **SPECIAL FORCES ATTEMPT TO HEAD OFF REBELS IN QUESA REGION**
7 **UNIVERSITIES ACCUSED OF DUMBING DOWN ENTRANCE EXAMS**

a) 5,000 men have been ordered to report to local bases for immediate posting to the front.
b) The aim is to push back the advance and to restore government control.
c) 2,000 people assembled calmly outside the Ministry and chanted slogans.
d) The riots had reached a level which could no longer be tolerated, the defence minister said.
e) Their work was now complete and had been a success, a spokesperson said.
f) Pass rates have increased by a huge 50% this year.
g) 250 downed tools and started an unofficial strike this morning.

**51.3** **Rewrite the underlined parts of these sentences, using a phrasal verb from the opposite page. Make any other necessary changes.**

1 The conservatives <u>won the election</u> in 2002.
2 A helicopter was <u>destroyed by enemy fire whilst in flight</u> yesterday.
3 My great-grandfather <u>became a soldier</u> when he was only 16.
4 The kidnappers <u>surrendered to the police</u> just after midday.
5 The rebels <u>successfully defended themselves</u> for six weeks.
6 The government has <u>ordered</u> a group of experts <u>to go</u> to assess the flood damage.
7 The government <u>crushed</u> the rebellion using massive force.
8 Mr Fleet is trying to <u>arouse</u> some enthusiasm for the concert he is trying to organise.
9 Hundreds of people <u>participated</u> in the celebrations outside the palace.
10 Ed <u>got a place on</u> the party's national committee.

**FOLLOW UP**

Phrasal verbs are very common in newspaper headlines – perhaps because they are often short and dramatic words. See how many you can find in any one copy of a newspaper. Make a note of any interesting ones.

# 52 Secrets and lies

## A News headlines

INVESTIGATION BEARS OUT[1] FRAUD CLAIM

1 proves that something that someone has said or written is true, or say that someone is telling the truth

COMPANY HUSHED UP[2] FINANCIAL SCANDAL

2 stopped the public from finding out about something bad that had happened

GOVERNMENT URGED TO LEVEL WITH[3] PUBLIC OVER HEALTH RISKS

3 (informal) tell the truth about something

PRIME MINISTER ACCUSED OF PAPERING OVER[4] CABINET DISAGREEMENT

4 hiding a difficulty to try to make people believe that there is no problem

MINISTERS TRIED TO COVER UP[5] ARMS SCANDAL, SAYS OFFICIAL REPORT

5 stop people from discovering the truth about something bad

AGENTS SPIED ON[6] UN DIPLOMATS: FORMER SPY BREAKS SILENCE

6 watched secretly in order to discover information about them

## B Email gossip

Hi Jim,

I wasn't at all surprised to hear that Ken and Maria are getting engaged, were you? The way they've been looking at each other was a real **give-away**[1], wasn't it? And Maria almost **let** the secret **out** a couple of weeks ago anyway, even though they continued to **make out**[2] that they were just good friends. They seem to be crazy about each other!

Steve

1 (informal) something that makes you aware of a fact that someone else was trying to keep secret
2 claim falsely that something is true

Dear Kim,

I need to **confide in**[3] you. I've been suspecting for a long time that one of my employees, George, has been stealing from the till at work, so I actually hired a private detective. He **dug up**[4] a few unpleasant facts, I'm afraid. George has had a number of convictions for theft already. But the detective hasn't managed to prove that he is stealing from us. So I've decided to just **play along**[5] and pretend I don't know, to see if I can **catch** him **out**[6], you know, just see if he **gives** anything **away**[7] without realising it. Am I doing the right thing, do you think, or should I confront him?

Rick

3 tell someone things that you keep secret from other people
4 discovered new facts about a person or situation after a lot of searching
5 (informal) pretend to agree with someone, or to do what someone wants for a short time, in order to get something from them or to avoid making them angry
6 discover that someone is lying or doing something wrong
7 lets someone know something that should be kept secret, often by mistake

# Exercises

**52.1** **Answer these questions about the headlines in A opposite.**

1 What was the aim of the investigation and what did it discover?
2 Why might the company have wanted to hush up the scandal?
3 What is the third headline implying about the government?
4 Why might the Prime Minister want to paper over what was happening in the Cabinet?
5 Does it sound as if the report supports or condemns the ministers' behaviour?
6 What has the former spy just admitted?

**52.2** **Match the beginning of each sentence with its ending.**

| | |
|---|---|
| 1 Fortunately, my research bore | a) in someone. |
| 2 Please just play | b) up a good scandal. |
| 3 I wish I could confide | c) out your secret. |
| 4 Journalists love to dig | d) on her. |
| 5 I'm so sorry I let | e) with her. |
| 6 We did all we could to hush | f) out my original hypothesis. |
| 7 My girlfriend begged me to level | g) along with the story I tell Mary. |
| 8 Tanya accused Josef of spying | h) up the scandal in the company. |

**52.3** **Correct the ten mistakes with particles in this paragraph.**

As journalists, it is our job to try to dig off stories that dishonest people are trying to cover over. Sometimes we are accused of spying at innocent people but surely it is our duty not to allow people to paper up their scandals. Often it is not at all difficult to learn secrets. People are often eager to confide with someone who is willing to lend a sympathetic ear. Or they let off a secret without realising it. Little things like a blush or a quick glance at someone else can be a real give-out to an experienced reporter. Of course, sometimes people try to make over that they have nothing to hide and then it can be a good idea to play on with them up to a certain point. Then you suddenly take them by surprise with an unexpected question and in this way you can often catch them across.

**52.4** **Which word could fit into all the sentences in each set? Look in your dictionary for any new meanings.**

1 The lawyer tried to ................ the accused out in a lie.
Be aware of exam questions designed to ................ you out.
Every year unexpected snowstorms ................ people out.

2 Helga likes to ................ out that she has a very important job.
Can you ................ out that small yacht on the horizon?
Who should I ................ this cheque out to?

3 Please take care not to ................ my secret out.
This skirt is too tight – I'll have to ................ it out.
Don't forget to ................ the cat out before you go to bed.

4 The way his hands were shaking ................ away his nervousness.
The company ................ away six new cars as part of their advertising campaign.
It was meant as a surprise but Irena ................ the game away.

# 53 Rules and laws

## A Obeying rules and laws

Judge: Well, Mr Smith. I am pleased to say the police have at last **caught up with**[1] you.
Mr Smith: But, I'm innocent, My Lord. Breaking the law would be **going against** my principles.
Judge: Well, several of your fellow criminals have **informed on**[2] you.
Mr Smith: Just wait till I see them!
Judge: They say you make a habit of persuading old ladies to **sign over**[3] their property to you.
Mr Smith: But they did it of their own free will.
Judge: I'm going to have to **impose** a substantial sentence **on**[4] you.
Mr Smith: But what if I promise to **abide by**[5] the law in the future?
Judge: Well, you certainly need to do that and, who knows, if you **adhere to**[6] the rules in prison, you might be **let out** early but I'm certainly not going to **let** you **off** your punishment.

1 managed to catch
2 given information to the police about someone who has done something wrong
3 give someone else legal rights to something
4 give someone a punishment
5 (formal) obey
6 (formal) obey

## B Describing rules and laws

### PROGRESS ON GAMBLING

The government has long been anxious to introduce a new law relating to gambling. The intention is to **toughen up**[1] the existing legislation, making all types of gambling **come under** the authority of the Gambling Control Body, giving the GCB considerable powers and **providing for**[2] the imprisonment of serious offenders. The initial proposals for the law were **thrown out**[3] at the committee stage. However, some modifications were made and the new proposals **went through** the committee stage last week. The next step is for them to be **voted on** in Parliament. It is expected that they will **get through** without difficulty, as there is general cross-party agreement that the current laws have too many loop-holes and should be **tightened up**[4]. Once passed, the new regulations will be **rolled out**[5] gradually over the coming year.

1 make more limiting and difficult to avoid
2 (formal) allowing to happen
3 rejected
4 made stricter
5 introduced

**TIP** Write sentences using phrasal verbs on little cards, missing out the preposition or particle. Write the missing word on the back of the card. Test yourself regularly using the cards.

# Exercises

**53.1** **Are you a good citizen? Complete this questionnaire and then answer the questions.**

## How law-abiding are you?

Work out your score then turn to page 157 to find out if you are a good citizen.

1 Have the police or a court ever ...................... (1) a fine on you? Yes: 0 No: 2
2 Do you ...................... (2) to speed limits? Rarely or never: 0 Mostly: 1 Always: 2
3 Would it go ...................... (3) your principles to take items from your place of work for your own private use? No: 0 Yes: 2 Depends on value: 1
4 Do you abide ...................... (4) parking laws? Rarely or never: 0 Mostly: 1 Always: 2
5 If you knew that a friend or family member had committed a crime, would you ...................... (5) on them? No: 0 Depends on how serious: 1 Yes: 2
6 If you park illegally in a foreign country because you genuinely don't understand the rules, do you think you should be ...................... (6) off or punished? Not punished: 0 Punished: 1

**Your total:**

**53.2** **Correct the mistakes with the phrasal verbs in these sentences.**

1 The new act went across Parliament last week and will become law on 1 January.
2 The anti-litter laws should be tightened in; as it is now, nobody is ever prosecuted.
3 He went on a two-year crime spree before the police finally caught up to him.
4 She avoided tax by signing out her property to her two sons.
5 The new law provides with gaol sentences of up to ten years for repeat offenders.
6 Building regulations come by local government rather than national or European law.
7 The bill was passed by the Lower Chamber but was thrown away by the Senate and never became law.
8 The bill will be voted to in Parliament next week and the government hopes it will get across without too much opposition. [two mistakes]
9 If trials prove successful, the government intends to roll in the scheme across the whole country next year.
10 He was sentenced to three years in prison but he'll probably be let off in 18 months.

**53.3** **Rewrite the underlined parts of these sentences, using a phrasal verb from the opposite page. Make any other necessary changes.**

1 The former CEO of Wilson & Wallace has been <u>released from prison</u> after serving a ten-year sentence.
2 If you don't <u>follow</u> the health and safety regulations, you will be punished.
3 The government plans to <u>make</u> the existing laws <u>more strict</u>.
4 The law reforming the Health Service <u>was passed by</u> Parliament with a large majority.
5 Henry's criminal activity was discovered when his neighbours <u>told the police about</u> him.

**53.4** **Here are some more phrasal verbs connected with rules and laws. Work out from the context what they mean and rewrite the sentences replacing the underlined phrasal expressions with a word or phrase that means the same.**

1 He was tried last week, found guilty and <u>sent down</u> for five years.
2 This government has <u>brought in</u> more new laws than any other in the last 50 years.
3 The new law will <u>come into force</u> in March.
4 The military authorities <u>put out</u> an order banning demonstrations in the area around the parliament buildings.

# 54 Technology

## A Computers

Several verbs related to computers are based on the verb *go*, meaning access or use something.

You can **go onto** a computer, the Internet, a website.
You can **go into** a menu, a programme, a different window.
You can **go to** an item on a menu, a particular web page or part of a page, or a link.

Note how phrasal verbs are used in these extracts from an online computer helpline.

***Query:*** How do I stop **pop-up adverts**[1] from **coming up** every time **I go onto** the Internet?
***Answer:*** **Go into** the tools menu on your browser and click 'disable pop-ups'.

***Query:*** When I try to **print off** more than one copy of a document, a warning light **comes on** on the printer or the printer just **goes off** altogether and I have to switch it on again.
***Answer:*** Try re-installing the printer driver. You can **call up** the information you need for your printer by opening the control panel and then **going to** 'printers', then clicking 'help'.

***Query:*** I want to **set up** a web cam. How do I do it?
***Answer:*** Firstly, plug the web cam into the back of your computer. Then, click on your taskbar at the bottom of your screen. A **pop-up menu**[2] will appear. Choose 'install new hardware' and follow the instructions.

***Query:*** How can I get my photos to **fade in** and **fade out**[3] when I show them on my computer?
***Answer:*** Just right-click on the folder and choose 'Slide show'. They'll fade in and out automatically.

***Query:*** There was a power cut the other day while I was working on my computer and a whole load of data I hadn't managed to save got **wiped out**[4]. How can I avoid this in future?
***Answer:*** You can buy a piece of equipment which will automatically provide **back-up** power.

1 unwanted advertisements which suddenly appear on the screen when you are online
2 a list of choices which appears on a computer screen
3 become gradually louder or brighter (**fade in**) or quieter or darker (**fade out**)
4 accidently removed from a computer

## B Other technical equipment

When the battery is low, the whole unit simply **plugs into** the mains supply to recharge.

**Tune into** any radio station anywhere in the world with Worldband software. You can **pick up** thousands of stations 24 hours a day.

No need to spend hours **wiring** everything **up**[1]. Bluetooth means you just switch on and connect!

1 connecting something to a piece of electrical equipment by using electrical wires

Most scanners take up to a minute to **warm up**[2]. The Zono 844B takes just 10 seconds.

2 start working so that it becomes warm enough to work well

Looking for a photocopier that doesn't **seize up**[3] every time you change the paper? The new Jentra 850 has a unique paper-flow controller.

3 stop moving or working in the normal way

# Exercises

## 54.1 Complete these sentences with phrasal verbs from A opposite.

1 At the end of a scene in a radio play the actors' voices often ...................... ...................... .
2 When you bought your new laptop, did you find it easy to ...................... ...................... ?
3 Could you ...................... ...................... three copies of the document, please?
4 The network crashed this morning and ...................... ...................... all my work.
5 When using this program, you can ...................... ...................... the dictionary whenever you need it.
6 If you click on any icon on the taskbar at the bottom of the screen, a ...................... menu appears on your screen.

## 54.2 Choose the correct word to complete these sentences.

1 With my new radio I can ...................... far more stations than I used to be able to get.
a) tune in b) pick up c) set up
2 If a machine stops moving or working normally, you can say that it has ...................... .
a) cut off b) wiped out c) seized up
3 Okay, if you want to create a template, go ........... Word and open the File menu.
a) onto b) in c) into
4 I'm going to have to get my printer repaired – it keeps going ........... for no apparent reason.
a) on b) off c) out
5 Please could you help me ...................... Internet access on my new computer?
a) set up b) tune in c) pick up
6 Whenever Dave is abroad he ...................... the BBC World Service to listen to the news.
a) seizes up b) tunes into c) goes onto

## 54.3 Are these sentences true or false about the computer that you usually work on?

1 Pop-ups come up every time you go on the Internet.
2 You create bullet points by going into the Format menu and clicking on Bullets and Numbering.
3 Your printer plugs into the back of your monitor.
4 You can pick up radio stations from all over the world.
5 It takes about a minute for your machine to warm up.
6 It makes an automatic back-up of files on a regular basis.

## 54.4 Complete each sentence in an appropriate way, using one of the phrasal verbs from the opposite page and any other words that you need.

1 The advantage of a Bluetooth connection is that you don't ........................................................................ .
2 You can print a document by selecting the print icon or by ........................................................................ .
3 It's quite easy to use a web cam once you have ........................................................................ .
4 Whenever I switch on my new computer it takes quite a long time ........................................................................ .
5 I can use this cable to listen to my MP3 player in the car by ........................................................................ .
6 If your printer is beginning to run out of ink, then a warning light ........................................................................ .

**FOLLOW UP** Find an article online about a computer, camera, mobile phone, MP3 player or other piece of technology that you are interested in. Does it contain any examples of phrasal verbs? If so, note them down in their context.

# 55 Food and drink

## A Eating

### Have fun with your food

***Readers' tips for enjoying mealtimes.***

It's better to have good big meals than just **pick at**[1] things all day.

Don't **gobble** your food **down**[2] – take your time, enjoy it. If you **wolf** it **down**[3], you won't even taste what you're eating.

Don't just **eat in**[4] every day; spoil yourself at least once a week by having a meal in a restaurant. Or if you feel like staying at home, **send out for**[5] something.

Have friends round and **serve up** something special.

For an easy meal, just buy lots of pizzas, **slice** them **up** and let everyone **help** themselves **to**[6] what they want.

Make sure you're aware of what foods **agree with** you and what don't. Avoid anything that **disagrees with**[7] you – even if it tastes good. You'll regret it later.

**Cut out**[8] **fry-ups**[9] and eat more salads – you're bound to feel healthier.

Eat lots of raw vegetables – they will **fill** you **up**[10] without making you **put on** weight.

1 eat small amounts
2 (informal) eat very fast
3 (informal) eat very fast
4 eat at home
5 phone a restaurant and ask for food to be delivered to you
6 put on a plate for oneself
7 makes you feel slightly ill or uncomfortable
8 stop eating
9 (UK, informal) quick meal made of fried food
10 make you feel that you've eaten enough

## B Drinking

| *phrasal verb* | *example* | *definition of phrasal verb* |
|---|---|---|
| **wash down** sth or **wash** sth **down** | Have a drink of milk to **wash down** the tablet. | help you swallow it |
| **drink to** sb/sth | Let's raise a glass and **drink to** the happy couple! | hold up your glass before drinking from it in order to wish someone success or happiness |
| **dip** sth **in** (sth) | She loves **dipping** a chocolate biscuit **in** her tea. | quickly put it in and take it out again |
| **soak up** | Cook the lentils until they **soak up** half the liquid. | absorb |
| **water down** | Neat whisky is very strong – you should **water** it **down**. | make it less strong by adding water or other liquid |
| **spill over** | Harry darling, hold your juice properly. It's **spilling over** the edge of the glass. | flow over the edge |

**TIP** A number of the words in B can also be used metaphorically. Anger can **spill over**, you can **soak up** an atmosphere and plans or suggestions can be **watered down**. Learning the literal and metaphorical uses together may help you to remember these expressions.

# Exercises

**55.1** **Complete these dialogues using phrasal verbs from the opposite page so that the second speaker agrees with and repeats more or less what the first speaker says.**

1 Tina: The kids eat so fast! I'm sure it can't be good for them.
Ron: Yes, they do tend to ...................... / ...................... their food ...................... .
(Give two possible answers.)

2 Vivian: Polly just eats tiny amounts, no wonder she's so thin.
Ed: Yes, she just ...................... ...................... her food like a bird.

3 Bill: Those prawns made me feel a bit sick.
Jenny: Yes, they ...................... ...................... me too. I don't feel too good either.

4 Arthur: I think we should stop eating burgers; they're not good for us.
Shona: You're right. We should ...................... them ...................... and eat more salads.

5 Ahmed: These trousers don't fit me any more. They must have shrunk.
Louise: No, I'm afraid you've ...................... ...................... a bit of weight.

6 Tim: Shall we eat at home tonight? We could order something from a takeaway.
Harriet: Yes, let's ...................... ...................... .We can ...................... ...................... for a pizza or something.

**55.2** **Read the remarks by different people and then answer the questions below.**

Roger: I enjoyed it, but I couldn't eat one bit more.
Liz: We toasted Kevin and wished him well in his new job.
Aine: The smoked salmon made me feel unwell. I shouldn't have eaten it.
Gavin: She gave me some sushi. It was the first time I'd ever tasted it.
Zubaida: I took a big slice of cake.

| | |
|---|---|
| 1 Who ate something that didn't agree with them? | |
| 2 Who helped themselves to something? | |
| 3 Who ate something that filled them up? | |
| 4 Who was served up something new? | |
| 5 Who drank to someone? | |

**55.3** **Complete the word puzzle.**

Across
2 Do you ................ your biscuits in tea?
3 We ................ the meal down with lemonade.
6 She's put ................ a lot of weight.
7 ................ the cake up and give everyone a piece.

Down
1 Oh no! The soup's about to ................ over the top of the pan!
3 This juice is too strong. I'll ................ it down.
4 Have some bread to ................ up the rest of the sauce.
5 Particle that goes with *water* and *wash*.

**55.4** **Name a food or drink that ...**

1 often disagrees with people
2 can be sliced up
3 is best watered down
4 fills you up
5 you should cut down on
6 people often send out for

# 56 Come

## A Typical meanings of *come* in phrasal verbs

You may have already met some phrasal verbs with *come* in this book or elsewhere. For example, **come in** [start speaking during a discussion (Unit 12) or, for the sea, come nearer to the beach or coast (Unit 47)], **come at** somebody [move towards someone in order to attack them (Unit 22)], **come at** something [think about something in a particular way (Unit 25)] **come down** [pass from one generation to another so that it continues (Unit 11) or, for a price or level, become lower (Unit 11)].

*Come* typically expresses movement and the particle shows the direction of the movement. **Come in** above suggests a person 'entering' a discussion. **Come at** someone suggests directing oneself at/towards someone and **come at** something suggests directing one's thoughts to a particular subject. **Come down** suggests moving through time (from the more distant past towards the present).

## B More phrasal verbs with *come*

Look at these extracts from two interviews for *Policy and Finance* magazine.

Interviewer: You are often seen as a survivor. How did you survive your difficult second term in government? Was it just luck?

Politician: Luck? No, luck doesn't **come into it**[1]. You have to *work* in politics. As you know, the party **came in for**[2] a lot of criticism on its tax policy and was also **coming under**[3] attack from pensioners' groups. We were **coming across**[4] as insensitive to ordinary people's needs and problems, so we needed new ideas. I **came up against**[5] critics in my own party, and it was a difficult period, but we **came through**[6] it because we were strong and determined to succeed.

1 (usually negative) have an influence
2 received (collocates with *criticism* or *praise*)
3 getting a lot of
4 being seen by others
5 faced
6 managed to get to the end of a difficult situation

Interviewer: You once **came out with**[1] a famous remark that surprised everyone: 'Capitalism is dead.' Do you still believe that?

Economist: I was misquoted. What I said was that in a period when new technology was **coming in** and replacing traditional employment patterns in the workplace, we needed to rethink our basic economics. Other economies which have combined capitalism with a caring social framework have **come off**[2] better in the long term. If our standards of employment and social care are to **come up to**[3] those of our neighbours, then we need something other than a traditional form of capitalism. And this is where a more cooperative approach **comes in**[4]. Our workers' general life-skills have **come on**[5] a long way since the days of mass manual labour and we have to involve them and their skills in a more democratic way. A new era has to **come into**[6] being or we will simply be left behind.

1 suddenly said
2 ended up in a good position (**come off better**) or bad position (**come off worse**) because of an argument or some kind of struggle
3 reach
4 is involved
5 improved
6 begin

**TIP** Look at the units which deal with the meanings conveyed by the particles (Units 10–16). These may help you learn the meanings of the phrasal verbs in Units 56–60.

# Exercises

## 56.1 Complete these sentences with phrasal verbs from A opposite.

1 Originally stories ................ ................ from one generation to the next through the spoken word rather than in writing.
2 The tide ................ ................ and goes out twice a day.
3 Prices tend to ................ ................ when the economy is experiencing a recession.
4 Surrealist artists ................ ................ their work very differently from artists of previous generations.
5 In a formal meeting you should wait until you catch the eye of the chairperson before ................ ................ to join a discussion.
6 The Russian revolutionary Trotsky died when someone ................ ................ him with an ice axe.

## 56.2 Complete these sentences with the correct particles.

1 Any original idea is bound to come ................ ................ a certain amount of opposition at first.
2 I prefer not to argue with Jenny because she usually comes ................ best.
3 The new licensing laws will come ................ force on 1 January.
4 The Chancellor is bound to come ................ attack for putting forward such a controversial proposal.
5 Small children say the funniest things – you never know what they are going to come ................ ................ next.
6 Sometimes your brother comes ................ as being a bit unfriendly.
7 I gave up football because I wanted a change. Age doesn't come ................ it.
8 Now I'd like to discuss the next stage of the project and this is where your plans come ................ .

## 56.3 Rewrite the underlined parts of these sentences, using a phrasal verb from the opposite page. Make any other necessary changes.

1 José's English has improved a lot since he met Diana.
2 Most people think Jack is confident and extrovert.
3 The Prime Minister has received a considerable amount of criticism lately.
4 Ida makes some very strange comments sometimes.
5 This history homework does not meet the standards we expect from our students.
6 We've had a difficult year but we've survived and are looking forward to the future now.
7 At this point I should like to invite Mariella Snow to enter the discussion.
8 I was afraid the dog was going to attack me.

## 56.4 Which phrasal verb with *come* fits each set of collocations? Use a dictionary to help you if necessary.

| | | | |
|---|---|---|---|
| 1 to not ...................................... | standard<br>expectations<br>scratch | 3 to ...................................... | scrutiny<br>attack<br>pressure |
| 2 to ...................................... | competition<br>a problem<br>prejudice | 4 to ...................................... | effect<br>being<br>force |

# 57 Get

## A Phrasal verbs with get

There are many phrasal verbs with *get*, some of which you may have already met in this book or elsewhere. For example, **get your act together** [become more organised (Unit 8)], **get around** [travel, of news or rumours (Unit 10)], **get by** [have just enough money to pay for the things you need but no more], **get** someone **down** [make someone depressed (Unit 11)] and **get off** [finish work (Unit 32)].

## B Phrasal verb collocations with get

| *collocation* | *meaning* |
|---|---|
| The children are very quiet. I hope they're not **getting up to mischief**. | doing something naughty |
| Now we're all here, let's **get down to business**. | start our work |
| I wish my parents would **get off my back**! I'm studying as hard as I need to. | stop nagging me |
| The football coach decided it was time for his team to **get back to basics**. | start again at the beginning |
| The business was a little slow to **get off the ground** but it's doing very well now. | get started |
| I just can't **get** the situation with Tom **out of my mind**. | stop thinking about |
| Doctors try to **get the message across** that too much salt is bad for you. | make people understand |
| You are far too soft on Jane. You let her **get away with murder**. | behave badly and not be criticised or punished |
| What happened between Dick and Karen? We must try to **get to the bottom of** it. | understand properly, not superficially |
| They've seen how popular the product is and now other companies want to **get in on the act**. | become involved |

## C Getting down to a good gossip

Alice: Hi, Jean! Haven't seen you for ages. What have you been **getting up to**[1] recently? Anything interesting?

Jean: Well, I've been **getting around**[2] quite a lot actually, mainly for work. I've been to Italy a couple of times and Ireland, visiting our offices. But I've also been **getting into**[3] golf recently and I managed to **get in**[4] a few rounds between meetings.

Alice: That's great. It's good if you can **get** something **out of**[5] the trips for yourself as well as for work.

Jean: That's right. In fact, I'm finding it quite hard to **get back into**[6] the ordinary office routine now.

Alice: Well, let's **get together** one evening soon and catch up properly on all the news.

1 doing
2 travelling to different places
3 becoming keen on
4 find time for
5 get benefit from
6 return to (after some time)

**TIP** Many phrasal verbs have a whole range of different meanings. There are, for example, about 20 different definitions for **get in** and **get into** in the *Cambridge Phrasal Verbs Dictionary*. If you come across a phrasal verb and it doesn't make sense with any meaning that you know, look it up online at www.dictionary.cambridge.org to see if it has a different meaning in that context.

# Exercises

**57.1** **Put the words in the correct order to make sentences.**

1 she got / together / her act / It's time / a job / found / and
2 not looking / always / to mischief / The children / when / get up / I'm
3 the bottom / of that / I must / strange letter / get to / I received
4 down / We / business / to / got / immediately
5 is too / Modern / complicated / life / to basics / should / get / We / back (two sentences)

**57.2** **Complete these dialogues using phrasal verbs from the opposite page so that the second speaker agrees with and repeats more or less what the first speaker says.**

1 Anna: Shirley always wants to be part of anything that involves publicity.
Ella: Oh yes, if publicity's involved she always wants to ............................................... ............................................... .

2 Alex: We'll just have to survive on less money now that I've lost my job.
Neela: Yes, don't worry I'm sure we'll ............................................................... .

3 Sue: Everyone soon found out about Harry's divorce. I'm amazed.
Vicky: Oh yes, the story soon ............................................................... .

4 Lindsay: It's often difficult to make people understand how important it is to protect the environment.
Gareth: Yes, it's hard to ............................................................... .

5 Adam: Lisa always seems to behave badly and never get criticised by anyone.
Astrid: Yes, she seems to be able to ............................................................... .

6 Emma: I just can't stop thinking about Maria.
Juan: I know. It's the same for me. I just can't ............................................................... .

**57.3** **Complete these sentences using the correct particles.**

1 Studying so hard really got me ...................... so I took a break to cheer myself up.
2 Look, just get ...................... my back, will you! I'm sick of you finding fault with me.
3 The project took a long time to get ...................... the ground, but we're moving now.
4 I hope I get something ...................... ...................... that summer course I've registered for; it's quite a lot of money to pay.
5 I'd like to get ...................... a game of tennis later today. Are you free around five?
6 Hi there. What have you been getting ...................... ...................... since I last saw you?
7 Mick has got ...................... photography recently; he spends all his time editing pictures on his computer.
8 Let's get ...................... for lunch one day. I've got loads to tell you.

**57.4** **Rewrite these questions, replacing the phrasal verbs with a word or phrase that means the same.**

1 When do you normally get off work?
2 Do you get around a lot?
3 Is there any time of the year when you find it hard to get back into the routine of your daily life?
4 What have you been getting up to recently?
5 What sort of things get you down?
6 Where do you usually get together with your friends?

**57.5** **Now answer the questions in 57.4.**

# 58 Go

## A Typical meanings of *go* in phrasal verbs

Look at these meanings of *go down* which you may have already met. Note that what they have in common is change from a bigger or more positive state to a smaller or more negative state.

| *phrasal verb* | *meaning* | *unit* |
|---|---|---|
| **go down** | if a computer **goes down**, it stops working | 11 |
| | become worse in quality | 19 |
| | if part of your body that is bigger than usual because of an illness or injury **goes down**, it starts to return to its usual size | 43 |

As these examples show, *go* typically carries meanings connected with movement, change or things happening. Here are some more examples:

We should **go back over** these figures. I think there's a mistake somewhere. [examine again]

The house **went for** €400,000, which was more than we expected. [was sold for]

The festival will **go ahead**, despite the bad weather. [happen]

I've been **going over** in my mind what happened the other day. I think we have a big problem. [thinking about something that happened or that was said]

Harry has decided to **go into** politics. I'm not sure I would vote for him! [become involved in]

Who would want to **go after** such a boring job? [try to get]

## B Other phrasal verbs with *go*

Look at the verbs with *go* in these short news clips.

The event **went off**[1] as planned and £2,000 was raised for charity.

The young mother **went through**[2] agony before her missing child was found.

Mr Drake said he had decided to **go over to**[3] the Green Party as he was disillusioned with his own party's policies on the environment.

**Going by**[4] the government's own statistics, they have failed to stop the rise in drug addiction.

Three candidates will **go forward** to the next round in the election for party leader.

Youths who **go around**[5] vandalising property should be forced to repair the things they have damaged.

The newspapers are really **going for**[6] Joss Rone. They seem determined to destroy his career.

1 happened in a particular way
2 experienced (used about an unpleasant or difficult situation or event)
3 leave one group or organisation and join another competing group or organisation
4 using as a reference
5 spend time (used about doing something that is unpleasant for other people)
6 strongly criticising

# Exercises

## 58.1 Look at A. Complete the text below using particles from the box.

| | | | | | |
|---|---|---|---|---|---|
| after | ahead | down | for | into | over |

It's been a terrible week. As you know, I'm planning to go ................ (1) teaching. On Monday I went ................ (2) a trainee teacher position that was advertised at a school in town but I didn't get it. I'm not sure why. I've been going ................ (3) the interview in my mind but I don't think I said anything too stupid. Then on Tuesday I fell off my bike and managed to twist my ankle. It was terribly swollen for a day or two but it's beginning to go ................ (4) now. It's my birthday party tomorrow. I hope you can come. Plans are still going ................ (5) for that, of course, although I don't suppose I'll be able to dance very much. I'm probably going to sell my bike, though. I hope it'll go ................ (6) at least £100, which will help me out till I manage to find a job.

## 58.2 Match the beginning of each question with its ending.

1 Are you planning to go after
2 Is the end-of-term concert going ahead
3 Why did you decide to go over
4 How much did their house go for
5 Did your engagement party go off
6 Could you help me go back
7 Has the swelling on your knee gone down
8 Which teams are going forward

a) when they finally managed to sell it?
b) over our business accounts?
c) yet?
d) in the school hall as usual this year?
e) to the semi-final?
f) to a different political party?
g) the boss's job when he leaves?
h) as well as you'd hoped?

## 58.3 Correct the mistakes with particles in these sentences.

1 Tony has been promised that his name will go over for a place on the board of directors next year.
2 Going for the weather forecast, there'll be snow tomorrow.
3 Harriet went on a terrible time during her husband's illness.
4 You really mustn't go across telling such terrible lies.
5 Horace has always wanted to go on law.

## 58.4 Which particle fits in each of these sets of sentences? Use a dictionary if necessary.

1 Pam really went ................ me in the office today.
They are selling their old computer but they don't expect it to go ................ much.
Please be quiet, children – and that goes ................ you too, Mick.
2 The standard of school leavers' English is going ................ .
The office computers have gone ................ again.
The bump on the boy's head looked alarming but it quickly went ................ .
3 Let's go ................ our plan of action for tomorrow again.
I keep going ................ what I said to him, wishing I could take my words back.
He started his political life as a Republican but later on went ................ to the Democrats.
4 I was nervous about playing in the concert but everything went ................ very well.
I didn't wake up when my alarm clock went ................ this morning.
Don't drink this milk – I think it's gone ................ .

# 59 Keep

## A Phrasal verbs with *keep*

In this book or elsewhere, you may have already met **keep in with** someone [be friendly with someone because they can help you (Unit 5)], **keep up** with something [be able to understand or deal with something that is developing very fast (Unit 25)] and **keep it up** [don't stop doing (Unit 31)]. This unit presents more of the many other phrasal verbs with *keep*.

## B Describing problems

My son has been **kept in**[1] at school several times recently but he won't tell me why. I can't understand why he should want to **keep** this **to**[2] himself. He normally tells me everything and doesn't **keep** anything **back**. Should I go behind his back and ask his teacher or should I **keep out of**[3] it and hope that he will tell me in his own time?

*I'm a medical student and up till now I've managed to **keep ahead** of the other students in my year. I really want to do well in my exams. However, now I have a problem with my flatmate. He always wants to spend hours discussing his problems with me and this is **keeping** me **from** my studies. What should I put first – work or friendship?*

I love my husband very much but there are two things about him that really annoy me. Firstly, he goes out to play darts every Friday evening but he always forgets his keys and I can't go to bed till he comes home. It is infuriating to be **kept up**[4] like this as I work on Saturdays. Secondly, he is very proud and never asks for help. So, if we're driving and we get lost, he'll **keep on**[5] until he finds a signpost or something, rather than just stop to ask someone the way. Should I try to change him or just accept these irritating habits?

1 made to stay at school as a punishment
2 keep something secret
3 not become involved
4 made to stay up late
5 continue in the same direction

## C Some advice

- **Keep off** sugary drinks if you want to stay slim.
- If you are on a diet, or on a budget, a bowl of homemade soup is a good and inexpensive way to **keep** your strength **up**[1].
- **Keep** your **music** down late at night or you'll annoy your neighbours.
- When answering an exam question, you will get better marks if you **keep to**[2] the point.
- When you buy a house, remember to budget for its **upkeep**[3] as this can be very costly.

1 not allow something that is at a high level to fall to a lower level
2 don't start writing about other topics
3 keeping a building in good condition

*Keep at it and you'll get on top of those phrasal verbs.*

# Exercises

**59.1** **Complete these emails using the correct particles.**

Hi Joan,

Keep this ................ (1) yourself, but I heard something very interesting the other day. You know how Lorna is always trying to keep ................ (2) with the boss and you know how she just tells everyone EVERYTHING (she can never keep anything ................ (3), can she?)? Well, she told me she's actually getting engaged to him! Can you believe it?

Meg

Hi there Jacko,

Thanks for the invitation to the week in France, but I think you're trying to keep me ................ (4) my studies, you bad man! Seriously, I really shouldn't take any more time off. My new year's resolution is to keep ................ (5) with my studies, so I'm trying to do five hours a day, five days a week. If I had a week off, I think I'd find it hard to keep ................ (6) the momentum.

Fran

Dear Chris,

Kate's had a row with Archie and she wants me to help sort it out. I think I should keep ................ ................ (7) it. What do you think? I find it hard to keep ................ ................ (8) all the ups and downs of their love life. I think they should solve their own problems, don't you?

Yvonne

**59.2** **Look at these brief notes giving people advice or warnings. Rewrite the underlined parts of the sentences, using a phrasal verb from the opposite page. Make any other necessary changes.**

1 Please <u>play</u> your music, TVs and radios <u>at a minimum volume</u> during the exam period.
2 Every household will be asked to contribute £5 a month towards the <u>maintenance</u> of the village recreation ground.
3 All team members are strongly advised to <u>refrain from drinking</u> alcohol during the training period. It is important to <u>maintain</u> your fitness to the highest level.

**59.3** **Which particle could fit into all the sentences in each set?**

1 There is one rule which we ask all club members to keep ........... .
I wish the lecturer would stop digressing and keep ........... the point.
Before your exams, make a revision timetable and try to keep ........... it.

2 I wish Dad wouldn't keep ........... at me about getting my hair cut.
Keep ........... until you reach the T-junction and then turn left.
My grandma kept ........... working until she was in her 80s.

3 Why don't you go to bed now? I really don't want to keep you ........... .
At university Jack did a course on ornithology but I don't think he's kept ........... his interest in birds.
Things change so quickly in Fay's life – it's hard to keep ........... with what's going on.

**59.4** **Answer the following questions.**

1 What sort of thing has kept you up late at night?
2 Were you ever kept in at school? If so, why?
3 What are you going to do to keep up your knowledge of phrasal verbs?

# 60 Take

## A Typical meanings of *take* in phrasal verbs

*Take* often carries a meaning of 'remove', as in:

We hope you will **take** many happy memories **away** from your stay here.

Phil's boss has agreed to **take** him **off** the night shift.

Helen **took** her parents **out** for a meal. (Unit 42)

*Take* also sometimes carries a meaning of doing something quickly or something happening quickly or abruptly, for example, **Take it away!** (Unit 31), **take aback** [surprise], **take off** (of a plane) and **take out** [kill or destroy in a military battle].

## B Organising a charity concert

I must say I was **taken aback**[1] when I saw how much cost was involved but I wanted it to be a memorable experience for people. A huge amount of time was **taken up**[2] with phone calls persuading sponsors to be involved, and so on. The **uptake**[3] was slow at first, but bit by bit we managed to persuade local companies and individuals to support us. The work didn't end when the concert was over. We spent a whole day **taking down**[4] the stage set and lighting and so on, but none of that **took away from**[5] the pleasure we got organising it. And I think the audience **took away**[6] something that will stay with them for a long time. Overall it was worth it – a great experience for all involved.

1 very surprised
2 used
3 number of people who committed themselves
4 removing by separating into pieces and taking the pieces away
5 made it seem less good or successful
6 remember [used about e.g. a memory, an impression, a message]

## C Other phrasal verbs with *take*

| *phrasal verb/noun* | *example* | *definition of phrasal verb/ noun* |
|---|---|---|
| **take** sb **away** | He **took** his mum **away** for a week to the coast. | take to a different place |
| **take** sb **off** sth | He was put in charge of security but he was **taken off** after just two weeks as he was not strict enough. | remove from a job |
| | The doctor **took** her **off** the pills as they were making her sick. | stop giving someone a particular type of medicine |
| **take out** sth / **take** sth **out** | I **took** a great DVD **out** of the library last week. | borrow |
| **take up** sth / **take** sth **up** | The tutor promised to **take** the problem **up** with the Head of Department. | discuss something or deal with something |
| **take along** sb/sth / **take** sb/sth **along** | I'd advise you to **take along** an umbrella. | take with you |
| **intake** | This year's **intake** have higher exam grades than last year's. | number of people that are accepted at a particular time by an organisation, especially a college or university |
| **take-off** | He does a brilliant **take-off** of Michael Jackson. | imitation |

# Exercises

**60.1** **Which of the phrasal verbs on the opposite page can have the following meanings?**

1 surprise someone ......................................................
2 detract from something ......................................................
3 leave an airport (of a plane) ......................................................
4 destroy a military target ......................................................
5 borrow (of a library book) ......................................................

**60.2** **Complete these sentences with the correct particles.**

1 My French cousin is coming to stay next week, so I plan to take her ................ when I visit my daughter at university.
2 When you're at the library, can you return this book and take ................ another one by the same author for me, please?
3 Personally, I took ................ a very good impression of France when I went there.
4 Joe was quite taken ................ to learn that his application had been unsuccessful.
5 Much of Nicky's time is taken ................ with dealing with customer complaints.
6 Grandma asked the doctor to take her ................ those tablets as she thought they were making her feel sick.

**60.3** **Rewrite the sentences using a phrasal verb or noun based on *take*. Remember to make all the changes to the sentences that are necessary.**

1 Martin does the best imitation of the Prime Minister that I have ever seen.
2 A ridiculous amount of my time is occupied by dealing with emails.
3 Even the rain could not detract from the beauty of the scene.
4 I was very surprised when I was told that I was no longer allowed to park in front of my own house.
5 Would you like me to raise your concerns with the manager?
6 We are expecting a particularly large group of students to arrive next week.
7 We decided it would be nicer to invite our aunt for a weekend in a hotel with us rather than having her stay with us.
8 The number of people wanting a place at the weekend seminar has been rather disappointing.

**60.4** **Rewrite these sentences so that the underlined words have the opposite meaning. Make any other changes that are necessary.**

1 Let's <u>put up</u> the decorations tomorrow.
2 The doctor has agreed to <u>put</u> my elderly aunt <u>on</u> some pills for her arthritis.
3 When she went into town Sheila <u>returned</u> some library books for her grandmother.
4 My favourite part of a flight is when the plane <u>lands</u>.
5 Norman's being there <u>added to</u> our enjoyment of the evening.
6 After Jack had been working in the kitchens for a week, he was <u>put on</u> washing-up duties.

**FOLLOW UP**

If you have now finished all the units in this book, congratulations! Remember to regularly revise the new phrasal verbs you have studied and try to use them in your own speaking and writing of English.

# Key

## Unit 1

**1.1** 1 I decided to <u>take up</u> gardening, so I went to the library, <u>took</u> a book <u>out</u> and <u>read up on</u> the subject. I <u>found out</u> so many interesting things, such as the best time to <u>plant</u> flowers <u>out</u> for the summer and how to grow vegetables. I've really <u>got into</u> it now and spend hours in the garden every weekend.

2 The other day we <u>went off</u> on a hike in the mountains. We <u>put</u> our wet-weather gear <u>on</u> as the weather forecast wasn't good. We <u>set off</u> early to avoid the rush hour and soon reached the starting point for our walk. The whole walk took about four hours and when we <u>got back</u> we were exhausted.

3 I have to <u>catch up on</u> my coursework this weekend as I've <u>fallen behind</u> a bit. I <u>worked on</u> till midnight last night but I still have loads to do. I have to <u>hand</u> one essay <u>in</u> on Tuesday and another one on Friday. I'm not sure whether I'll make it but I'll try.

**1.2** 1 out of 2 down 3 out 4 in

**1.3** 1 intake
2 breakout
3 off-putting
4 outspoken
5 broken-down

**1.4** 1 d 2 e 3 a 4 b 5 c

## Unit 2

**2.1** 1 no object needed
2 object needed: If you're ready to leave now I can drop **you** off at your office. Remember, without an object, drop off means 'fall asleep'.
3 no object needed
4 object needed: My son is so good at English that I think the teachers should move **him** up to the class above.
5 object needed: I associate **this music / that perfume / Juliet** with that evening we spent together in Rome.
6 no object needed

**2.2** 1 I can pick you up from work and then drop you off at the airport. *Or* I can pick you up from the airport and then drop you off at work.
2 The teacher said that she would not put up with such rudeness from her class.
3 The floods have cut off several villages in the mountains. *Or* (but less likely as it is quite a long object) The floods have cut several villages in the mountains off.
4 If your handwriting doesn't improve, the examiners will mark you down.
5 Margot always seems to cope cheerfully with all her problems.

**2.3** 1 I'll have to ask my nephew to **sort** my Internet connection **out**. *Or* .... to **sort out** my Internet connection.
2 I was so tired after work that I **dropped off** in the train on the way home.
3 I was **marked down** because my essay was far too long.
4 Bill has no right to **look down on** me – I'm no worse than he is.
5 Lisa doesn't **get on** (well) with one of her flatmates.
6 You have to **face up to** the fact that you will probably never see each other again.
7 Maria has got a new job **looking after** an old lady.
8 If you **deprive** the children **of** sleep, they won't be able to concentrate at school.
9 In Lapland we had to **contend with** some difficult driving conditions.
10 The road to our house **branches off** (the main road) just after the petrol station.

**2.4** *Possible answers:*
1 I'm **looking forward to** visiting my aunt in New York for a couple of weeks.
2 I've got to **catch up on** some maths I missed when I was off school on Monday.
3 My mother **picks** me **up**.
4 My favourite album is *Sergeant Pepper's Lonely Hearts Club Band* and I like it because I **associate** it **with** being a student.
5 I feel stressed when I have too many different things to **contend with** at the same time.
6 I usually **drop off** as soon as my head touches the pillow.

**Follow up**
This is how the *Cambridge Advanced Learners' Dictionary* deals with these verbs:
**associate *sth* with *sth*** phrasal verb
**deprive** verb [T] [T = transitive]
**contend with *sth*** phrasal verb
**face up to *sth*** phrasal verb

Collocations highlighted by examples in *Cambridge Advanced Learners' Dictionary*:
risks **associated with** smoking
**deprive** someone **of** freedom/rights/sleep
**contend with** problems / someone's death
**face up to** the fact that

## Unit 3

**3.1**
1 onset
2 overkill
3 back-up
4 input
5 warm-up
6 letdown
7 standby

**3.2** 1 The police opened the container and arrested two **stowaways**.
2 There was a **breakdown** in negotiations with union members (after a couple of hours).
3 There was a management **buyout** of the company in 2003.
4 There was a **walkout** (by the workers) last night and the factory was forced to close.
5 The military **build-up** is continuing on both sides of the border.

**3.3**
1. There has been a stand-**off** for several days now in the talks between the government and the rebels. Neither side will make any concessions.
2. Last year there were 15,000 new Internet business start-**ups**, most of which only survived for a few months.
3. After years without releasing a CD, Sonia Flame has staged a come**back** with her new collection of love songs.
4. Jess: Have you decided where you're going this summer?
   Kelly: Not really. It's a toss-**up** whether it'll be Italy or Greece.
5. I met Chris and we just had a knock**about** on the tennis courts for half an hour.

**3.4**
1. Output
2. lookout
3. downpour
4. outbreak
5. Lift-off
6. a break-in

## Unit 4

**4.1**
1. There was a **worn-out** carpet on the stairs.
2. The newsletter has a list of **forthcoming** activities at the tennis club.
3. What's happened? You're looking very **downcast!**
4. Unlike her sister, Emily is very **outgoing.**
5. I find the cover of this novel very **off-putting**, don't you?
6. It doesn't matter what time of day it is, Tilly always looks **tired out**.
7. We are not in the habit of going to such **overpriced** restaurants.
8. When you meet my boss I think you'll find him surprisingly **outspoken.**

**4.2** 1 a **fold-up** chair 2 a **broken-down** car 3 a **built-in** oven 4 a **foldaway** bed

**4.3** *Possible answers:*
1. An advantage of having a live-in nanny might be that the children look on her as one of the family; a disadvantage might be that the parents do not get much privacy.
2. A foldaway bed would be particularly useful in a small room, especially one that is also used for entertaining visitors.
3. A job requiring tact might not be suitable for a very outspoken person – a diplomat, for example, or a beautician.
4. You might want to give a watered-down version of something that happened to you to your parents if you think they might not like the whole truth.
5. A job in show business requires you to be outgoing – an actor, singer or TV presenter, for example.
6. A difficult social problem would tend to be ongoing – for example, the problem of poverty or of discrimination.
7. If you are having a meal in a restaurant, you might find it off-putting if someone at the next table smokes or talks very loudly.
8. You might think that meals, clothes or cosmetics are often overpriced.

**4.4**

| | |
|---|---|
| **broken-down** | not working |
| candid | **outspoken** |
| continuing | **ongoing** |
| diluted | **watered-down** |
| **downcast** | miserable |
| dynamic | **go-ahead** |
| exhausted | **tired out** |
| extrovert | **outgoing** |
| **forthcoming** | future |
| obsolete | **outdated** |
| **off-putting** | repellent |
| shabby | **worn out** |

Note that *worn out* can also mean exhausted.

**4.5** *Possible answers:*

1 If the union doesn't accept our terms, what should we have as the position **that we will agree to if we cannot get our main aim?**
2 Clare always feels **ignored / lonely** when her brother's friends come round to play.
3 Sophie is usually chatty but her brother is not very **talkative / communicative.**
4 You shouldn't get **so upset / in such a state** about every little thing.
5 Zak met me at the airport with arms **open wide ready to embrace** me.

## Unit 5

**5.1**

1 Collocation means the way words combine with each other.
2 a, c and e
3 They are things that are written.
4 Because it will help you to be able to use them appropriately in your own speaking and writing.
5 You might want to note down:
whether it collocates with positive or negative things or both
whether it collocates with people or things as objects
whether it collocates with people or things as subjects
whether it collocates with particular types of situation

**5.2**

1 appropriate
2 appropriate
3 not appropriate – *hit upon* is used about good ideas; in this context it would be better to say, 'You can always rely on Joe to **come up with an idea** that will never work.'
4 appropriate
5 appropriate
6 not appropriate – though it would be appropriate to talk about the need to **keep in with your bank manager**

**5.3**

| | |
|---|---|
| 1 after | 5 off |
| 2 into; off | 6 off |
| 3 through | 7 in with |
| 4 with | 8 with |

**5.4**
1 Helena **sailed through** her driving test.
2 I've really **gone off** coffee.
3 The wind is **easing off/up** now. *Or* The wind has **eased off/up** now.
4 If I have a problem, I find a walk by the sea often helps me to **hit upon/on** a solution.
5 Masses of people **streamed into** the shop as soon as it opened, hoping to find a bargain in the sale.
6 His argument is **riddled with** holes.

## Unit 6

**6.1**

> Dear Mr Janes,
>
> Thank you for your letter of 23 May 2005 **complaining** about the bad service you experienced at this hotel. I promise you we will **investigate** the problem at once and **respond** to you as soon as possible. We always try to **achieve/meet** the highest standards of service, and if we have failed to **meet/achieve** those standards we will immediately seek to **remedy** the situation. Meanwhile we hope you will **continue** making Miromana Hotels your first choice for all your business and leisure travel.
>
> Yours sincerely,
>
> G. H. Logan (General Manager)

**6.2**
1 Will you **look after** Aunt Jessie while I go and get the children's supper ready?
2 He **went into** the subject in great detail in his lecture.
3 When the President died his son **took on** the title of Great Leader.
4 I like her. Do you think I should **ask her out**?
5 During the war he **went over to** the enemy side and was killed in action.
6 She **bought up** all the shares in the company in 2004.
7 The local newspaper **put out** a story about a strange animal seen in the city park.
8 I think I'll **call in on** my grandmother on the way home from work.
9 The deal **fell through** at the last minute.
10 I managed to **get by** on about €50 a day when I was travelling.

**6.3**

| computers and technology | academic lectures/writing | money and business |
|---|---|---|
| back up, boot up, hack into, log in, print off, scroll down | base upon, gloss over, put forward, sum up | bail out, carry forward, sell up, square up, take over, turn over |

**6.4**
1 Despite his family's poverty, Alan never **wants for anything**.
2 You must inform the police if you have evidence **which bears upon** the case. (Note that ... *which bears on the case* is also possible but *upon* sounds particularly formal.)
3 Jack will have to **call upon** all his ingenuity to resolve the situation. (Note that ... *to call on all his ingenuity* ... is also possible but *upon* sounds particularly formal.)
4 The president **ascribes** his party's victory **to** his leadership.
5 The manager will **attend to** your enquiry without delay.

## Unit 7

**7.1** *Possible answers:*

1 later than expected
2 They've risen.
3 aggressively
4 He wants to read the agenda and make sure it is correct. Perhaps also prepare what they are going to say.
5 more
6 go straight into the proposal without any planning
7 not pay any attention to them, not consider their proposal

**7.2**

1 It's not good for children to spend too much time **glued to the** TV.
2 Choosing a university course **boils down to** deciding what you want to do with your life.
3 I arrived at the stadium early and watched the other spectators **flooding in.**
4 Laura **dragged herself away from** the window and returned to her desk.
5 Sam was staring at Fiona, **drinking in** every word she said.
6 George **brushed off / swept aside** all objections to his plan, saying they were unimportant.

**7.3**

1 stands by
2 soldier on
3 fished out
4 nosing around
5 eat into
6 brushed off *or* swept aside
7 struck out
8 sandwiched between

**7.4** *Possible answers:*

1 If someone warms up an audience they make it more receptive and friendly, more relaxed (perhaps by telling some jokes). Coldness in English equates with unfriendliness and warmth with friendliness. Warming up people and warming up food both have the idea of making something pleasanter.
2 If someone falls into a job they get it very easily and without making any effort. So both falling into a hole and falling into a job have the idea of something happening by chance.
3 If you climb down in an argument you admit that you were wrong. So both uses of climb down suggest moving back to the level of other people from a position in which you were separated from others.

## Unit 8

**8.1**

1 the baby
2 get on like a house on fire
3 let off steam
4 to spite their face
5 take the sting out of something
6 run rings round somebody; go round in circles

**8.2**

1 off; nose; spite; face
2 put; roots
3 ran rings
4 sting; of
5 round; circles
6 throw; baby
7 get; house
8 letting off

**8.3** After a year of travelling, I decided to ~~put~~ my act together and get a job. A friend who worked for a bank put in ~~some good words~~ for me. In fact he ~~pushed in~~ all the stops and arranged for me to have lunch with the CEO. I got ~~on the wrong feet~~ by saying I wasn't ready to ~~plant~~ down roots yet; I think they were looking for someone to make a long-term commitment. I should have kept quiet!

| |
|---|
| 1 get |
| 2 a good word |
| 3 pulled out |
| 4 off on the wrong foot |
| 5 put |

**8.4** 1 her heels in
2 for lost time
3 smell the coffee
4 his own
5 the heat
6 your mind

## Unit 9

**9.1** 1 top-up  2 copied; in  3 hug-in  4 scroll

**9.2** 1 bump off
2 chill out
3 kick off
4 chill out
5 bumped off
6 kick off

**9.3** 1 c  2 d  3 a  4 b

**9.4** 1 clap
2 b
3 dumb up
4 He thinks they need some extra training.
5 Suggested rewrites:
   a The company intend to launch/distribute the new version of the software in April 2012.
   b We were very lucky and got the last flight out before the hurricane struck.
   c We investigated the data very thoroughly / went very deep into the data and found some very interesting statistics.

## Unit 10

**10.1** 1 banging
2 floating
3 run
4 switched
5 ask
6 fly
7 lying
8 clowning

**10.2** 1 ask around
2 lying around/about / floating around/about
3 gets around/about
4 bosses; about/around
5 clowns around/about

**10.3** 1 lying/pottering/playing/clowning around/about; lying around/about; switched around
2 play/clown around/about; bossing us around/about; run around/about
3 work around
4 skirt around (Note that skirt around can also be used to describe physical movement, e.g. We decided to skirt around the city centre to avoid the rush-hour traffic.)
5 banging around/about; flying around/about. (Note that it would also be possible to say that *all sorts of rumours have been going around/about among the neighbours*.)

### Follow up
*Possible answers:*

| *phrasal verb* | *meaning* | *example* |
|---|---|---|
| **crowd around** | surround someone or something, standing close together | Please don't **crowd around** the desk. Stand in an orderly queue. |
| **knock** sth **about/ around** / **knock about/around** | if people knock a ball about, they hit or kick it to each other for fun | We knocked a ball about in the park after work. |
| **turn around** | turn so that you are facing the opposite direction | I saw him walk up to the door but then he hesitated, **turned around** and walked away again. |
| **turn** sth **around** | make something unsuccessful (e.g. a business) become successful | Paul has made a very successful career out of **turning** failing businesses **around**. |
| **roll about/around** | laugh a lot | Kathy is very funny. Her stories had us all **rolling around**. |
| **blunder about/ around** | move in an awkward way (often because you can't see where you're going) | When the lights went off we were all **blundering around** in the darkness. |

## Unit 11

**11.1** 1 Linda Trotsky 2 Peter Hind 3 Harry Irving 4 Joe Reece 5 Freda Calvo

**11.2** *Suggested answers:*
1 The computers suddenly **went down** this morning, so we're doing everything manually at the moment.
2 I'm sorry I'm so irritable. Things have been **getting me down** lately.
3 Shall I **put you down** (on my list) to sponsor me for the charity walk?
4 This event will **go down** in history as the worst catastrophe this country has ever suffered.
5 The company had to **shut down** all their machines during the 24-hour strike at the factory.
6 The salesman **came down on the price**, and after that we even managed to **knock him down** by a further 10%.
7 Many everyday remedies for minor ailments have **come down to us** from our ancestors.

**11.3** 1 slam the phone down
2 have it put down (rather than *put it down*, since you would probably not do it yourself)
3 tie it down
4 depressed
5 turn it down

**11.4** 1 a and c 2 b and c 3 a, b and c 4 b and c

## Unit 12

**12.1**
1 cash in on
2 come in / cut in
3 pitch in
4 usher in
5 boxed in
6 lead-in
7 factor in
8 squash in
9 build in
10 set in

**12.2**
1 My new curtains are excellent – they don't **let** any light in.
2 Tina, can you **show** Mr Hill in as soon as he arrives, please?
3 Having the meeting on the 28th would **fit** in better with our plans than the 30th.
4 Our office in Buenos Aires has **brought** in a lot of new business this year.
5 When you are planning the course, make sure you **build** in enough free time.
6 It's rude to **cut** in when someone else is in the middle of speaking. (Note that *come in* does not fit as well in this context as it does not sound so abrupt and potentially rude as *cut in*.)
7 If everyone **pitches** in, we'll soon get the job done.
8 If I move up, then Rachel should be able to **squash** (**fit** is also possible here) in at the end of the bench.

**12.3** 1 squashed 2 fitted 3 pitched 4 set 5 let

**12.4**
1 **bring in** customers / profits / ~~a loss~~ / business
2 a **lead-in** to a discussion / ~~a bargain~~ / a lesson
3 a recession / rain / ~~a new product~~ **sets in**
4 **usher in** ~~a price increase~~ / a new era / changes

## Unit 13

**13.1**
1 Kersty's mother to Kersty's father: Kersty's 21 now and should make her own decisions. I think we should **back off** and let her run her own life.
2 Newsreader: The Prime Minister has **shrugged off** leadership threats from within his party, saying that they are only rumours.
3 Mother to father: I think we should let the kids run round in the garden for a bit, let them **work off** some of their energy so that they sleep tonight.
4 Father to Petra: Petra, you MUST pay your electricity bill. If you don't, they'll **cut you off** and you won't have any heating.
5 Ken to Nick: Oh no! Dave wants to come back with us to Pete's house. He's such a drag! How can we **shake him off**?
6 Chairperson: I'd like to just **round off** the meeting by giving a vote of thanks to the committee for all their work this year.
7 The last 100 metres to the top of the hill just **finished me off**. I had to sit down and rest for an hour.
8 I don't want you in my room any more, so just **shove off**!

**13.2**

| | |
|---|---|
| When I come home from work, I love to just kick ~~away~~ my | off |
| shoes and relax for the evening. It's great to ~~let~~ off worrying | leave |
| about work and round ~~up~~ the day with a nice meal. If I | off |
| ~~have off~~ a couple of days it's even better. I usually go off to | have a couple of days off |
| our country cottage. I can just ~~light~~ off completely. I love it. | switch |
| I never stay there long, because after a while I feel a bit ~~stood~~ | cut |
| off from all my friends and social life back in the city. | |

**13.3**

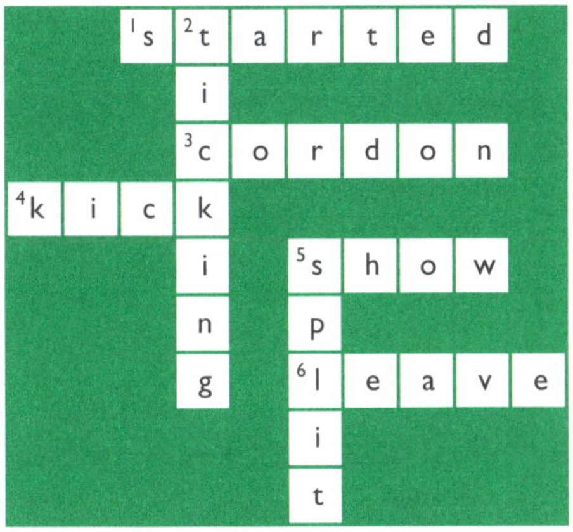


## Unit 14

**14.1** 1 B 2 D 3 I 4 N 5 B 6 I 7 D

**14.2** 1 a or b 2 b, c, or d 3 a, c or d

**14.3**
1 Try to **focus on** what is really important and to ignore what is not essential.
2 Now we've had a bit of a rest, it's time to **press on** again.
3 I'm **counting/depending/relying on** you to let me know when my talk has gone on for long enough.
4 Your grandmother will always **live on** in your memory.
5 This is a quiet neighbourhood where noisy behaviour is **frowned (up)on**.
6 After the first few pages of the book, I decided I couldn't be bothered to **read on**.
7 Please stop **harping/going/droning on** about Sheila. Your relationship is over, so just forget her.
8 I am worried about my son's behaviour. He is so easily **led on** by his friends.

**14.4**
1 focus
2 spring
3 dwell
4 press
5 lead (Note that **egg on** has a similar meaning.)
6 frowned
7 depend
8 going/droning/harping

**14.5** *Suggested answers:*
1 You can count/rely/depend on James.
2 Dad will ramble/drone on for hours about European history.
3 Many political reputations are hanging (up)on / riding on the outcome of next week's election.
4 Josh never stops going on (and on) / harping on about the litter in the office car park. It irritates me.
5 While tidying my room, I happened (up)on an old diary of mine from 1985.

## Unit 15

**15.1**
1 She shared the apples out / shared out the apples among the four children.
2 He sorted things / the situation out. *Or* He sorted out the situation.
3 She picked out the best ones / picked the best ones out.
4 He kicked Sam out of the restaurant. *Or* He threw Sam out of the restaurant.
5 It juts out over the terrace.

**15.2**
1 I don't have any money so you can **count** me **out** from the shopping trip.
2 I **shared** the mints **out** / **shared out** the mints among my friends in the car.
3 We need to **sort out** this mess about the misprinted tickets pretty soon.
4 He really **lashed out at** me when I suggested he'd got it wrong.
5 Look at those big rocks **jutting out** from the sea.
6 **Pick out** the good strawberries and leave the rotten ones in the box.

**15.3**
1 I opened the door and heard somebody **yell out** (*or* **shout out / cry out / scream out**) from the staircase below.
2 My position as regards the committee is that I **want out.**
3 He always **draws out** the discussion / **draws** the discussion **out** with arguments about political ideology.
4 When we got back to our campsite, the campfire had **gone out.**
5 **Spread** the leaflets **out** on the table.
6 The burglars **cleaned us out** (completely).

**15.4** 1 c  2 d  3 a  4 b

## Unit 16

**16.1**
1 finish up *or* eat up
2 pep up
3 shore up
4 pick them up
5 propped up
6 jazz it up
7 wrap up
8 lift up

**16.2**
1 stand
2 split
3 set
4 land
5 bought
6 show
7 blown
8 sticking

**16.3** 1 blow up  2 shore up  3 set up (Note that **fix up** is also possible.)  4 open up

## Unit 17

**17.1** 1 c  2 e  3 d  4 a  5 b

**17.2** 1 Reeta  2 Terry  3 Noreen  4 Jenna  5 Jack

**17.3**
1 out
2 back
3 along/up
4 in
5 back/off
6 over
7 apart/aside
8 up

**17.4**
1 You'd get far more done if you didn't fritter **away** so much time.
2 The children tried to spin their game **out** so they didn't have to go to bed.
3 Jack might lose his job if he doesn't pull his **socks** up.
4 We must discuss what we need to do leading up **to** the opening of the new branch.
5 Let's try to **set** some time apart next month to discuss progress on the project.

**17.5**
1 We've had to **bring** the meeting **forward** to this Tuesday as Kerry will be away next week.
2 Ivor always **drags out** any discussion. *Or* Ivor always **drags** any discussion **out.** (Note **draw out** is also possible.)
3 I think we should **space** our meetings **out** a bit more. *Or* I think we should **space out** our meetings a bit more.
4 I thought I had ages to prepare for my exams but they have **crept up on** me in no time at all.
5 I think we should try to **eke out** the printing paper. *Or* I think we should try to **eke** the printing paper **out.**

## Unit 18

**18.1** 1 h 2 f 3 i 4 b 5 c 6 a 7 d 8 e 9 g

**18.2**
1 Bill puts the problems down to the government but I attribute them **to** the general world economic situation.
2 To a large extent, how a person accounts for the problems in their lives seems to depend largely **on/upon** their own parents' attitudes to difficult situations.
3 I believe the new legislation will contribute to a general improvement in the standard of living but Ben thinks it will result **in** increased poverty for most people.
4 The desire for reform has come **out of** a general desire to improve the situation but I suspect the proposed changes may rebound on the government.
5 The proposals are rooted in an appropriate awareness of the problems that exist but I do not feel that what is proposed adds up **to** a coherent programme of action.

**18.3**
1 The school's rituals and traditions are **rooted in** its long history.
2 My father **puts** the problem **down to** a decline in moral values.
3 How do you think the changes will **impact on/upon** your business?
4 The economic recession inevitably **resulted in** increased unemployment.
5 How would you **account for** the recent increase in violent crime?
6 Ken's criticism of Anna may **rebound on** him now that she's his boss!
7 I do not feel that the writer's analysis of the problem **adds up**.
8 Some unforeseen problems have **come out of** the change in legislation.

**18.4** *Author's answers:*
1 I'd put global warming largely down to increased air and road travel.
2 I think a dramatic change in social values has led to the current increase in violent crime in most societies.
3 I'd account for it by saying that girls tend to be more inclined to work harder at school than boys – though of course there are plenty of exceptions.
4 I'd attribute the success of the MP3 player to the huge amount of music it can hold and to its attractive design.
5 I'd point to the prevalence of materialistic attitudes as one main cause of social problems today.
6 My own interest in English stems from the fact that I had very good English teachers when I was at school.
7 I think that mobile phones have resulted in more communication between people – it's so much easier to keep in touch with friends and family.
8 For me the main thing that contributes to the difficulty of phrasal verbs is the fact that one verb – like, say, *make out* – can have so many different meanings.

## Unit 19

**19.1**
1 around
2 makeover
3 perked
4 down
5 shake
6 tinkering

**19.2**
1 up
2 makeover
3 with
4 around/about
5 up
6 around
7 ease
8 round
9 going
10 back
11 turnaround

**19.3**
1 Turn it into a spare bedroom.
2 Change over.
3 They should go over to the new accounts system.

**19.4** 1 I don't like the layout of this office – let's **change** the furniture **around/round.**
2 Our teacher has been working us very hard but she has promised to **ease up** if we all do well in our next test.
3 The government needs to do something drastic about education in this country; **tinkering with** the system will not be enough.
4 Suzie had made a lot of progress with her exercise programme but then it got busy again at work and she **went back** to her old habits and stopped going to the gym.
5 When Gary was appointed manager of the company he was determined to **shake** things **up** as he was convinced that major change was essential.
6 If you get tired of driving, let me know and we can easily **change over/round.**

## Unit 20

**20.1** 1 b 2 c 3 d 4 a 5 b

**20.2**
1 reminds
2 conjure/stir/summon/call
3 flooding
4 associate
5 coming
6 blocked
7 put
8 stick/stay
9 store
10 conjure/summon/call

**20.3** In each case the play on words depends on the literal meaning of the basic verb in the phrasal verb.
1 To stir up memories means to make memories, often unpleasant ones, appear in your mind. A cook stirs ingredients e.g. the ingredients for a cake or batter for pancakes.
2 Conjure up memories means to make you remember things from the past. A magician traditionally conjures a rabbit out of a hat.
3 Call up memories means to evoke memories or make someone remember something. Another meaning of call up is to require young men to become soldiers.
4 If a memory sticks with you, then you don't forget it. Glue is used to stick something to something else. The first meaning of stick here is metaphorical and the second is literal.
5 If memories come flooding back you suddenly remember a lot of things very clearly. When pipes burst – this typically happens if they freeze and then the ice melts – then there will be a flood.

**20.4** *Author's answers:*
1 I associate my childhood with the colour green because I spent so much time playing in the garden at home.
2 The smell of lavender reminds me of my childhood because we had a lot of lavender growing in our garden.
3 The pop music of the 1970s always conjures up memories of my youth.
4 I would like to block out the memory of school dinners, particularly of the awful macaroni cheese we were forced to eat.
5 I think that music makes memories come back to me more powerfully, although smells can also be very potent.

## Unit 21

**21.1** 1 It would depend on whether you wanted to buy or sell US dollars.
2 Unhappy, because they are complaining about something you have done.
3 sprouting or springing
4 True. See the left-hand page, section A.
5 You begin to feel less confident.
6 It becomes less strong.

**21.2** 1 opens 2 apart 3 on 4 up 5 breaks 6 out

**21.3**
1 When you**'ve finished with** the scissors, could you pass them to me? (Note the change to present perfect tense.)
2 They **wound up** the business in 2004 after a year of low sales.
3 Okay, so who's **magicked** the bottle opener **away** / **magicked away** the bottle opener? It was here a minute ago!
4 We've had some setbacks but we'll **press on**.
5 I only **got up to** page 12 of the book before I got bored and stopped reading it.

**21.4**
1 Wind up means to finish/terminate something. It is also what you do to a non-electric clock or watch to make it work.
2 Sprout up means to suddenly appear. A Brussels sprout is also a vegetable.
3 Press on means to continue in a determined way. Dry cleaners also press clothes (remove creases by using an iron or a pressing machine).
4 Spring up means to appear suddenly. A trampoline has springs, which contract and expand, making it possible for a person to bounce up and down on it.
5 Training shoes are worn by athletes when running. To run out of money means to have no money left.

## Unit 22

**22.1**
1 up
2 rage
3 around
4 out (or over)
5 up
6 off
7 back
8 off

**22.2** There was a terrible bust-**up** at work today. The departmental manager came into the office in a terrible temper. He flew **at** his PA and when people tried to calm him down, he rounded **on** them. I don't know what had got into him. He pushes everyone **around*** a lot but he's not normally quite so aggressive. I tried not to get dragged **into** it, but when it seemed as if he might actually hit someone, then I felt it was time to do what I could to break things **up**.
* push over would mean literally push people onto the floor

**22.3** *Possible answers:*
1 When I tried to enter the house, the dog flew at **me**.
2 No object required
3 They threatened to bump **him** off if he told anyone about the robbery.
4 Because she had learned some judo as a child, Tina found it much easier to fight off **her attacker** / to fight **her attacker** off.
5 I was completely taken by surprise when someone suddenly came at **me** from behind.
6 After only ten seconds in the ring, Henry's opponent had knocked **him** out.

**22.4**
1 Paul tried to **drag me into** the argument but I managed to stay out of it.
2 The old man thought the boys were trying to break into his house, so he **set his dog on them**.
3 The aim of the organisation is to **wipe out** cruelty to children.
4 Although he is small, James is strong and he quickly managed to **knock his attacker out**.
5 Uncle Walter can **flare up** (very quickly) if you say the wrong thing.
6 The witness saw the thief **come at** the woman just as she was opening her car door.
7 The government is determined to **stamp on** (or **out**) smoking in public places.
8 The robbers came running out of the bank, **pushing over** an old lady who was in their path.
9 Older people often find it harder to **fight off** colds and other infections than younger people do.

## Unit 23

**23.1**

| *making noise* | *reducing noise* |
|---|---|
| belt out | die down |
| boom out | trail off |
| blast out | keep down |

**23.2** 1 trailed 2 belting 3 blasting 4 keep 5 boomed 6 died

**23.3** 1 b 2 c 3 a 4 c 5 b 6 a 7 c 8 c

**23.4**
1 You would not enjoy it: droning on means continuing for a long time in a boring, monotonous way.
2 True
3 up
4 away
5 ring out
6 came over

## Unit 24

**24.1** This party **stands** for equality for all.
We do not hesitate to **come** out strongly against any case of injustice.
We **stick** by our principles at all times and never **cave** in to threats or pressure from the opposition.
We **side** with the underdog and do not **defer** to those who are wealthy and powerful.

**24.2**
1 The runners were cheered on by the spectators as they headed for the finishing line.
2 You can rely on Tim to stick up for his little sister. *Or* You can rely on little Tim to stick up for his sister.
3 My grandfather swears by raw garlic as a way of protecting himself from catching colds.
4 My mother would never have tried bungee jumping if we hadn't egged her on.
5 She wanted to go to an all-night party but her mother wouldn't hear of it.
6 The discovery of gas in the North Sea buoyed up the British economy for some years. *Or* The discovery of gas in the North Sea for some years buoyed up the British economy.

**24.3** 1 stick 2 side 3 cheer 4 buoy

**24.4**
1 My preferred course of action would be to **go** with what Ivan has recommended.
2 He began his political life as a Conservative but crossed **over** to the Labour Party when he realised that he would be more likely to get a seat in Parliament that way.
3 correct
4 correct
5 I shall have to defer **to** your superior knowledge of the situation.
6 My mother **swears** by a daily spoonful of honey to keep healthy all year long.
7 Josh is not usually naughty himself but he is quick to egg others **on**.
8 correct

## Unit 25

**25.1**

1 grappling
2 rough
3 talk
4 bounce
5 reflect
6 occurred
7 cottoned
8 hit
9 break
10 piece
11 thrash

**25.2**

1 up; on
2 out
3 up; on
4 with
5 around
6 with
7 at
8 in

**25.3** *Possible answers:*

1 bounce off, bat around, play with, hit on an idea
2 piece together
3 thrash something out, grapple with, break something down

## Unit 26

**26.1**

1 The basic meaning is collecting up animals who have ranged over a wide area of land, e.g. a sheepdog rounds up sheep or a cowboy rounds up cattle. With a different meaning, round up (a number / a total) also refers to raising a number or total to the nearest whole number, e.g. The bill was £9.20 so we rounded it up to £10 and gave the waiter a £10 note. See Unit 27.
2 a cushion
3 pile up
4 looking for something important among things which are not so important
5 Some of the uses of 'up' do have similar meanings. In *prop up*, *pile up* and *stack up* the particle suggests up rather than down. In *gather up*, *round up* and *line up*, the particle suggests 'together'.

**26.2** 1 stack up 2 round up 3 separate out

**26.3**

1 up
2 after
3 up
4 away
5 among
6 towards
7 up
8 up

**26.4** *Possible answers:*

1 You would **fix up** a meeting.
2 They are required to **space out** the desks.
3 You might put a book under the short leg to **prop up** the table.
4 You might need to **separate out** paper, glass, food waste, etc. into different containers.
5 The photographer usually **lines** the pupils **up** before taking the photograph.
6 A sofa could **double up as** a bed if someone stays over.
7 You **gather** all the papers **up** and then throw or tidy them away.
8 You might agree to wear a red carnation so you will **know** each other **from** all the other people in the station.
9 Could you **see about** decorating the room, perhaps, while I get the food prepared?
10 It might be sensible to **sift through** the papers first to ensure that nothing important is thrown away.

## Unit 27

**27.1**
1 The total cost of our holiday amounted **to** nearly £500.
2 The bill came to £22.20 each, so we rounded it **up** to £25 to include a tip.
3 Helena has **put** on a lot of weight recently.
4 It will take Joe some time to build **up** his strength again after such a long illness.
5 The college hoped that the advert would push **up** enrolments for its new course.
6 The new fertiliser claims to **bump** up agricultural yields considerably.

**27.2** 1 e 2 b 3 a 4 c 5 f 6 d

**27.3**
1 The new manager intends to cut costs by making the business smaller in some way – very possibly by sacking some staff.
2 It was a good place for a picnic because there were fewer trees there so there might have been a bit of sunlight, more space to sit down, etc.
3 The number of hits on the website in June must have been much the same as the number of hits in May.
4 Young people are now clearly less interested in politics than they used to be.
5 The speaker sounds as if s/he feels reasonably happy about Jim and what he does at home in that he seems to do more than his share of the gardening even if he does less than his share of the housework.

**27.4**
1 knock down
2 fall off / tail off
3 amount to
4 tail(ing) off / fall(ing) off
5 slimming down
6 push up / build up
7 put on
8 adds up

## Unit 28

**28.1**
1 Some people were going to buy our flat but at the last moment the sale **fell through**.
2 Steve **prides** himself **on** his organisational skills.
3 The company was able to **capitalise on** the unusually wet weather by promoting its inexpensive umbrellas.
4 The England team lost the trophy in 2004 but **won** it **back** the following year.
5 It's been a difficult year for us but we have **come out** of it with renewed vigour.
6 Leila **succeeded in** passing her driving test at her first attempt.
7 Darren **lost out** to his brother in the finals of the tennis tournament.
8 They had a long battle in court to prove their innocence but finally they **won through**.

**28.2**
1 doomed
2 carry
3 pack
4 sail
5 rise
6 get
7 pulled
8 succeeded

**28.3** 1 b 2 a 3 c 4 c 5 a 6 b

**28.4** Oliver has always wanted to become an engineer but it was quite difficult for him to get a place at college. He didn't get in at his first attempt, losing **out** to applicants with better exam grades. However, at his second try he succeeded **in winning** a place. He then sailed **through** all his first-year exams, but failed some of his exams in the second year, as he started spending a lot of time on the rugby pitch, playing for the college first team, rather than in the library. Then his team fell **behind** in the college league after three games, so he wasn't too happy and he did even less work, and as a result he failed three exams. However, he's always prided himself **on** being able to revise very efficiently when he's really under pressure, and in the third year he did enough to pull himself **through**. His friends were amazed that he managed to carry it **off**, as they were sure he could not have packed **in** enough study in such a short time to get **through** the exams. But Oliver knew that he had only just got **by/through** and he resolved to organise his life much better after leaving college.

## Unit 29

**29.1**

1 clear
2 hanging
3 break
4 landed
5 walk
6 spill
7 caught
8 smooth
9 resort
10 make

**29.2**

1 When the doctors examined the dead man, they found his body was **riddled with** disease.
2 I just **grasped at** the first opportunity to get out of my boring job and do something more exciting. I wasn't prepared to just **live with** it / **resign myself to** it; I had to make a change.
3 I **fell back on** / **had to resort to** my knowledge of map reading from my days as a boy scout to help us find a way out of the valley.
4 I'm sorry, I've **botched things up** and caused a lot of problems for everyone.
5 A healthy diet and plenty of exercise is the best way to **safeguard against** heart disease.
6 Her life is difficult. Her husband died. Now she just has to **bear up** and try to carry on as best she can.
7 I'm afraid we just have to **resign ourselves to** the fact that we are going to have to sell the house.
8 She tried very hard to **clear up** / **iron out** the misunderstandings between the two groups.

## Unit 30

**30.1**

1 flirt with something
2 reason with someone
3 mull something over
4 decide on something / work something out
5 do someone out of something
6 size up someone or something
7 tie someone down
8 single someone out

**30.2**

1 You need a coin.
2 No, they haven't.
3 A drum is a musical instrument that is beaten. In the past the drummer in an army used to play rousing military music to encourage soldiers to fight and this may be the origin of drum up meaning attract support or business.
4 It took them some time to arrive at that decision – often they were originally against the idea and/or they had to be persuaded to it.

**30.3**

1 work; out
2 single; out
3 push; through
4 tie; down
5 arrive at
6 drum up
7 play on
8 toss for
9 mull; over
10 playing; off against

**30.4**

1 Everyone is trying to dissuade me from taking the job but I'm tending **towards** accepting it.
2 You'll need to take time to **size** up the situation before you decide what to do.
3 Wicked Uncle Fred succeeded in **doing** his brother out of his rightful inheritance.
4 correct
5 It took Lily ages to get her father to **come** round to the idea of her training as a bus driver.
6 correct – **decide upon** is also possible in more formal registers
7 The advert plays **on** people's desire to appear young and attractive.
8 I don't want to do the washing-up either. Get a coin and we'll **toss for** it.

## Unit 31

**31.1**

1 Go for it!
2 Grow up!
3 Go on!
4 Come off it! / Come on!
5 Hang in there! / Keep it up!
6 Wake up!
7 Knock it off! / Cut it out!
8 Dream on!

**31.2**

1 Roll
2 pipe
3 hang
4 Drink
5 ahead
6 Shut
7 go
8 eat
9 take

**31.3**

1 Come along!
2 Calm down!
3 Get off!
4 Watch out!
5 Go easy on it!
6 Listen up!

## Unit 32

**32.1**

1 fling yourself into something
2 step aside, pack something in, get off
3 ease off, coast along
4 slog away, beaver away, plug away, knuckle down
5 beaver away (a beaver is an animal with sharp teeth and a large flat tail – it lives in a dam which it builds across a river)
6 farm out and get bogged down (a bog is a piece of very wet land – if you step in a bog it can be easy to get stuck there so that you cannot move out)

**32.2** 1 Louise always **flings herself into** her work.
2 I really think that it is time you **knuckled down** to your studies.
3 As a research scientist, you just have to keep **plugging away** at your experiments and eventually you'll get results.
4 If this morning's meeting goes smoothly, I should be able to **get off** by 1 pm.
5 The meeting was going well until we got **bogged down in** the details of the sales conference party.
6 I'm not sure exactly what I'm going to say in my speech but I'm sure I'll be able to **cobble something together** by tomorrow morning.
7 There comes a time when it is best for an older manager to **step aside** and let a younger person take over.
8 I always say that if you start a job, you should **see it through**.

**32.3** I'd hate a job where I could just coast **along** without needing to think about what I was doing. I'd far rather keep busy and really don't mind how much I have to slog **away** each day. I'd soon pack **in** any job that didn't keep me working hard. I fling myself **into** everything I do. Even when I was at school, I used to beaver **away** at my homework as soon as I got home from school. My brothers certainly never used to knuckle **down to** work in the way I did.

**32.4** 1 I can't stand the sight of blood, so I'm not really **cut out for** nursing.
2 If you hate your job so much, why don't you just **hand in** your notice?
3 When several workers were unfairly dismissed, the trade union official decided it was time to **call everyone/people out** on strike.
4 As a PA I spend most of my time **running round** after my boss.
5 We've had a very busy few months at work but things are beginning to **ease off** now.
6 Liam is very good at his job, so I can't understand why he always gets **passed over (for promotion)** while less able people get promoted.
7 Our company has started doing a lot of outsourcing, which means that we **farm out** jobs that we previously used to do ourselves.
8 Ever since she was a little girl she has wanted to **go in for** medicine.

## Unit 33

**33.1** 1 e 2 d 3 f 4 a 5 b 6 c

**33.2**
1 through
2 through; through
3 off
4 off
5 behind
6 towards
7 across
8 against

**33.3** *Suggested answers:*
1 As each person arrived she (asked their name and) **checked them off** on her list.
2 She picked up her favourite novel and **buried herself in** it.
3 He decided to **major in** economics (for his degree).
4 His tutor **moved him up** to a higher class.
5 What sort of grades do you need to **get into** university in your country?
6 I applied to Oxford University but I didn't **get in**.

**33.4** *Possible answers:*
1 What would you like to do when you leave/finish school?
2 Why did you give up / stop studying French/law (or the name of any other subject)?
3 Did Sally finish/complete her degree/course?
4 Do you fancy going to see a film this evening? (Or anything else suggesting a leisure activity. Note that **snowed under** is an informal way of saying that you have a huge amount of work to do.)

**33.5** *Author's answers:*
1 I usually sailed through my exams – apart from maths!
2 It depends on the subject – sometimes I'd get started early, sometimes I wouldn't really buckle down to it until a week before.
3 Yes, teachers often used to mark me down for bad handwriting. I used to think this was really unfair and that they should just think about the content of my work. However, now I am a teacher and have to mark badly written work, I understand why they marked me down!
4 In the UK, taking part in extra-curricular activities, such as sport or music, having work experience and good references, showing you have good organisational or leadership skills, possibly also having good contacts can count towards getting into some universities.

## Unit 34

**34.1** 1 to 2 to 3 from 4 to 5 of 6 up 7 on/upon 8 at

**34.2** *Possible answers:*
1 The research team **consists of** two Americans, two Russians and a Swede.
2 Immigrants to the UK have to **contend with** a whole range of problems.
3 The headteacher would like to **interest** more pupils **in** studying maths at university.
4 The examinations board **insists upon/on** its instructions being followed to the letter.
5 It is essential that society should **invest in** the education of its future citizens.
6 The change in the law **resulted in** a more efficient welfare system.
7 The government is keen to **improve upon/on** the country's system of transportation. (Note that it is also possible to say to improve the country's system of transportation without any preposition. Adding *upon* or *on* makes the writing a little more formal and also suggests that the system of transportation is already reasonably good.)
8 The writer's philosophy is **founded upon/on** a firm belief in socialist principles.
9 Some critics have **objected to** the poet's occasionally coarse use of English.

**34.3** What best **sums the present situation up** – give examples / quotes.

**34.4**
1 The teaching materials will **cater for** historians as well as economists.
2 The recent problems in the company are bound to **detract from** its reputation.
3 The policy of clearing the hillsides of trees appears to have **resulted in** an increased danger of flooding.
4 The football team **consists of** three players from France, one from Sweden and two from Russia.
5 Many people **objected to** being moved from their houses to high-rise flats.
6 Being **deprived of** your freedom is a very difficult punishment to endure.
7 In her article, the writer frequently **refers to** a research study carried out in Canada in 2005.
8 The book is **aimed at** undergraduate students who have little previous knowledge of the subject.
9 For me, this song **sums up** the atmosphere in rural England in the 1960s. (Note that *up* would not be put after the object in a sentence like this becuse the object is very long.)
10 Much of the book is **devoted to** the writer's experiences in the United States.

**Follow up**

*Possible answer:*

Soviet education was **founded upon** the belief that all children could succeed, given the right support. The school system was **based upon** the teachings of Marx and Lenin and it **aimed at** providing the best education possible for all pupils, regardless of their social background. It must be remembered that, at the beginning, Soviet education had many problems to **contend with**. As well as widespread illiteracy and a low level of resources, there were plenty of people who **objected to** the new Soviet regime, saying that citizens were being **deprived of** basic freedoms. Yet, although many people are critical of other aspects of Soviet society, it cannot be denied that the authorities **invested** a great deal **in** the education system. This **catered** well **for** Soviet youth, most of whom **profited from** the education they received. Teachers were respected professionals who **devoted** themselves **to** their pupils, doing all they could to **interest** them **in** their lessons and **insisting upon** high standards in the classroom. To summarise, if we **refer to** most contemporary accounts of the Soviet education process, we find that it **resulted in** a well-educated population.

## Unit 35

**35.1**

1 headed
2 turned
3 set
4 look
5 deal
6 breaking
7 brought
8 aimed
9 buy
10 firmed
11 hiving
12 turning
13 brought

**35.2**

1 Our business has had lots of success in Europe but now we'd like to break into **the US**.
2 Have you heard? Hilary has been asked to head up **the new department**.
3 Arsenal has signed up **a young Brazilian footballer**.
Arsenal has signed **a young Brazilian footballer** up.
4 Her father made his fortune by dealing in **modern art**.
5 Get your people to call my people to firm up **arrangements**. (Note that 'Get your people to call my people to firm arrangements up' is also possible, though less frequent. We are more likely to use this structure when we are saying a time afterwards, e.g. We'll firm the arrangements up next week.)
6 The new factory is already turning out **10,000 pairs of shoes** a week. *Or* The new factory is already turning **10,000 pairs of shoes** out a week.
7 The Alpha model is aimed at **the lower end of the market**.
8 The company is planning to bring out **a new sports car** soon. *Or* The company is planning to bring **a new sports car** out soon.

(Note that when the object phrase is quite long, e.g. in 3 and 6, the phrasal verb is more likely to be kept together rather than separated.)

**35.3** *Possible answers:*
We must **set up** a meeting early in the New Year. [make arrangements for]
Can you help me **set up** the apparatus for the experiment? [get the equipment ready]
A good breakfast **sets** you **up** for the whole day. [prepares you]

Someone **broke into** my car last night and stole the radio. [forcibly entered]
When James caught sight of the bus approaching, he **broke into** a run. [started]
I don't want to **break into** my savings unless I really have to. [start using]

The government is hoping to **bring in** some new legislation relating to education. [introduce]
When you're writing your essay try to **bring in** some good phrasal verbs. [include]
They **brought in** a consultancy firm to help sort out the business. [hired/involved]

That blue dress **brings out** the colour of your eyes. [makes more noticeable]
Her new friends have certainly succeeded in **bringing** her **out** of herself. [helping her to behave in a more confident, less shy way]

A lot of people **turned out** to the concert. [came to]
It **turned out** that he had known the truth all the time. [happened]
His father **turned** him **out** when he heard what he'd done. [made him leave home]

## Unit 36

**36.1**
1 run through, gobble up, set back, clean out, roll in
2 put by, put aside, pay in
3 work off , square up
4 a) square up b) bail out c) clean out d) gobble up
5 rent out

**36.2**

| | |
|---|---|
| 1 bail | 6 square |
| 2 forward | 7 renting |
| 3 cleaned | 8 pay |
| 4 put | 9 back |
| 5 up | |

**36.3**
1 c – **off** my student debts.
2 g – **back** all our profits into the business.
3 h – **aside/by** each month for a rainy day.
4 f – **up** enough money for me to buy a car.
5 b – **into** some money on your gran's death.
6 a – **back** more than I had anticipated.
7 d – **into** my savings for as long as I can.
8 e – **through** enormous sums of money.

**36.4**
1 I never had much money when I was a student but I managed to **live** (**spending as little as possible**) somehow.
2 If everyone **contributes**, then we should be able to afford a nice leaving present for Juliet.
3 Harold's **been receiving large quantities of** money ever since he had that brilliant idea for a website.
4 At the bakery it was Amanda's job to **count the money taken by the shop** at the end of every day.
5 Adrian **risked** (**through a gamble**) a ridiculous amount **on** a horse race and, needless to say, he lost it all.

**36.5** *Possible answers:*

1 It probably set me back about €1,000.
2 They put money aside for a big expense such as a car, a house, a holiday or for a rainy day, i.e. when they might need money unexpectedly.
3 A car typically gobbles up money because you have to pay for petrol, repairs, road tax, etc.
4 I think it's worth breaking into savings for a really good holiday.
5 I'd probably ask my parents or my brother to bail me out if I had financial problems.

## Unit 37

**37.1**
1 clearing away
2 pushing; to
3 stopping up
4 plumping up
5 drawing up *or* pulling up
6 mopping up

**37.2**
1 You put them away.
2 You wash them down.
3 You mop it up.
4 You should chuck them away or put them out in the rubbish (in the recycling bin, of course).
5 You might put a shelf up / put up a shelf.
6 You'd stop up the hole / stop the hole up.

**37.3** 1 e 2 g 3 d 4 b 5 f 6 h 7 a 8 c

**37.4** *Possible answers:*

1 I didn't hear you come in because I'd **got the TV / radio / my music on** rather loud.
2 My husband tends to make a mess when he's cooking and leaves me to **clean / clear up after** him.
3 When you go to bed, please don't forget to **lock up / put the rubbish out**.
4 The bookcase was too big for our new flat, so we had to **part with it / chuck it away**.
5 Anita is untidy. There are always lots of things **cluttering up** her room.
6 Our hall hasn't been decorated for years – it's time we **did/smartened it up**.
7 Living in a student hostel was odd for Ali at first but he soon **settled in**.
8 If I lay the table, you can **clear away** after the meal.
9 You'll make the room look nicer if you **plump up the cushions** on the sofa.
10 It took me all day to **clear up after** those wild, crazy kids and get the place **straightened up** again.

## Unit 38

**38.1**
1 trousers
2 get down to some work
3 trousers, a dress, a skirt
4 unzip
5 a plant, perhaps
6 a coat, a skirt, a dress
7 a) making them looser b) making them tighter
8 fancy dress

**38.2** 1 b 2 c 3 a 4 b 5 c 6 d 7 c 8 b

**38.3**
1 We were surprised when we arrived at the party because the host was wearing a kind of Superman **getup** with a mask, cape and blue bodysuit.
2 My daughter's only 13 but she already wants to get **dolled up** in make-up and high-heeled shoes.
3 Now that I'm pregnant I can't **get into** any of my clothes.
4 Those trousers look a little tight around the waist. Shall I **let them out** a bit for you?
5 (Father to little child) You'd better **zip** your jacket **up**, darling, it's cold outside.

**38.4** *Possible answers:*
1 from older brothers or sisters or cousins
2 Once I went out with one black shoe on and one brown shoe on.
3 I'm afraid I have, especially in the spring as I often seem to put on weight in the winter.
4 It depends, but I'm probably more inclined to pull on the first thing I find.
5 I'd get them taken up because I'm not much good at sewing myself.
6 Yes, I have. Once I dressed up as a woman from the Middle Ages and once I dressed up as a character from a Chekhov play.

## Unit 39

**39.1**
1 Alex: No, but **I've heard of her**.
2 Anna: I wasn't. They've been **going out together** for two years.
3 Will: Yeah, he was **flirting with her** all evening.
4 Fiona: No. I tried to **strike up** a conversation with him, but he wasn't very friendly.
5 Freda: Yes, I **warmed to him** straight away in fact. He's very nice.
6 Diane: Yes, you could say it was tennis that **brought us together**.

**39.2**
1 I've never met Carol Goff, but I know **of** her because Charles works with her.
2 I had an email last month from Tony, but I haven't heard **from** him since then.
3 I think Joe is cheating **on** me. Somebody saw him out with another woman.
4 Mrs Looney fusses ever so much **over** her two sons, even though they're adults.
5 Irena spent all evening flirting **with** her friend's brother.
6 I'm afraid my son is getting mixed **up with** some bad company at university.
7 Marek struck **up** a conversation with the person sitting next to him and the flight passed quickly.
8 Rosa told me about your bust-**up** with Tony.

**39.3**
1 bad
2 c
3 It spoils or damages their relationship.
4 b
5 butter them up
6 c
7 an undesirable one
8 Both are possible.

## Unit 40

**40.1**
1 screwed
2 toughen
3 getting
4 bored
5 had
6 outspoken
7 grown
8 descend

**40.2**
1 across; out
2 through
3 on; for
4 up
5 out

## Unit 41

**41.1**
1 brimming
2 summon
3 perk
4 give
5 hankering
6 work
7 gone
8 snap

**41.2**
1 choke back *or* fight back
2 come over
3 bowl over
4 shake up
5 run away with
6 feel up to

**41.3**
1 choke back *or* fight back
2 bowled over
3 hanker after/for
4 brim with

**41.4**
1 Dolly
2 Geoff
3 Anna
4 Olga
5 Hannah
6 Aaron
7 Bert
8 Emma

**41.5**
1 Gina let it all **spill out** / her feelings **spill out**.
2 Grandma isn't **feeling up to** a long flight.
3 We must not allow our feelings to **run away with us**.
4 You mustn't **give in to** those feelings of insecurity.
5 A feeling of tiredness suddenly **came over everyone**.
6 Our sympathies **go out** to all the victims of the disaster.

## Unit 42

**42.1**
1 deal; move
2 letdown
3 blew
4 shoot
5 passing
6 rolled

**42.2**
1 That it was good quality before but it is not so good any more.
2 That they have become very involved in bird-watching and do it a lot.
3 What you did.
4 Members of the family would all come to one place and meet each other socially.
5 Just spend time together doing nothing special.
6 (b) go out with you and pay for you. *Take someone out* can mean to kill them in a military context, of war etc. If you go with someone to show them the way out of a building, you *show them out*.

**42.3**
1 Ed
2 Tina
3 Louise
4 Ralph
5 Hilary
6 Li
7 Dana
8 Shirley

## Unit 43

**43.1**
1 Patient: I think I've **picked up** a chest infection. I'm coughing and wheezing a lot.
2 Patient: Well, **I broke out in a rash** on my neck about a week ago.
3 Patient: Well, I had an ear infection about a month ago. It seemed to **clear up** when I took the antibiotics you gave me but now it's **flared up** again.
4 Patient: Well, okay, but my nose is **bunged-up** all the time. Can you give me something for it?
5 Patient: Well, I sprained my ankle a week ago and the swelling just hasn't **gone down** and it's still painful.
6 Patient: Well, Doctor, I just seem to feel absolutely **tired out / worn out / wiped out / done in** all the time. I simply have no energy to do anything.

**43.2**
1 Natasha
2 Grace
3 Dan
4 Janice
5 Harry
6 Ray
7 Rajiv
8 Kenji

**43.3** 1 e 2 c 3 a 4 f 5 g 6 d 7 b

## Unit 44

**44.1** 1 d 2 a 3 e 4 f 5 b 6 c

**44.2** *Possible answers:*
1 You need to loosen up / warm up.
2 You may screw up your eyes.
3 It may take you some time to thaw out.
4 You have to pick yourself up.
5 You turn around (*or* **swing around** perhaps if you do it very quickly).
6 They tense up.
7 They waste away.
8 You may double up (in pain).

**44.3** I'm rather worried about my neighbour. I saw her the other day in the garden and she was doubled **up** in pain. She also looks as if she is wasting **away**. I asked her about it and she said she was just trying to lose some weight, but she clearly didn't like my talking about it and I could sense her tensing **up**. I think she's probably been doing far too much exercise. She spends hours outside bending **down** to touch the ground or spreading **out** her arms and swinging them in circles. I can see that she's screwing **up** her face in pain and I long to tell her to relax a bit.

**44.4**
1 You must be freezing – do come inside and **thaw out**.
2 Look at me – now **turn round**.
3 The little girl was (lying) **curled up** on her bed with her thumb in her mouth.
4 When the teacher turned his back, the boy **stuck** his tongue **out** at him.
5 If you don't eat more, you'll **waste away**.
6 The stand-up comic was so good that we spent the evening **doubled up** (laughing).

**44.5** In each case the play on words depends on another meaning of the base verb.
1 Double means two or twice and obviously there are two twins.
2 A screw is a piece of metal used by carpenters to fix things together.
3 Tense is a grammatical term which you are certainly familiar with as a student of English.
4 A taxi driver picks people up to drive them somewhere.

## Unit 45

**45.1**
1 It's so boring listening to Uncle Bill **holding forth** about the morals of young people today.
2 I'll try to **engage** your father **in** conversation so he won't notice you leaving.
3 I wish my parents would stop **going on at** me all the time.
4 OK, before everyone starts working, I'd like to quickly **run through** the instructions (again).
5 The personnel manager **glossed over** salary progression during our interview.

**45.2** 1 They asked her a lot of questions.
2 He would not have been pleased with his performance.
3 He didn't have to stop and think. He spoke very quickly, almost without pausing for breath.
4 She spoke less after Brian arrived.
5 It was difficult for the detective to get the girl to tell her the truth.
6 He wanted to find out if the editor thought it would be a good idea to write the kind of article he had in mind.
7 It's dreadful because he just talks without listening to others or even giving them much chance to speak.
8 She told them a little about it but did not give them too many details, probably in case it worried them.

**45.3** 1 put
2 on
3 led
4 sound
5 out
6 bombarded
7 clammed
8 blurted

**45.4** 1 Jim was so rude – he **interrupted** the conversation I was having with Susan about her new job and started to ask her questions about her son.
2 I don't know how you'll manage to **give a reason for** (**make it appear that it was not your fault**) the scratch on your father's car.
3 I wish he'd stop **talking endlessly about** the weather – it's so boring.

## Unit 46

**46.1** 1 in on
2 away
3 on
4 into; up
5 up on

**46.2** 1 piled
2 tripped
3 push
4 stand
5 clear
6 stumbled
7 bowling
8 double

**46.3** 1 Draw back means to move away because you are surprised or afraid, and artists 'draw' pictures.
2 Bowl along means to travel quickly, and the proper word for throwing a ball in cricket is 'bowling'.
3 Squash up means to move closer together in order to make space for someone else, and 'squash' can also be a kind of juice drink.
4 Double back means to turn and go back in the direction you came from; identical twins could be called 'doubles'.
5 Stole is also the past tense of 'steal' meaning to take something without the owner's permission. The robbers were probably stealing money from the bank.

**46.4** 1 hang 2 drop 3 draw 4 double
*Possible sentences:*
1 I think we should **hang back** and let the family guests go into the reception first.
2 I was walking with Rita and chatting to her but then I **dropped back** to talk with Charlie, who was a bit behind everyone else.
3 We approached the man to help him but then **drew back** as he looked very aggressive.
4 As the mist came down we decided it would be best to **double back** and abandon the walk.

## Unit 47

**47.1**
1 feed on
2 prey on
3 die out
4 eat away at
5 washing away
6 dry up
7 pull down
8 break; off
9 pulling up
10 send out
11 offshoots
12 cutting down (or chopping down)
13 digging up

**47.2**
1 It would freeze over.
2 It might dry up.
3 overcast
4 Because the tide comes in and goes out.
5 Dogs might help them to flush the robbers out.

**47.3**
1 As night fell, the stars **came out**.
2 The sun **went in** and the temperature fell suddenly.
3 Cats (both large and small) **pick up** their young with their teeth to move them around.
4 It was lovely and sunny this morning but now the sky is **overcast** / it is **overcast**.
5 Many wild animals and plants are on the verge of **dying out**.

**47.4**
1 moved in
2 chased; out
3 taken over
4 bring up
5 watching over
6 fend for

## Unit 48

**48.1** 1 off 2 down 3 on 4 down

**48.2** How you mark these sentences will in some cases be a matter of personal preference.

1 Your pipes at home freeze up while you are on a skiing holiday.
☹ You are likely to be unhappy about this as pipes that freeze up will probably later burst and cause a lot of damage.
2 You receive a letter that makes your face cloud over.
☹ You are likely to be unhappy.
3 You are walking by the sea when fog rolls in.
☹ Most people probably don't like it when it becomes foggy because it spoils the view but some people may enjoy it.
4 You can hear the rain beating down outside as you sit by a big log fire.
☺ You are probably happy because you are warm and cosy when it is wet outside but you may feel unhappy if – say – you know you have to go out later on.
5 You are on a long country walk and the rain holds off.
☺ You are probably happy – unless you are the kind of person who enjoys rain.
6 You have to give a speech at a friend's wedding and you freeze up.
☹ You are unhappy because you have become too nervous or anxious to give your speech.
7 You breeze through an important exam.
☺ You are happy because you very easily manage to do well in the exam.
8 You storm out of a meeting.
☹ You are likely to be unhappy because you left the meeting in an angry manner.
9 A group of friends start to freeze you out.
☹ You are likely to be unhappy because your friends seem to want to exclude you from their group.
10 You are sitting on the beach and the sun is beating down.
☺ Most people probably like this, but I for one don't like sitting in very hot direct sunshine.

**48.3** *Possible answers:*

1 The sun is breaking through the clouds.
2 The rain is pelting down (and that person will get very wet).
3 The windscreen has fogged/misted up.
4 The lock has frozen up.
5 The sun is beating down.
6 The smoke from the chimney is blotting out the sun.

**48.4** *Possible answers:*

1 breezed in (as if nothing had happened)
2 misting over
3 mist/fog/steam up
4 break through (the clouds)
5 holds off
6 rolling in (from the sea/hills/moors)
7 breeze through (it)
8 freeze up

## Unit 49

**49.1**

| | | |
|---|---|---|
| 1 set | 6 dotted | 11 in |
| 2 stretches | 7 off | 12 reduced |
| 3 steeped | 8 run-down | 13 off |
| 4 bursting | 9 boarded-up | 14 off |
| 5 soaking | 10 onto | 15 up |

**49.2**

1 New housing developments are encroaching **on** (or, more formal, *upon*) the countryside on the edge of town.
2 Those climbing red roses really set that old white cottage **off**, don't they?
3 The architects made a large-scale mock-**up** of the new shopping centre.
4 The plain lines of the marble walls are **off**set by the ornate windows; together they produce a harmonious building.
5 This plan shows how the area will be **laid** out when it is redeveloped.
6 Signs have gone **up** round the area to be demolished warning the public to keep away.
7 The 1960s buildings do not blend **in** very well with the older houses around them.
8 The whole area is steeped **in** history.

**49.3** *Possible answers:*

1 I think the Palace of Congresses in the Kremlin in Moscow blends in very well with the cathedrals and other old buildings there.
2 I live in Cambridge and the old city centre is often bursting with tourists, particularly in summer.
3 Cambridge, particularly the ancient university there, could certainly be said to be steeped in tradition.
4 My house backs onto a primary school.

## Unit 50

**50.1** 1 picked 2 cut 3 change 4 rev 5 pull

**50.2** *Possible answers:*

1 The police officer is **flagging a car down / flagging down a car.**
2 The driver is **picking up a hitchhiker / picking a hitchhiker up.**
3 The aeroplanes are **stacked up over an airport.**
4 The tyre has **blown out.**
5 The car is **branching off the main road.**
6 The car has been **blocked in.**

**50.3**

1 The police flagged down a lorry and found ten stowaways on board.
2 I was woken by a car revving up outside my bedroom window.
3 That car nearly caused an accident by cutting in on us.
4 I was very frightened when my tyre blew out on the motorway.

**50.4**

1 stow away
2 knocked over
3 blocked; in
4 pulled; over (*or* flagged; down)
5 cast away
6 branches off
7 pick; up
8 stacked up

**Follow up**

*Author's answer:*

I had a wonderful holiday once driving down the Rhone Valley with a friend and her husband. We **set off** from Switzerland, where they were living at the time, in their British car which had the steering wheel on the right-hand side. The problem was that her husband, the only driver among us, couldn't stand having another car in front of him. If a car **picked up** enough speed to pass us, he insisted on immediately **pulling out** to overtake it. Yet, because he was on the right-hand side of the car, he didn't have a clear view of the road ahead so he'd **cut in** ahead of the car he'd overtaken in an alarming way to avoid crashing into the oncoming traffic. In the end we were **flagged down** by a policeman who **told** him **off** for driving in such a dangerous way. Although we saw some great places, I was quite relieved when we **got back** to Switzerland without having had any serious accidents.

## Unit 51

**51.1**

1 root out
2 put out
3 pick up
4 leaked out
5 confide in
6 worm; out of
7 stake out
8 sound; out
9 ferret out
10 get out
11 writing; up

**51.2** 1 c 2 e 3 d 4 a 5 g 6 b 7 f

**51.3**

1 The conservatives **got in** in 2002.
2 A helicopter was **shot down** yesterday.
3 My great-grandfather **joined up** when he was only 16.
4 The kidnappers **gave themselves up** just after midday.
5 The rebels **held out** for six weeks.
6 The government has **sent in** a group of experts to assess the flood damage.
7 The government **put down** the rebellion using massive force.
8 Mr Fleet is trying to **whip up** some enthusiasm for the concert he is trying to organise.
9 Hundreds of people **joined in** the celebrations outside the palace.
10 Ed **got onto** the party's national committee.

## Unit 52

**52.1** *Possible answers:*

1 Its aim was to find out whether claims of fraud were correct or not – and it discovered that the claims were justified.
2 By hushing up a scandal, the company is trying to keep it secret – which suggests that it is a scandal which might harm the reputation of the company in some way.
3 It is implying that the government is not being entirely honest with the public about possible health risks.
4 Because he does not want knowledge of the internal disagreements to become public in case they lose public support. In other words he is trying to hide this information in the same way in which wallpaper is sometimes used to paper over cracks in a wall.
5 It sounds as if it condemns their behaviour – this is suggested by 'cover up'.
6 He has given information about the way in which secret agents spied on diplomats.

**52.2** 1 f 2 g 3 a 4 b 5 c 6 h 7 e 8 d

**52.3** As journalists it is our job to try to dig **up** stories that dishonest people are trying to cover **up**. Sometimes we are accused of spying **on** innocent people but surely it is our duty not to allow people to paper **over** their scandals. Often it is not at all difficult to learn secrets. People are often eager to confide **in** someone who is willing to lend a sympathetic ear. Or they let **out** a secret without realising it. Little things like a blush or a quick glance at someone else can be a real give-**away** to an experienced reporter. Of course, sometimes people try to make **out** that they have nothing to hide and then it can be a good idea to play **along** with them up to a certain point. Then you suddenly take them by surprise with an unexpected question and in this way you can often catch them **out**.

**52.4**
1 catch
2 make
3 let
4 gave

(Note that *give the game away* (= tell someone something that should be kept secret) is slightly different from the other examples in this set, in that it is a fixed expression or an idiom.)

## Unit 53

**53.1**
1 imposed
2 adhere
3 against
4 by
5 inform
6 let

[You may be curious to know how the scores were judged in the original magazine article: 0 – 3 Call yourself an outlaw!; 3 – 6 You're good, but not very good; 7 – 10 You're a model citizen. Congratulations!]

**53.2**
1 The new act went **through** Parliament last week and will become law on 1 January.
2 The anti-litter laws should be tightened **up**; as it is now, nobody is ever prosecuted.
3 He went on a two-year crime spree before the police finally caught up **with** him.
4 She avoided tax by signing **over** her property to her two sons.
5 The new law provides **for** gaol sentences of up to ten years for repeat offenders.
6 Building regulations come **under** local government rather than national or European law.
7 The bill was passed by the Lower Chamber but was thrown **out** by the Senate and never became law.
8 The bill will be voted **on** in Parliament next week and the government hopes it will get **through** without too much opposition.
9 If trials prove successful, the government intends to roll **out** the scheme across the whole country next year.
10 He was sentenced to three years in prison but he'll probably be let **out** in 18 months.

**53.3**
1 The former CEO of Wilson & Wallace has been **let out** after serving a ten-year sentence.
2 If you don't **abide by / adhere to** the health and safety regulations, you will be punished.
3 The government plans to **toughen up / tighten up** the existing laws.
4 The law reforming the Health Service **got through** Parliament with a large majority.
5 Henry's criminal activity was discovered when his neighbours **informed on** him.

**53.4**
*Suggested answers:*
1 He was tried last week, found guilty and **sent to prison** for five years.
2 This government has **introduced / made** more new laws than any other in the last 50 years.
3 The new law will **become official / take effect** in March.
4 The military authorities **issued / made public** an order banning demonstrations in the area around the parliament buildings.

## Unit 54

**54.1**

| | |
|---|---|
| 1 fade out | 4 wiped out |
| 2 set up | 5 call up |
| 3 print off | 6 pop-up |

**54.2**
1 b 2 c 3 c 4 b 5 a 6 b

**54.3**
These statements are all true for the writer but whether they are for you will depend on your own computer – and on how you have set it up.

**54.4**
*Possible answers:*
1 The advantage of a Bluetooth connection is that you don't **have to wire everything up**.
2 You can print a document by selecting the print icon or by **going to the File Menu and choosing Print**.
3 It's quite easy to use a web cam once you have **set it up / got it set up**.
4 Whenever I switch on my new computer it takes quite a long time **to warm up**.
5 I can use this cable to listen to my MP3 player in the car by **plugging it into the car radio**.
6 If your printer is beginning to run out of ink then a warning light **usually comes on**.

## Unit 55

**55.1** 1 gobble/wolf; down
2 picks at
3 disagreed with
4 cut; out
5 put on
6 eat in; send out

**55.2** 1 Aine  2 Zubaida  3 Roger  4 Gavin  5 Liz

**55.3**

| | | | | | | | | | | | |
|---|---|---|---|---|---|---|---|---|---|---|---|
| | | [1] s | | | | | | | | | |
| [2] d | i | p | | | [3] w | a | [4] s | h | e | [5] d | |
| | | i | | | a | | o | | | [6] o | n |
| | | l | | | t | | a | | | w | |
| | [7] s | l | i | c | e | | k | | | n | |
| | | | | | r | | | | | | |

**55.4** *Possible answers:*
1 Shellfish often disagree with people.
2 A tart can be sliced up.
3 Alcoholic drinks are sometimes best watered down.
4 Rice or potatoes fill you up.
5 I should cut down on cakes and biscuits.
6 In Britain people often send out for curry or for pizza.

## Unit 56

**56.1**

| | |
|---|---|
| 1 came down | 4 came at |
| 2 comes in | 5 coming in |
| 3 come down | 6 came at |

**56.2**

| | |
|---|---|
| 1 up against | 5 out with |
| 2 off | 6 across |
| 3 into | 7 into |
| 4 under | 8 in |

**56.3** 1 José's English has **come on** a lot since he met Diana.
2 **Jack comes across as** confident and extrovert.
3 The Prime Minister has **come in for** a considerable amount of criticism lately.
4 Ida **comes out with** some very strange comments sometimes.
5 This history homework does not **come up to** the standards we expect from our students.
6 We've had a difficult year but we've **come through (it)** and are looking forward to the future now.
7 At this point I should like to invite Mariella Snow to **come in**.
8 I was afraid the dog was going to **come at** me.

**56.4** 1 come up to  2 come up against  3 come under  4 come into

## Unit 57

**57.1**
1 It's time she got her act together and found a job.
2 The children always get up to mischief when I'm not looking.
3 I must get to the bottom of that strange letter I received.
4 We got down to business immediately. / We immediately got down to business.
5 Modern life is too complicated. We should get back to basics.

**57.2**
1 get in on the act
2 get by
3 got around
4 get the message across
5 get away with murder
6 get her out of my mind

**57.3**
1 down
2 off
3 off
4 out of
5 in
6 up to
7 into
8 together

**57.4** *Suggested answers:*
1 When do you normally **finish** work?
2 Do you **travel** a lot and **do things away from home or from your normal place of work**?
3 Is there any time of the year when you find it hard to **return to** the routine of your daily life?
4 What have you been **doing** recently?
5 What sort of things **make** you **feel depressed**?
6 Where do you usually **meet** your friends **socially**?

**57.5** *Author's answers:*
1 I normally get off work at about 5 o'clock in the evening.
2 I get around quite a bit – particularly in the summer months.
3 I find it hard to get back into the routine of my daily life after my summer holiday.
4 I've been away on a trip to the Czech Republic.
5 Grey, damp days get me down.
6 My friends and I usually get together at a café in town.

## Unit 58

**58.1**
1 into
2 after
3 over
4 down
5 ahead
6 for

**58.2** 1 g 2 d 3 f 4 a 5 h 6 b 7 c 8 e

**58.3**
1 Tony has been promised that his name will go **forward** for a place on the board of directors next year.
2 Going **by** the weather forecast, there'll be snow tomorrow.
3 Harriet went **through** a terrible time during her husband's illness.
4 You really mustn't go **around** telling such terrible lies.
5 Horace has always wanted to go **into** law.

**58.4** 1 for 2 down 3 over 4 off

## Unit 59

**59.1**
1 to
2 in
3 back
4 from
5 ahead
6 up
7 out of
8 up with

**59.2** 1 Please **keep your** music, TVs and radios **down** during the exam period.
2 Every household will be asked to contribute £5 a month towards the **upkeep** of the village recreation ground.
3 All team members are strongly advised to **keep off** alcohol during the training period. It is important to **keep** your fitness **up** to the highest level.

**59.3** 1 to 2 on 3 up

**59.4** *Possible answers:*
1 Noisy neighbours have occasionally kept me up.
2 I was once kept in for not having done my homework.
3 I'm going to regularly revise the units in this book and am also going to make a point of noting down any examples of phrasal verbs I find when I'm reading English.

## Unit 60

**60.1** 1 take someone aback
2 take away from
3 take off
4 take out
5 take out

**60.2** 1 along
2 out
3 away
4 aback
5 up
6 off

**60.3** 1 Martin does the best **take-off** of the Prime Minister that I have ever seen.
2 A ridiculous amount of my time is **taken up** with dealing with emails.
3 Even the rain could not **take away from** the beauty of the scene.
4 I was **taken aback** when I was told that I was no longer allowed to park in front of my own house.
5 Would you like me to **take up** your concerns **with** the manager? *Or* Would you like me to **take** your concerns **up** with the manager?
6 We are expecting a particularly large **intake** of students next week.
7 We decided it would be nicer to **take** our aunt **away** for the weekend rather than having her stay with us.
8 The **uptake** of places for the weekend seminar has been rather disappointing.

**60.4** 1 Let's **take down** the decorations tomorrow.
2 The doctor has agreed to **take** my elderly aunt **off those** pills for her arthritis.
3 When she went into town Sheila **took out** some library books for her grandmother.
4 My favourite part of a flight is when the plane **takes off**.
5 Norman's being there **took away from** our enjoyment of the evening.
6 After Jack had been working in the kitchens for a week, he was **taken off** washing-up duties.

# Mini dictionary

This Mini dictionary includes the definitions of the phrasal verbs and related noun and adjective forms that are practised in this book. Note that many of the phrasal verbs have other meanings which do not appear here. Refer to a good dictionary such as the *Cambridge Dictionary of Phrasal Verbs* for a full list of English phrasal verbs.

*The numbers in the Mini dictionary are **Unit** numbers not page numbers.*

**abide by sth** to accept or obey an agreement, rule, or decision *53*
**accede to sth** *formal* to agree to something that someone has asked for [e.g. request, demand], often after disagreeing with it *6*
**account for sth** to explain the reason for something or the cause of something *18*
**add up (sth) *or* add (sth) up** to calculate the total of two or more numbers *1*
**add up** to be a reasonable or likely explanation for something *18*
**add up** to increase and become a large number or amount *27*
**add up to sth** to have a particular result or effect *18*
**adhere to sth** *formal* to obey a rule or principle *53*
**(not) agree with sb** if a type of food or drink does not agree with you, it makes you feel slightly ill *55*
**aim at sth/doing sth** to intend to achieve something, or to be intended to achieve something *34*
**aim sth at** to intend something to influence someone, or to be noticed or bought by someone *35*
**amount to sth** to become a particular amount *27*
**arrive at sth** to achieve an agreement or decision, especially after thinking about it or discussing it for a long time *30*
**ascribe sth to sth** *formal* to believe or say that something is caused by something else *6*
**ask around** to ask several people in order to try to get information or help *10*
**be asking for sth** *informal* to behave stupidly in a way that is likely to cause problems for you *6*
**couldn't ask for sb/sth** if you say that you couldn't ask for someone or something better, you mean that that person or thing is the best of their kind *6*
**ask out sb *or* ask sb out** to invite someone to come with you to a place such as the cinema or a restaurant, especially as a way of starting a romantic relationship *6*
**associate sth with sth** to connect someone or something in your mind with someone or something else *2, 20*
**attend to sb/sth** to deal with a situation or problem *6*
**attribute sth to sth** *slightly formal* to believe or say that something is the result of something else *18*
**average out at sth** to have as the average number *27*
**back off** to stop being involved in a situation, especially in order to allow other people to deal with it themselves *13*
**back onto sth** if a building backs onto something, its back faces that thing *49*
**back up (sth) *or* back (sth) up** to make a copy of computer information so that you do not lose it *6*
**back-up** *n* support, help or something that you have arranged in case your main plans or equipment go wrong *3, 54*
**bail out sb/sth *or* bail sb/sth out** to help a person or organization by giving them money *6, 36*
**balance out** to make things equal *27*
**bang about/around** to move around a place, making a lot of noise *10*
**bang down sth *or* bang sth down** to put something down with force, often because you are angry *23*
**base sth on/upon sth** if you base something on particular facts or ideas, you use those facts or ideas to develop that thing *6, 34*
**bat around sth *or* bat sth around** to talk about a plan or idea and to discuss different ways of dealing with it *25*
**bear out sth/sb *or* bear sth/sb out** to prove that something that someone has said or written [e.g. claim, theory] is true, or to say that someone is telling the truth *52*
**bear up** to deal with a very sad or difficult situation in a brave and determined way *29*
**bear on/upon sth** *formal* to be directly connected to something *6*
**beat down** if the sun beats down, it shines strongly and makes the air very hot *48*
**beat down** if the rain beats down, it comes down in large amounts with force *48*
**beaver away** *informal* to work hard at something for a long time, especially something you are writing *32*
**belt out sth *or* belt sth out** *informal* to sing or to play a musical instrument very loudly *23*
**bend down** to move the top part of your body towards the ground *44*

**blast out (sth)** *or* **blast (sth) out** to produce a lot of noise, especially loud music *23*
**blend in/into sth** if something or someone blends in, they look or seem the same as the things or people around them and so you do not notice them *49*
**block in sb/sth** *or* **block sb/sth in** to put a car or other vehicle so close to another vehicle that it cannot drive away *50*
**block out sth** *or* **block sth out** to stop yourself from thinking about something unpleasant because it upsets you *20*
**blot out sth** *or* **blot sth out** if smoke or a cloud blots out the sun, it covers it and prevents it from being seen *48*
**blow out** if a car tyre blows out, it suddenly bursts *50*
**blow out sb** *or* **blow sb out** *British informal* to disappoint someone by not meeting them or not doing something that you had arranged to do with them *42*
**blow up sth** *or* **blow sth up** to make something seem much worse or much better than it really is *16*
**blunder about/around** to move in an awkward way, usually because you cannot see where you are going *10*
**blurt out sth** *or* **blurt sth out** to say something suddenly and without thinking, especially because you are excited or nervous *45*
**boarded-up** *adj* covered with pieces of wood *49*
**be bogged down** to become so involved in the details of something that you cannot achieve anything *32*
**boil down to sth** *slightly informal* if a situation or problem boils down to a particular thing, that is the main reason for it *7*
**bombard sb with sth** to direct a lot of something [e.g. questions, letters] at one person *45*
**boom out (sth)** to speak in a loud voice, or to make a loud noise *23*
**boot up (sth)** *or* **boot (sth) up** if a computer boots up, or if someone boots a computer up, it is turned on so that it is ready to use *6*
**bore into sb** if someone's eyes bore into you, they look at you very hard and make you feel nervous *40*
**boss about/around sb** *or* **boss sb about/around** to tell people what they should do all the time *10*
**botch up sth** *or* **botch sth up** *informal* to spoil a piece of work by doing it badly *29*
**bottom out** if a situation, level, or rate that is getting worse bottoms out, it reaches the lowest point and remains at that level or amount, usually before improving *21*
**bounce sth off sb** *informal* to tell someone about an idea or plan in order to find out what they think of it *25*
**bowl along (sth)** *British informal* to move quickly and energetically *46*
**bowl over sb** *or* **bowl sb over** to surprise or please someone a lot *41*
**box in sb** *or* **box sb in** to prevent someone from doing what they want to do *12*
**branch off** if a road or path branches off, it goes in another direction *2, 49*
**branch off** to leave a main road by turning onto a smaller road *50*
**breakaway** *adj* a breakaway group is a group of people that stop being part of another group, often because they disagree with them *1*
**break down** if a machine or vehicle breaks down, it stops working *1, 4*
**break down sth** *or* **break sth down** to divide information or a piece of work into smaller parts so that it is easier to understand or deal with *25*
**break down** if a discussion, system or relationship breaks down, it fails because of a disagreement or problem *29*
**breakdown** *n* when talks between two groups of people fail because of a disagreement or problem *3*
**break-in** *n* when someone manages to get in a building by using force, usually in order to steal something *3*
**break into sth** to become involved in a type of business or activity that is difficult to become involved in *35*
**break into sth** to start to use an amount of money or food that you have been saving *36*
**break off sth** *or* **break sth off** to separate a part from a larger piece *47*
**break out in/into sth** if you break out in a sweat, it suddenly appears on your skin *43*
**breakout** *n* when someone escapes from prison *1*
**breakout** *n* when something dangerous and unpleasant, like war, disease or fire, suddenly starts *3*
**break through (sth)** if the suns breaks through or breaks through the clouds, it starts to appear from behind the clouds *48*
**break up sth** *or* **break sth up** if an event breaks up a period of time, it makes it more interesting by being different to what you are doing for the rest of the time *17*
**break up (sth)** *or* **break (sth) up** if an occasion when people meet [e.g. meeting, party] breaks up, or if someone breaks it up, it ends and people start to leave *21*
**break up (sth)** *or* **break (sth) up** if a fight breaks up, or if someone breaks it up, the people in it stop fighting or are made to stop fighting *22*
**breeze in/into swh** to walk in quickly and confidently *48*
**breeze through sth** *slightly informal* to succeed in something [e.g. exam] very easily *48*

**brim with sth** to have or show a lot of a good emotion or good quality *41*
**bring forward sth *or* bring sth forward** to change the date or time of an event so that it happens earlier than planned *17*
**bring in sth *or* bring sth in** to earn or make a particular amount of money *12*
**bring in sth *or* bring sth in** if a government or organization brings in something new [e.g. law, rule], they make it exist for the first time *53*
**bring in sb/sth *or* bring sb/sth in** if something, for example a company, brings people or business in, it attracts people, often encouraging them to buy products or services *35*
**bring out sth *or* bring sth out** to produce something to sell to the public *35*
**bring out sth *or* bring sth out** to make a particular quality more noticeable *40*
**bring together sb *or* bring sb together** to cause people to be friendly with each other, especially people who have argued with each other or who would not usually be friendly with each other *39*
**bring up sb *or* bring sb up** to look after a child and educate them until they are old enough to look after themselves *47*
**broken-down** *adj* if a machine or vehicle is broken-down it no longer works *4*
**brush off sb/sth *or* brush sb/sth off** to refuse to listen to what someone says, or to refuse to think about something seriously *7*
**brush down/off sb/sth *or* brush sb/sth down** to use a brush or your hand to remove something *7*
**buckle down** to start working hard *33*
**build in sth *or* build sth in** to include something as part of a system *12*
**build up (sth) *or* build (sth) up** to increase in amount, size, or strength, or to make something increase in amount, size, or strength *3, 23, 27*
**build up sb *or* build sb up** to make someone healthier and stronger after an illness, especially by making sure that they eat a lot *43*
**build-up** *n* when something increases in amount, size or strength *3*
**built-in** *adj* if something is built-in, it is made so that it fits into part of a wall or room *4*
**bump sb off *or* bump off sb** *informal* to kill someone *9, 22*
**bump off sb *or* bump sb off** if you are bumped off the Internet, you lose your connection to it *9*
**bump up sth *or* bump sth up** *informal* to increase the size or amount of something [e.g. price] by a large amount *27*
**bunged-up** *adj slightly informal* blocked nose *43*
**buoy up sth *or* buoy sth up** to support something and help to make it more successful *24*
**burn out *or* burn yourself out** *informal* to have to stop working because you have become ill or very tired from working too hard *43*
**burst out sth** if you burst out laughing or crying, you suddenly start to laugh or cry *23*
**be bursting with sth** to be very full with something *49*
**bury yourself in sth** to give all your attention to something *33*
**bust-up** *n informal* an angry argument *22*
**bust-up** *n informal* a break in a relationship *39*
**butter up sb *or* butter sb up** *informal* to be very nice to someone so that they will do what you want them to do *39*
**buy out sb/sth *or* buy sb/sth out** to buy part of a company or building that belonged to someone else so that you own all of it *3, 35*
**buy up sth *or* buy sth up** to quickly buy a lot of something, often all that is available *6, 16*
**buyout** *n* the buying of a company, especially by the people who previously managed it or worked for it *3*
**call in (on)** *British and Australian* to visit a place or person for a short time, usually while you are going somewhere else *6, 42*
**call on/upon sth** *formal* to use something, especially a quality that you have, in order to achieve something *6*
**call out sb *or* call sb out** to order workers to strike (= to refuse to work because of an argument with an employer) *32*
**call up sth *or* call sth up** if something calls up a memory or an idea, it makes you remember or think about it *20*
**call up sb *or* call sb up** to order someone to join the army, navy, or airforce *51*
**call up sth *or* call sth up** to find and show information on a computer screen *54*
**calm down (sb) *or* calm (sb) down** to stop feeling upset, angry, or excited, or to make someone stop feeling this way *31*
**capitalise on sth** to use a situation in order to achieve something good for yourself *28*
**not care for sth/sb** *formal* to not like something or someone *41*
**carry forward sth *or* carry sth forward** to include an amount of money in a later set of calculations *6, 36*
**carry off sth *or* carry sth off** to succeed in doing or achieving something difficult *28*
**cash in on sth** to make money from an event or situation, or to get some other advantage from it, often in an unfair way *12*
**cash up** *British and Australian* to count all the money taken by a shop or business at the end of the day *36*
**be cast away** to be on an island with no other people after swimming from a ship that is sinking *1, 50*

**cast-offs** *n* clothes which have been given to somebody else because the first owner cannot use them any more *38*
**catch on** *slightly informal* to understand something, especially after a long time *25*
**catch out sb *or* catch sb out** to discover that someone is lying or doing something wrong *52*
**catch up on/with sth** to do something you did not have time to do earlier *2*
**catch up with sb** if someone in authority [e.g. police, tax officials] catches up with you, they discover that you have been doing something wrong and often punish you for it *53*
**be caught up in sth** to become involved in an activity or situation which prevents you from moving or making progress *29*
**cater for sb/sth** to provide all the things that people need or want in a particular situation *34*
**cave in** to agree to something that you were against before, after someone has persuaded you or threatened you *24*
**change around/round sth *or* change sth around/round** to move objects such as furniture into different positions, or to change the appearance of a room by moving furniture into different positions *19*
**change down** *British and Australian* to put a vehicle into a lower gear (= part of a machine that controls the speed of a vehicle), usually in order to go slower *50*
**change over/round** if two people change over, each one starts to do what the other one was doing before, or each one moves to where the other one was standing or sitting before *19*
**chase sb/sth off/out *or* chase off/out sb/sth** to run after a person or an animal in a threatening way in order to make them leave *47*
**chatter away** to talk continuously *23*
**cheat on sb** *informal* to behave in a dishonest way towards your husband, wife, or usual sexual partner by having a sexual relationship with someone else *39*
**check off sth *or* check sth off** to look at each item on a list, or to write something next to each item on a list, in order to make sure that everything or everyone on it is correct, present, or has been dealt with *33*
**cheer on sb *or* cheer sb on** to shout encouraging words at someone, especially a person or team in a race or competition, or to receive encouraging words or shouts *24*
**chill out** *informal* to relax completely *9*
**chip in (sth) *or* chip (sth) in** *slightly informal* to give an amount of money, especially when a group of people are giving money to pay for something together *36*
**chirp away** if a bird chirps away, it sings continuously *23*
**choke back/down sth *or* choke sth back/down** to force yourself not to show your feelings *41*
**chuck away/out sth *or* chuck sth away/out** *informal* to get rid of something that is not needed anymore *37*
**clam up** *informal* to become silent or to refuse to speak about something, usually because you are shy or afraid *45*
**clean out sth *or* clean sth out** to steal everything from a place *15*
**clean out sb *or* clean sb out** *informal* if someone cleans you out, they take or use all the money you have, or if something expensive cleans you out, you spend all the money you have on it *36*
**clean up after sb** to remove dirt someone has made, or to make a place tidy by putting things back where they belong *37*
**clean up your act** to start to behave better *8*
**clear sth away *or* clear away sth** to remove things in order to make a place tidy *37*
**clear out** *informal* to leave a place *46*
**clear up sth *or* clear sth up** to give or find an explanation for something, or to deal with a problem or disagreement *29*
**clear up** if an illness clears up, or if medicine clears an illness up, the illness goes away *43*
**clear up after sb** to remove dirt someone has made, or to make a place tidy by putting things back where they belong *37*
**click-through** *adj* (rate) the number of people who click on an online ad to get to the target site as a percentage of all the people who look at the ad *9*
**climb down** to admit that you are wrong *7*
**climb down** if you climb down from a tree, you go back down to the ground *7*
**close off sth *or* close sth off** to put something across the entrance to something, in order to prevent people from entering it *49*
**cloud over** if someone's face clouds over, they suddenly look unhappy or worried *48*
**clown about/around** to act in a silly way *10*
**clutter up sth *or* clutter sth up** to fill something in an untidy or badly organised way *37*
**coast along** to do only the things that you have to do without trying to go faster or be more successful *32*
**cobble together sth *or* cobble sth together** to make something quickly and not very carefully *32*
**come across sth/sb** to discover something by chance, or to meet someone by chance *1*
**come across** if an idea or an emotion comes across in writing, film, music, or when someone is speaking, it is expressed clearly and people understand it or notice it *33*
**come across** to behave in a way which makes people believe that you have a particular characteristic *40, 56*
**come along** to start to exist, happen, or be available *1*

**cordon off sth *or* cordon sth off** if people in authority [e.g. police] cordon off an area, they put something around it in order to stop people from entering it *13*

**cotton on** *informal* to begin to understand a situation or fact *25*

**cough up (sth) *or* cough (sth) up** *informal* to provide money for something, especially when you are not very willing to do this *36*

**count against sb/sth** to make someone or something more likely to fail *33*

**count on/upon sth** to expect something to happen, and make plans which depend on this thing happening *14*

**count out sb *or* count sb out** *informal* to not include someone in an activity *15*

**count towards sth** to be part of what is needed in order to complete something or achieve something *33*

**cover up (sth) *or* cover (sth) up** to stop people from discovering the truth about something bad *52*

**cover-up** *n* if someone stops people from discovering the truth about something bad *1*

**cream off sb *or* cream sb off** to separate the cleverest or most skilful people from a group and treat them differently *33*

**creep up on sb** to move closer to someone, usually from behind, without being seen by them *46*

**creep up on sb** if a date or an event creeps up on someone, it seems to come or happen sooner than they were expecting *17*

**cross off sth *or* cross sth off (sth)** to remove a word from a list by drawing a line through it *33*

**cross over** to start to support a different, often opposing, person or group *24*

**crowd around/round (sth/sb)** to surround something or someone, standing very close to them *10*

**curl up** to lie or sit with your back curved and your knees close to your stomach *44*

**cut down sth *or* cut sth down** if you cut down a tree or bush, you make it fall to the ground by cutting it near the bottom 47

**cut in (on) (sth)** to interrupt what someone is saying by saying something yourself *12, 45*

**cut in** to suddenly drive in front of someone, not leaving enough space between the two vehicles *50*

**Cut it out!** *informal* something that you say in order to tell someone to stop doing something which is annoying you *31*

**cut off sth *or* cut sth off** to stop the supply of something such as electricity, gas or water *2, 13*

**cut off your nose to spite your face** to do something because you are angry, though it may cause you more problems *8*

**cut out sth *or* cut sth out** to stop eating or drinking something, usually in order to improve your health *55*

**be cut out for sth** to have the right qualities for something, especially a job *32*

**dash off** *informal* to leave a place quickly *5*

**deal in sth** to buy and sell particular goods as a business *35*

**deal with sth** to take action in order to achieve something, or in order to solve a problem *42*

**decide on/upon sth/sb** to choose something or someone after thinking carefully *30*

**defer to sb/sth** *formal* to accept someone else's opinion because they know more than you or are more important than you *24*

**depend on/upon sth/sb** to need the help or support of something or someone in order to survive or continue as before *14*

**depend on/upon sth/sb** if something depends on a particular situation, condition, or person, it is influenced by them or cannot change without them *18*

**deprive sb/sth of sth** to take something important away from someone *2, 34*

**descend to sth/doing sth** to behave badly in a way that other people would not expect you to *40*

**detract from sth** to make something seem less good than it really is or than it was thought to be *34*

**devote sth to sth/doing sth** to use all of something, for example your life or your time, for a particular purpose *34*

**die away** if something, especially a sound, dies away, it gradually becomes less strong or clear and then stops *2, 23*

**die down** if something, especially noise or excitement, dies down, it gradually becomes less loud or strong until it stops *23*

**die out** to become more and more rare and then disappear completely *47*

**dig up sth *or* dig sth up** to remove something from the ground *47*

**dig up sth *or* dig sth up** to discover new facts about a person or situation after a lot of searching *52*

**dig your heels in** to refuse to do what others try to persuade you to do *8*

**dip sth in (sth)** to quickly put something into something else and then take it out again, especially biscuits in tea or coffee *55*

**disagree with sb** if a type of food disagrees with you, it makes you feel slightly ill or uncomfortable *55*

**dive in/into sth** to start doing something suddenly without thinking about it *7*

**do in sb *or* do sb in** *informal* to make someone extremely tired *43*

**do in sb *or* do sb in** *informal* to attack or kill someone *30*

**do out sth *or* do sth out** *British & Australian* to decorate or clean a room *37*

**do sb out of sth** *informal* to stop someone from getting or keeping something, in a dishonest or unfair way *30*

**do up sth** ***or*** **do sth up** to wrap something [esp. present] in paper *26*

**do up sth** ***or*** **do sth up** to repair something, or to improve the appearance of something, especially a building *49*

**do yourself up** *slightly informal* to make yourself look more attractive *30*

**do without (sth/sb)** to manage without something or someone *30*

**doll yourself up** *informal* if a woman dolls herself up, she tries to make herself more attractive than usual by putting on special clothes and make-up *38*

**doom sb/sth to sth** to make someone or something sure to fail or suffer in a particular way *28*

**dot sth with sth** if a place is dotted with something, it has many of them, all over the place *49*

**double back** to turn and go back in the direction that you have come from *46*

**double (sb) over/up** to suddenly bend your body forwards because you are laughing a lot or you are in pain *44*

**double up as sth** if something designed for one purpose can double up as something else, it can also be used for something else *26*

**downcast** *adj* sad and depressed *4*

**downpour** *n* a sudden, heavy fall of rain *3*

**drag sb away from** *informal* to make somebody stop doing something, so that they can do something else *7*

**drag sb/sth into sth** to talk about or bring someone or something into a difficult or unpleasant situation, especially when that person or thing is seen as being connected with the situation *22*

**drag out (sth)** ***or*** **drag (sth) out** to continue for longer than is necessary, or to make something do this *17*

**drag sth out of sb** to make someone tell you something that they do not want to tell you *45*

**draw back** to move away from someone or something, usually because you are surprised or afraid *46*

**draw out sb** ***or*** **draw sb out** to help someone who is shy to feel more confident *40*

**draw out sth** ***or*** **draw sth out** to make something continue for longer than is usual or necessary *15*

**draw up sth** ***or*** **draw sth up** to move a piece of furniture [esp. chair] near to something or someone *37*

**Dream on!** something that you say in order to tell someone that what they are hoping for is not possible and will not happen *31*

**dress up (sb)** ***or*** **dress (sb) up** to put on someone else's clothes to make yourself look like someone else, or to make someone do this, usually as a game *38*

**drill down** to examine something closely *9*

**drink in** to look at, listen to, or experience something with all your attention and to enjoy it very much *7*

**drink to sb/sth** to hold up your glass before drinking from it in order to celebrate something or to wish someone success or happiness *55*

**drink up (sth)** ***or*** **drink (sth) up** to completely finish your drink *31*

**drone on** to talk for a long time in a very boring way *14, 23*

**drop back** if you are moving forward in a group of people and you drop back, you move to a position nearer the back *46*

**drop by** *British & Australian informal* to make a short visit to someone in their home, usually without arranging it before *42*

**drop off** to fall asleep *2, 43*

**drop off sb/sth** ***or*** **drop sb/sth off** to take someone to a place that they want to go to, or to deliver something to a place, usually in a car, often when you are going somewhere else *2*

**drop out** to not do something that you were going to do, or to stop doing something *15*

**drop out** if a student drops out, they stop going to classes before they have finished their course *33*

**drown out sth** ***or*** **drown sth out** if a loud noise drowns out another noise, it prevents it from being heard *23*

**drum up sth** to increase interest in something or support for something *30*

**dry out (sth)** ***or*** **dry (sth) out** to make something dry, or to become dry *47*

**dry up** if a supply of something dries up, it ends *21*

**dry up** to stop speaking when you are acting or making a speech, especially because you suddenly forget what to say next *45*

**dry up** if an area of water [esp. river, lake] dries up, the water in it disappears *47*

**dumb down sth** ***or*** **dumb sth down** to make something [e.g. textbook, curriculum] simpler and easier to understand *9, 51*

**dumb up sth** ***or*** **dumb sth up** to make something less simple and harder to understand *9*

**dwell on/upon sth** to think or talk about a particular subject for too long *14*

**ease off/up** to start to work less or to do things with less energy *32*

**ease off/up** to gradually stop or become less *5*

**ease off/up** to start to treat somebody less severely than before *19*

**eat away at sb** if a memory or bad emotion [e.g. bitterness, shame] eats away at someone, they think about it a lot and it makes them very unhappy *20*

**eat away at sth** to gradually destroy something by continuously damaging it or taking little parts of it away *47*

**eat in** to have a meal at home, not in a restaurant *55*

**eat into sth** to use or take away a large part of something valuable [e.g. savings, profits, leisure time, business] *7*

**eat up sth** *or* **eat sth up** to eat all the food you have been given *16*

**Eat up!** something that you say to someone, especially a child, in order to tell them to eat their food *31*

**egg on sb** *or* **egg sb on** to encourage someone to do something, often something that is wrong, stupid, or dangerous, or to be encouraged to do something *24*

**eke out sth** *or* **eke sth out** to use something slowly or carefully because you only have a small supply of it *17*

**encroach on/upon sth** to gradually cover more and more of an area of land *49*

**engage sb in sth** if you engage someone in conversation, you try to start a conversation with them *45*

**expand on/upon sth** to give more details about something you have said or written *45*

**explain away sth** *or* **explain sth away** to give a reason for something bad happening which makes other people think that it is not so bad or that it is not your fault *45*

**face up to sth** to accept that a difficult or unpleasant situation exists *2*

**factor in sth** *or* **factor sth in** to include something when making a calculation or when trying to understand something *12*

**fade in** if the sound or picture of a film or recording fades in, or if you fade it in, it becomes gradually louder or brighter so that you can hear it or see it clearly *54*

**fade out** if the sound or picture of a film or recording fades out, or if you fade it out, it gradually becomes quieter or less clear until you cannot hear or see it any more *54*

**fall apart** if an organization, system, or agreement falls apart, it fails or stops working effectively *21*

**fallback** *adj* a fallback position is something you use when other things have failed, or when there are no other choices *4*

**fall back on/upon sth** to use something when other things have failed, or when there are no other choices *29*

**fall behind (sb)** to fail to remain level with a group of people that is moving forwards *33*

**fall behind (sb)** to fail to score as many points as another team or player in a competition *28*

**fall in** if a structure [e.g. roof, ceiling] falls in, it drops to the ground because it is weak or damaged *49*

**fall into sth** to start doing something, often without intending to *7*

**fall into sth** to accidentally arrive in a hole *7*

**fall off** if the amount, rate, or quality of something falls off, it becomes smaller or lower *27*

**fall through** if a plan or agreement falls through, it fails to happen *6, 28*

**farm out sth** *or* **farm sth out** to give work to other people instead of doing it yourself *32*

**feed on/upon sth** if an animal feeds on a particular type of food, it usually eats that food *47*

**feel up to sth/doing sth** to feel physically and mentally strong enough to do something *41*

**fend for yourself** to take care of yourself without needing help from other people *47*

**ferret out sth** *or* **ferret sth out** to find something after searching for it *51*

**fight back sth** *or* **fight sth back** to try hard not to show an emotion, or to try hard not to let your emotions control what you do *41*

**fight off sb/sth** *or* **fight sb/sth off** to use violence so that something or someone goes away *22*

**fill up sb** *or* **fill sb up** if food fills someone up, it makes them feel as if they have eaten enough *55*

**finish off sb** *or* **finish sb off** to make someone so tired, weak, or unhappy that they are unable to continue what they were doing *13*

**finish up (sth)** *or* **finish (sth) up** to eat or drink all of what you are eating or drinking *16*

**finish with sth** to stop using or needing something *21*

**firm up sth** *or* **firm sth up** to make something [e.g. agreement, details, prices] more definite or less likely to change *35*

**fish out sth** *or* **fish sth out** *informal* to pull or take something out of a bag or pocket, especially after searching *7*

**fit in** to be able to be done between other activities *17*

**fit in with sth** if one activity or event fits in with another, they exist or happen together in a way which is convenient *12*

**fix up sth** *or* **fix sth up** to arrange something [esp. meeting] *26*

**flag down sth** *or* **flag sth down** to make a vehicle stop by waving at the driver *50*

**flare up** if someone flares up, they suddenly become very angry *22*

**flare up** if a disease that you had before flares up, you suddenly get it again *43*

**flash back** if your mind or thoughts flash back to something that happened to you in the past, you suddenly remember that thing *20*

**flashback** *n* an occasion when you suddenly remember something vividly that happened to you in the past *20*

**flatten out** if the rate of something flattens out, or if something flattens it out, it stops increasing and decreasing and begins to stay at the same level *27*

**fling off sth *or* fling sth off** to remove very quickly *38*

**fling yourself into** to start to spend a lot of your time and energy doing something *32*

**flirt with sb** to talk and behave towards someone in a way that is sexually attractive and which shows that person that you are sexually attracted to them *5, 39*

**flirt with sth** to consider doing something, or to be interested in something for a short period of time *5, 30*

**be floating about/around** if you say something is floating around, you mean that you have seen it somewhere but you do not know exactly where it is *10*

**flood back** if memories flood back, you suddenly remember very clearly a lot of things about an experience or period in the past *20*

**flood in/into sth** to arrive or enter somewhere in very large numbers or amounts *7*

**flush out sb/sth *or* flush sb/sth out** to force a person or animal to come out of the place they are hiding in *47*

**fly about/around (swh)** if rumours fly around, they are made in a way which makes people excited *10*

**fly at sb** to attack someone suddenly and violently *22*

**fly into sth** if someone flies into a particular state [e.g. rage, temper, panic] they are suddenly in that state *22*

**focus (sth) on/upon sth** to give a lot of attention to one particular activity, situation or idea *14*

**fog up** if something made of glass [e.g. windscreen, glasses] fogs up, or if something fogs it up, it becomes covered with small drops of water and you cannot see through it any more *48*

**fold up (sth) *or* fold (sth) up** to make something [e.g. cloth, paper, chair] into a smaller, neater and usually flatter shape by folding it, or to be able to be folded in this way *26*

**fold-up** *adj* a fold-up chair can be made into a smaller, neater and flatter shape by folding it *4*

**foldaway** *adj* a foldaway bed has parts that can be folded so that it is smaller and can be stored somewhere *4*

**forthcoming** *adj* a forthcoming event, action, or product is one which will happen or become available soon *4*

**be founded on/upon sth** to be based on a particular idea or belief *34*

**free up sth *or* free sth up** to make time or money available for a particular use by not using it in another way *17*

**freeze out sb *or* freeze sb out** to make someone feel that they are not part of a group by being unfriendly towards them, or to stop someone from being included in an arrangement or activity *48*

**freeze over** if water freezes over, it becomes covered with ice *2, 47*

**freeze up** if something [e.g. pipe, lock] freezes up, it becomes blocked with ice and stops working *48*

**fritter away sth *or* fritter sth away** to waste something [esp. money, time] by using it in a careless way for unimportant things *17*

**frown on/upon sth** to believe that something is wrong and that you should not do it *14*

**fry-up** *n* a quick meal made of fried food *55*

**fuss over sb/sth** to pay too much attention to someone or something, especially because you want to show that you like them *39*

**gain on/upon sb/sth** to get nearer to someone or something that you are chasing *46*

**gang up** *informal* to form a group to act against someone else *6*

**gather up sth *or* gather sth up** to collect several things, especially from different places, and put them together *26*

**gear sth to/towards sth/sb** to design something so that it is suitable for a particular purpose, situation, or group of people *26*

**get across sth *or* get sth across** to successfully communicate an idea to other people *57*

**get around** if news or information gets around, a lot of people hear about it *10, 57*

**get around** to travel to a lot of different places *57*

**get away with sth/doing sth** to succeed in not being criticized or punished for something wrong that you have done *57*

**get back into sth** to begin doing something again after not doing it for a period of time *57*

**get by** to have just enough money to pay for the things that you need, but nothing more *6, 57*

**get by** to have or know just enough of something to be able to deal with a particular situation but not have or know as much as you would like *1, 28*

**get down to sth/doing sth** to start doing something seriously and with a lot of your attention and effort *57*

**get sb down** to make someone feel unhappy *11, 57*

**get in** to succeed in getting a place at a school, college, or organization *33*

**get in** if a political party or a politician gets in, they are elected *51*

**get in sth *or* get sth in** to manage to do something even though you do not have much time because you are busy doing other things *57*

**go down** if part of your body that is bigger than usual because of an illness or injury goes down, it starts to return to its usual size *43, 58*
**go easy on sth** to not take or use too much of something *31*
**go for sth** if something goes for a particular amount of money, it is sold for that amount *58*
**Go for it!** something that you say to encourage someone to try and achieve something *31*
**go forward** if someone's name goes forward, it is suggested that that person should compete for an elected position or a job *58*
**go in** *informal* if a fact or piece of information goes in, you understand it and remember it *25*
**go in** if the sun or moon goes in, it becomes hidden behind a cloud *47*
**go in for sth** to choose a particular type of work as your job *32*
**go into sth** to describe, discuss, or examine something in a detailed way *6*
**go into sth** to click on a menu or a programme or a different window when using a computer *54*
**go into sth** to start an activity, or start to be in a particular state or condition *58*
**go off sb/sth** to stop liking someone or something *5, 41*
**go off** *British & Australian* to become worse in quality *42*
**go off** if a light or machine goes off, it stops working *54*
**go off** to happen in a particular way *58*
**go on** to continue to exist or happen *4*
**go on** to talk in an annoying way about something for a long time *14*
**Go on!** something that you say to tell someone that you do not believe what they have just told you *31*
**go on at sb** to criticize someone continuously *45*
**Go on then!** something that you say to encourage someone to do something *31*
**go on to sth** to start to do something after you have finished something else *33*
**go on to swh** to go to a particular place after going somewhere else *42*
**go onto sth** to use a computer or the Internet, or to visit a website *54*
**go out** if something which is burning [e.g. fire] goes out, it stops burning *15*
**go out** if the sea or the tide (= movement of the sea in and out) goes out, it moves away from the beach *47*
**go out to sb** if your thoughts or sympathies go out to someone, you feel very sorry for them when they are in a difficult situation *41*
**go out together** to have a romantic relationship *39*
**go out with sb** to have a romantic relationship *39*
**go over sth** to think about something that has happened or something that was said *58*
**go over to sth** to leave one group or organization and join a group or organization that is competing against them *6, 58*
**be going round in circles** to use a lot of time and effort with no results *8*
**go through** if a law, plan, or deal goes through, it is officially accepted or approved *53*
**go through sth** to experience an unpleasant or difficult situation or event *58*
**go to (swh)** to click on a menu item or visit a particular web page when using a computer *54*
**go up** if a shout [e.g. cheer, cry, groan] goes up, a lot of people make that noise at the same time *23*
**go up** if a building or sign goes up, it is built or it is fixed into position *49*
**go with sth** to accept a plan or an idea, or to support the person whose ideas you agree with *24*
**go-ahead** *adj* using new methods and ideas to succeed *4*
**gobble down/up sth** *or* **gobble sth down/up** *informal* to eat very quickly *55*
**gobble up sth** *or* **gobble sth up** *informal* to use a lot of something, especially money *36*
**grapple with sth** to try to deal with or understand a difficult problem or subject *25*
**grasp at sth** to quickly use or accept an opportunity to do or have something, especially because you are unhappy with the present situation *29*
**grate on sb/sth** if something, especially someone's voice or way of behaving, grates on you, it annoys you *23*
**grow out of sth** if a child grows out of an interest, way of behaving, or illness, they stop having or doing it because they have become older *40*
**Grow up!** *informal* something that you say to an adult in order to tell them to stop behaving stupidly *31*
**gun down sb** *or* **gun sb down** to shoot someone and kill or seriously injure them, often when they cannot defend themselves *11*
**be gunning for sb** *informal* to try to harm someone or cause trouble for them *6*
**hack into sth** to get into someone else's computer system without permission in order to look at information or do something illegal *6*
**hand in sth** *or* **hand sth in** to tell your boss officially that you do not want to do your job anymore *32*
**Hang about!** something that you say to tell someone to stop doing or saying something *31*
**hang about/around/round with sb** *informal* to spend time with someone *6*
**hang back** to not move forwards, usually because you are shy or afraid *46*
**hang in there** to continue to try to do something, even though it is very difficult *31*

**hang on to/onto sth/sb** to keep someone or something *21*
**hang on/upon sth** to depend on something *14*
**hang out** *informal* to spend a lot of time in a particular place, or to spend a lot of time with someone *42*
**hang over sb/sth** if a problem or threat hangs over a person or situation, it exists and makes people worry about what is going to happen *29*
**hanker after/for sth** to want something very much, especially something you know you should not want *5, 41*
**happen on/upon sb/sth** to find something or meet someone without planning to *14*
**harp on** to talk continually about something in a way that other people find boring or annoying *14*
**have sth against sb/sth** to dislike or disagree with someone or something for a particular reason *41*
**have sb down as sth** to think that someone is a particular type of person, especially when they are not in fact like that *40*
**have off sth** ***or*** **have sth off** to spend time away from work *13*
**have on sth** ***or*** **have sth on** if you have clothes or shoes on, you are wearing them *38*
**have on sth** ***or*** **have sth on** if you have an electrical device [e.g. television, radio, iron] on, it is operating so that you can use it *37*
**head off sth** ***or*** **head sth off** to prevent a difficult or unpleasant situation from happening *51*
**head up sth** ***or*** **head sth up** to be in charge of an organization *35*
**heal over** if a wound heals over, new skin grows over it *43*
**hear from sb** to receive news or information from someone, usually by letter or telephone *39*
**have/had heard of sb/sth** to know a little about someone or something because you have read, seen, or been told something about them before *39*
**not hear of sth** ***or*** **not hear of sb doing sth** to not allow something, or not allow someone to do something *24, 31*
**help sb to sth** to put food onto a plate for yourself *55*
**hinge on/upon sth** to depend on something or be very influenced by it *14*
**hit on/upon sth** to have a good idea, especially one that solves a problem *5, 25*
**hit out** to strongly criticise something or someone *7*
**hive off sth** ***or*** **hive sth off** to separate one part of a company from the rest *35*
**hoard away sth** ***or*** **hoard sth away** to put a supply of something in a safe place so that you can use it in the future *26*
**hold back sb/sth** ***or*** **hold sb/sth back** to prevent something from working effectively, or to prevent someone or something from making progress *1*
**hold down sb** ***or*** **hold sb down** to limit the freedom of a group of people *1*
**hold forth** to talk about a particular subject for a long time, often in a way that other people find boring *45*
**hold off** to not start, although you expect it to *48*
**hold out** to continue to defend yourself against an enemy or attack *51*
**hold out for sth** to wait until you get what you want and to refuse to accept anything less *1*
**hold over sth** ***or*** **hold sth over** to delay something and to arrange to do it at a later time *17*
**hook up** *US informal* to meet someone for a particular purpose *42*
**huddle up** to move closer to other people, or to hold your arms and legs close to your body, usually because you are cold or frightened *44*
**hug-in** *n* when lots of people embrace each other *9*
**hurry along** to make someone do something more quickly, or to make something happen more quickly *17*
**hush up sth** ***or*** **hush sth up** to stop the public from finding out about something bad that has happened *52*
**impact on/upon sth/sb** *slightly formal* to have a noticeable effect on *18*
**impose sth on/upon sb** *formal* to force a group of people to accept something, or to give someone a punishment [e.g. fine, ban] *53*
**improve upon/on sth** to do something in a better way or with better results than when it was done before *34*
**inform on sb** to give information about someone who has done something wrong to a person in authority, especially the police *53*
**input** *n* contribution to a system to help it operate *3*
**insist on/upon sth/doing sth** to demand something and to make it clear that you will not accept anything else *34*
**intake** *n* the number of people who begin to study at a school, or who join an organization at a particular time *1, 60*
**interest sb in sth** to try to persuade someone that they want something *34*
**invest sth in sth** to use a lot of time or effort trying to achieve something or trying to make something successful *34*
**iron out sth** ***or*** **iron sth out** to find a way of solving small difficulties or problems, or to find a way of ending a disagreement *29*
**jazz up sth** ***or*** **jazz sth up** to make something more attractive or interesting *16*

**join in (sth)** to become involved in an activity with other people *51*
**join up** to join the army, navy, or airforce *51*
**jut out** to stick out from a surface or beyond the edge of something *15*
**keep (sb) ahead** to continue to be more advanced and successful than other people, or to make sure that someone is more advanced or successful than other people *59*
**keep back sth *or* keep sth back** to not tell someone everything you know about a situation or an event that has happened *59*
**keep down sth *or* keep sth down** if you keep the noise of something [e.g. music, voice] down, you stop it from becoming too loud *23*
**keep sb/sth from doing sth** to prevent someone from doing something, especially work, by spending time with them *59*
**keep sb in** to make a child stay at school or at home, especially as a punishment *59*
**keep in with sb** *British & Australian* to continue to be friendly with someone, especially because they can help you *5, 59*
**keep (sb) off sth** to not eat, drink or use something that can harm you *59*
**keep on** *slightly informal* to talk in an annoying way about something for a long time *14*
**keep on doing sth** to continue to do something, or to do something again and again *59*
**keep out of sth** to not become involved in something *59*
**keep to sth** if you keep to the point, you do not write or talk about other topics *59*
**keep sth to yourself** to keep something secret *59*
**keep sb up** to make someone go to bed later than they usually do *59*
**keep up sth *or* keep sth up** to not allow something that is at a high level to fall to a lower level *59*
**keep up** to be able to understand or deal with something that is happening or changing very fast *25, 59*
**keep it up** to continue to do something, especially to work hard or to do good work *31, 59*
**kick off** if a game of football or American football kicks off, it starts *9*
**kick off** *British informal* to start making trouble *9*
**kick off (sth)** *informal* to start *13*
**kick off sth *or* kick sth off** to remove your shoes by shaking your feet *13*
**kick out sb *or* kick sb out** to force someone to leave a place or an organization *15*
**knock sb about/around** *informal* to hit or kick someone several times *10*
**knockabout** *n British informal* when two or more people hit or kick a ball to each other for pleasure but not in a serious way, sometimes to warm up before a game *3*
**knock down sth *or* knock sth down** to destroy and remove a building or part of a building [esp. wall] *2*
**knock down sb/sth *or* knock sb/sth down** to reduce a price, or to persuade someone to reduce the price of something that they are selling *11*,
**knock down sb *or* knock sb down** to cause someone to fall to the ground by pushing or hitting them *1*
**Knock it off!** *informal* something you say to tell someone to stop doing something which is annoying you *31*
**knock out sb *or* knock sb out** to make someone become unconscious or to make someone fall asleep *22, 43*
**knock over sb *or* knock sb over** to hit someone with a vehicle and injure or kill them *50*
**know sth from sth** to know the difference between something and something else, so that you can recognize either of them *26*
**know of sb/sth** to have heard of someone or something and to be able to give some information about them, but not very much *39*
**knuckle down** to start to work or study hard, especially if you have not been working very hard before *32*
**land (sb) in sth** to be in a difficult situation, or to cause someone to be in a difficult situation or an unpleasant place [e.g. prison] *29*
**land up** *informal* to finally be in a particular place, state, or situation, especially without having planned it *16*
**lash out** to criticize someone or something in an angry way *15*
**lay out sth *or* lay sth out** to design the way in which a house, city, or garden is built or created *49*
**lead into sth** if a subject you are talking about or a discussion leads into another subject or discussion, it is the reason why you start talking about the second subject or start the second discussion *45*
**lead-in** something that introduces something else *12*
**lead on sb *or* lead sb on** to make someone do something bad by encouraging them or annoying them until they do it *14*
**lead to sth** if an action or event leads to something, it causes that thing to happen or exist *18*
**lead up to sth** if a period of time or a series of events leads up to an event or activity, it happens until that event or activity begins *17*
**leak out** if secret information leaks out, people who should not know this information find out about it *51*
**lean towards sth/doing sth** to support, or begin to support, a particular set of ideas or a particular political party *24*

**leap out at sb** if something leaps out at you, you notice it immediately *25*
**leave behind sb *or* leave sb behind** to make progress much faster than someone else *33*
**leave off (sth/doing sth)** to stop, or to stop doing something *13*
**left out** *adj* if someone feels left out, they are unhappy because they have not been included in an activity or conversation *4*
**let in** if something lets in water, air, or light, it allows water, air, or light to enter it through a hole or opening *12*
**let off sb *or* let sb off** to not punish someone who has committed a crime or done something wrong, or to not punish someone severely *53*
**let off steam** to talk or act in a way that helps get rid of strong feelings *8*
**let out sth *or* let sth out** to make a piece of clothing wider by removing the sewing from the side edges and then sewing closer to the edge of the material *38*
**let out sth *or* let sth out** to tell someone about something which was supposed to be a secret *52*
**let out sb/sth *or* let sb/sth out** to allow a person or animal to leave somewhere, especially by opening a locked or closed door *53*
**let down sth *or* let sth down** to make a piece of clothing longer by removing the sewing from the bottom folded edge and then sewing closer to the edge of the material *38*
**letdown** *n* something which is not as good as you thought it would be *3, 42*
**level off/out** if a rate or amount levels off, it stops rising or falling and it stays at the same level *27*
**level with sb** *informal* to tell the truth about something *52*
**lie about/around (swh)** if things are lying around, they are untidily left in places where they should not be *10*
**lift up sth *or* lift sth up** to move something from a lower to a higher position *16*
**lift-off** *n* the moment when a spacecraft leaves the ground *3*
**light up (sth) *or* light (sth) up** if your face or eyes light up, or if something [e.g. smile] lights them up, you suddenly look very happy or excited *40*
**line up sth *or* line sth up** to move something in order to make it straight or level with something else *26*
**listen out for sth** to make an effort to hear a noise which you are expecting *23*
**Listen up!** *informal* something you say to tell people to listen to what you are going to say *31*
**live-in** *adj* a live-in nanny lives at the home of the children she cares for *4*
**live on** to continue to exist *14*
**live with sth** to accept a difficult or unpleasant situation and continue with your life while it exists *29*
**lockout** *n* when workers are prevented from entering their place of work until they agree to particular conditions given by the employer *1*
**lock up (sth) *or* lock (sth) up** to lock all the doors and windows of a building when you leave it *37*
**log in/into sth** to connect a computer to a system of computers by typing your name or password, usually so that you can start working *6*
**look after sb/sth** to take care of someone or something by doing what is needed to keep them well or in good condition *2, 6*
**look after sth** to be responsible for dealing with something *35*
**look down on sb/sth** to think that someone is less important than you, or to think that something is not good enough quality for you to use *2*
**look for sth/sb** to try to find something or someone, either because you have lost them or because you need them *2*
**look forward to sth/doing sth** to feel pleased and excited about something that is going to happen *1, 2*
**lookout** *n* a person who looks at what is happening in the area around them, especially in order to watch for any danger *3*
**loosen up (sth) *or* loosen (sth) up** to prepare your body muscles for a physical activity by stretching and doing simple exercises *44*
**lose out to** to be less successful than *28*
**luck out** *US informal* to be very lucky *9*
**magic away sth *or* magic sth away** to make something disappear so quickly that it seems as if you have used magic *21*
**major in sth** *US & Australia* to study something as your main subject at university *33*
**make out sth** to claim falsely that something is true *52*
**make up for sth** if someone makes up for something bad that they have done, they do something good so that the bad thing does not cause a problem any more *29*
**make up for lost time** to do something to compensate for not doing it previously *8*
**make up your mind** to make a decision about something *8*
**makeover** *n* a set of changes that are intended to make a person or place more attractive *19*
**mark down sb *or* mark sb down** to give someone a lower result in an exam or competition because they have made a mistake or done something wrong *2, 33*
**melt-up** *n* when a financial market is overheated, causing prices to rise *9*
**mess about/around with sth** *informal* to try to change or improve something, usually with bad results *19*

**mist over** if your eyes mist over, they become filled with tears which stop you from seeing clearly *48*
**mist over/up** if something made of glass [e.g. windscreen, glasses] mists up, or if something mists it up, it becomes covered with small drops of water and you cannot see through it any more *48*
**be mixed up with sb** to be involved with someone who has a bad influence on you *39*
**mock-up** *n* a model showing how something will look when it is built *49*
**mop up (sth) or mop (sth) up** to use a cloth to remove a liquid that has been dropped or that has spread *37*
**move away** to leave the place or area where you live and go and live in another place *42*
**move in** to begin living in a new house or area *47*
**move (sb) in/into (swh)** to go to a place to deal with a difficult situation *51*
**move on** to move forward in one's life and not look back to the past *42*
**move up (sb) or move (sb) up** if a student moves up, or if a teacher moves them up, they are put in a higher level or class *2, 33*
**muck up sth or muck sth up** *informal* to do something very badly *6*
**mull over sth or mull sth over** to think carefully about something for a long time, often before making a decision *30*
**nod off** *informal* to fall asleep when you do not intend to go to sleep *43*
**nose about/around (swh)** *informal* to look around a place, often in order to find something *7*
**object to sb/sth/doing sth** to feel or say that you oppose or dislike something or someone *34*
**occur to sb** if a thought or idea occurs to you, it comes into your mind *25*
**off-putting** *adj* slightly unpleasant or worrying so that you are discouraged from getting involved in any way *1, 4*
**offset** *adj* if something is offset by something else it is compensated for *49*
**offshoot** *n* plant which has developed from a larger plant *47*
**ongoing** *adj* if a problem is ongoing, it continues to be a problem *4*
**onset** *n* the moment at which something unpleasant starts *1, 3*
**open off sth** if an area opens off another area, you can enter one from the other directly *49*
**open up (sth) or open (sth) up** if a country or area opens up, or is opened up, it becomes easier to travel around it or sell things to it *16*
**open up (sth) or open (sth) up** to create a new opportunity or possibility *21*
**outbreak** *n* a sudden beginning of something, especially something unpleasant *3*
**outdated** *adj* old-fashioned and therefore not as good or as fashionable as something that is modern *4*
**outgoing** *adj* if someone is outgoing, they are friendly and energetic and find it easy and enjoyable to be with others *1, 4*
**outlook** *n* the likely future situation *3*
**output** *n* an amount of something, produced by a person, machine, factory or country *3*
**outspoken** *adj* if someone is outspoken, they express their opinions even though other people might be offended by them *1, 4, 40*
**outstretched** *adj* if someone's arms are outstretched they are held out in front of the person's body, often in order to greet someone *4*
**overcast** *adj* if the sky is overcast, it is grey and covered in cloud *47*
**overkill** *n* when there is more of something than is needed *3*
**overpriced** *adj* too expensive *4*
**pack in sth or pack sth in** *informal* to manage to do a lot of activities in a period of time *28*
**pack in sth or pack sth in** *informal* to stop doing something, especially a job *32*
**paper over sth** to hide a disagreement or difficulty and try to make people believe that there is no problem *52*
**part with sth** to give something away, usually when you do not want to *37*
**pass by (swh)** *British* to visit somewhere for a short time, usually while you are going somewhere else *42*
**pass sb by** if an event or opportunity passes you by, you do not notice it or you do not get any advantage from it *17*
**pass off** *British & Australian* if an event passes off in a good way, it happens in that way *51*
**pass on sth or pass sth on** to give a disease to another person or animal *43*
**pass over sb or pass sb over** to not give someone a job or a higher position and give it to someone else who is younger or less experienced *32*
**patch up sth or patch sth up** to try to improve your relationship with someone after an argument *39*
**pay sth into sth** to put money into a bank account, often to save money for a particular purpose *36*
**peal out** when bells ring loudly, they peal out *23*
**pelt down** *informal* to rain very heavily *48*
**pep up sth/sb or pep sth/sb up** *informal* to make something more interesting or attractive, or to make someone feel more active or energetic *16*
**perk up (sb) or perk (sb) up** to suddenly become happier or more energetic, or to make someone feel this way *41*
**perk up** if something perks up, it improves or becomes more exciting *19*

**peter out** if an energetic activity or a strong emotion peters out, it gradually becomes less energetic or strong until it stops completely *21*
**phish for sth** to fish for financial information (to fraudulently obtain this information through dishonest websites) *9*
**pick at sth** to eat only a small amount of a meal because you are not hungry or because you are feeling ill *55*
**pick out sth/sb** ***or*** **pick sth/sb out** to choose one thing or person or several things or people from a large group *15*
**pick up sth/sb** ***or*** **pick sth/sb up** to lift something or someone by using your hands *1, 16*
**pick up sth/sb** ***or*** **pick sth/sb up** to collect someone who is waiting for you, or to collect something that you have left somewhere or that you have bought *1, 2*
**pick up sth** ***or*** **pick sth up** to buy something cheaply *1*
**pick up sth** ***or*** **pick sth up** to learn a new skill or language by practising it rather than being taught it *1*
**pick up sth** ***or*** **pick sth up** if a device picks up a signal or programmes broadcast by a radio station, it receives them *1, 54*
**pick up (sth)** ***or*** **pick (sth) up** to start something again [e.g. story, relationship] from the point where you had stopped *1*
**pick up** if something [e.g. business, economy, trade] picks up, it improves or increases after a bad period *1*
**pick up** if the wind picks up, it becomes stronger *1*
**pick up sth** ***or*** **pick sth up** to learn interesting or useful information [e.g. idea, tip, gossip] from someone or something *25, 51*
**pick up sth** ***or*** **pick sth up** to get an infectious illness from someone or something *43*
**pick yourself up** to stand up again after you have fallen *44*
**pick up** to lift something by using a bill (birds) *47*
**pick up sth** if you pick up speed, you suddenly start to go faster *50*
**pick up after sb** *informal* to put things back in the place they are kept after someone has untidily left them in the wrong place *26*
**pick up on sth** to react to something that you have noticed or something that has happened *16*
**piece together sth** ***or*** **piece sth together** to try to understand a situation or to try to discover the truth about something by collecting different pieces of information and considering them at the same time *25*
**pile into swh** to enter a place or vehicle quickly and not in an organised way *46*
**pile out (of)** to leave a place or vehicle quickly and not in an organised way *46*
**pile up (sth)** ***or*** **pile (sth) up** to become a pile, or to make a lot of things into a pile by putting them on top of each other *26*
**pin down sb or pin sb down** to force someone to stay in a horizontal position by holding them *11*
**pipe down** *informal* to talk more quietly, or to stop complaining *31*
**pitch in** to help with work that needs to be done *12*
**play along** to pretend to agree with someone, or to do what someone wants for a short time, in order to get something from them or to avoid making them angry *52*
**play around** to behave in a stupid way *10*
**play sb off against sb** to encourage one person or group to compete against or argue with another, hoping that you can get some advantage from this situation *30*
**play on/upon sth** if someone plays on your fears or weaknesses, they use them to try and make you do what they want, often in a way that is unfair *30*
**play with sth** if you play with the idea of doing something, you consider it, but usually do not do it *25*
**plough back sth** ***or*** **plough sth back** to put money that you have earned into a business, in order to make the business bigger or better *36*
**plug away** *informal* to work hard at something for a long time *32*
**plug into sth** if a piece of electrical equipment plugs into a supply of electricity or another piece of electrical equipment, it works by being connected to that supply of electricity or that piece of equipment *54*
**plump up sth** ***or*** **plump sth up** to make something [e.g. cushion, pillow] rounder and softer, especially by shaking it *37*
**point to/towards sth** if one thing points to something else, it makes it seem likely that it is true *18*
**poodle around** to wander around in a relaxed way *9*
**pop up** if something pops up, it suddenly appears, often when you are not expecting it *54*
**pop-up** *adj* a pop-up menu is a list of choices which appears on a computer screen when the user requests it *54*
**pore over sth** to study or look carefully at something, especially a book or a document *5, 33*
**potter about/around (swh)** *British & Australian* to spend time in a pleasant, relaxed way, often doing small jobs in or around the house *10*
**pour down** to rain heavily *3*
**predispose sb to/towards sth** *formal* predisposing someone to something makes it more likely that that thing will happen *6*

**preside over sth** *formal* to be in charge of an event or situation and have official responsibility for it *6*
**press on** to continue doing something in a determined way *14, 21*
**prey on/upon sth** to catch for food *47*
**pride yourself on/upon sth/doing sth** (always reflexive) to be proud of a quality you have or of something you do *28, 40*
**print off sth *or* print sth off** to print a particular number of copies of something *6, 54*
**profit from sth/doing sth** to get an advantage from something *34*
**prop up sth *or* prop sth up** to make something stay in a particular position by putting something underneath or against it *26*
**prop yourself up** to support yourself by leaning on or against something *16*
**provide for sth** *formal* if a law or agreement provides for something, it allows it to happen or exist *53*
**pull down sth *or* pull sth down** to destroy a structure because it is not wanted anymore *47*
**pull on sth** to put on clothes quickly *38*
**pull out sth *or* pull sth out** to remove something from a hole or the ground *47*
**pull out** to drive to a different part of the road, usually a part where the vehicles are travelling faster *50*
**pull out all the stops** to do everything you can *8*
**pull over sb/sth *or* pull sb/sth over** if the police pull someone who is driving a car over, they order them to drive the car to the side of the road and stop *50*
**pull (sb) through (sth)** to succeed in dealing with a difficult period of your life, or to help someone else to do this *28*
**pull sth to** to close a door or window by pulling it towards you *37*
**pull up** to move a piece of furniture [esp. chair] near to something or someone *37*
**pull your socks up** to make an effort to improve *17*
**push sb about/around/round** to tell someone what to do in a rude or threatening way *22*
**push on** to continue travelling somewhere *46*
**push over sb/sth *or* push sb/sth over** to push someone or something so that they fall to the ground *22*
**push through sth *or* push sth through** to make a plan or suggestion be officially accepted *30*
**push sth to** to close a door or window by pushing it *37*
**push up sth *or* push sth up** to increase the amount, number, or value of something *27*
**put aside sth/sb *or* push sth/sb** to save money for a particular purpose *36*
**put away sth *or* put sth away** to put something in the place where it is usually kept *37*
**put back sth *or* put sth back** to change the date or time of an event so that it happens later than planned *17*
**put by sth *or* put sth by** to save an amount of money in order to use it later *36*
**put down sb *or* put sb down** to put someone's name on a list or document, usually in order to arrange for them to do something *11*
**put down sth *or* put sth down** to use force to stop people opposing the government *51*
**put down roots** to settle down and make a relationship more permanent *8*
**put down sth *or* put sth down** to kill an animal because it is very old or very ill *11*
**put sth down to sth** to think that a problem or bad experience is caused by something else *18*
**put forward sth *or* put sth forward** to state an idea or opinion, or to suggest a plan, so that it can be considered or discussed *6*
**put in a good word for someone** to say good things about someone to people in authority *8*
**put on sth *or* put sth on** if a person or animal puts on weight, they become heavier *27, 55*
**put out sth *or* put sth out** to produce information [e.g. statement, warning, press release] and make it available for everyone to read or hear *6, 51, 53*
**put out sth *or* put sth out** to put something outside the house, especially so that it can be collected *37*
**put sb on sth** to give someone a particular type of medical treatment or food *43*
**put sth behind sb** if you put an unpleasant experience behind you, you forget it so that it does not affect your life *20*
**put sb through sth** to pay for someone to study at college or university *33*
**put sth to sb** to ask someone a question, or to state an opinion to someone which they are likely to disagree with *45*
**put up sth *or* put sth up** to fasten a piece of furniture [e.g. shelves, cupboard] to a wall *37*
**put up with sb/sth** to tolerate unpleasant behaviour or an unpleasant situation *2*
**rake in sth *or* rake sth in** *informal* to earn large amounts of money, especially without doing much work *36*
**ramble on** to talk or write for a long time about things that are not interesting to other people *14*
**rank (sth) among sth** to have a particular position in a list that has been arranged in order of quality *26*
**read on** to continue reading and read the next part of something *14*
**reason with sb** to try to persuade someone not to do something stupid by giving them good reasons not to *30*
**rebound on/upon sb** if a negative action rebounds on someone, it has a bad effect on the person who did it and they do not achieve what they were trying to achieve *18*

**reduce sth to sth** to destroy something that has been built [e.g. building, city] *49*

**reel off sth** ***or*** **reel sth off** to say a long list of things quickly and without stopping *45*

**refer to sb/sth** if writing or information refers to someone or something, it describes or is about that person or thing *34*

**reflect on/upon sth** *slightly formal* to think very hard about something, or to express your thoughts about something in what you say or write *25*

**relate to sth** to be connected to a particular subject, or to be about a particular subject *34*

**rely on sth/sb** to need something or someone in order to survive, be successful, or work correctly *14*

**remind sb of sb/sth** to cause someone to think of someone or something *20*

**rent out sth** ***or*** **rent sth out** if you rent out something that you own [e.g. house], you allow someone to pay you money so that they can use it *36*

**resign yourself to sth** to accept that something we do not want to happen will happen *29*

**resort to sth/doing sth** to do something bad in order to achieve what you want, often because it is the only thing you can do to achieve it *29*

**result in sth** to cause something to happen, or to make a situation exist *18*, *34*

**rev up sth** ***or*** **rev sth up** to make a vehicle's engine work faster while the vehicle is not moving *50*

**be riddled with sth** be full of something, especially something bad or unpleasant *5*, *29*

**ride on sth** if something important [e.g. reputation, money] rides on something else, it depends on it *14*

**ring out** if a noise [e.g. gunshot, bells, voice] rings out, it can be heard loudly and clearly *23*

**rise above sth** to not allow something bad that is happening or being done to you to upset you or to affect your behaviour *28*

**roll about/around** *informal* to laugh a lot about something *10*

**roll in** if money or requests for money [e.g. bills] roll in, they arrive in large numbers *36*

**roll in** if bad weather [e.g. clouds, fog] rolls in, it appears in large amounts *48*

**Roll on sth!** *British informal* something that you say in order to show that you are looking forward to a time or event *31*

**roll out sth** ***or*** **roll sth out** to make a new product, service or system available for the first time *9*, *53*

**roll (sb/sth) over** to turn from lying on one side of your body to the other side, or to make someone or something turn from one side to the other *1*

**roll up sth** ***or*** **roll sth up** to fold the edges of a piece of clothing that you are wearing [e.g. sleeves, trousers] in order to make them shorter *38*

**roll up** to arrive somewhere, often in large numbers *42*

**be rooted in sth** to be based on, or caused by *18*

**root out sth/sb** ***or*** **root sth/sb out** *informal* to search and find something or someone that is difficult to find *51*

**rough out sth** ***or*** **rough sth out** if you rough out a drawing or an idea, you draw or write the main parts of it without showing the details *25*

**round down sth** ***or*** **round sth down** to decrease a number to the nearest whole amount *27*

**round off sth** ***or*** **round sth off** to do something as a way of finishing an event or activity in a satisfactory way *13*

**round on/upon sb** to suddenly turn and attack someone, or shout at them angrily *22*

**round up sb/sth** ***or*** **round sb/sth up** to find and gather together a group of people or animals *26*

**round up sth** ***or*** **round sth up** to increase a number to the nearest whole amount *27*

**run about** to run and play *10*

**run around/round after sb** *informal* to do a lot of things for someone else, especially when they should be able to do more for themselves *10*, *32*

**run away with sb** if something [e.g. emotions, imagination, enthusiasm] runs away with someone, it makes them do or think stupid things *41*

**run-down** *adj* shabby, in disrepair *49*

**run into sth** if you run into difficulties or problems, you begin to experience them *29*

**run out** if a supply of something runs out, there is none left because it has all been used *21*

**run over sb/sth** ***or*** **run sb/sth over** to hit someone or something with a vehicle and drive over them, injuring or killing them *7*

**run over sth** to quickly read something or repeat something in order to remember it or to make sure that it is correct *7*

**run over** to continue past the expected finishing time *7*

**run rings round** to outwit and be cleverer than people *8*

**run through sth** if you run through money, you spend a lot of it very quickly *36*

**run through sth** to explain or read something to someone quickly *45*

**safeguard against sth** to do things that you hope will stop something unpleasant happening *29*

**sail through (sth)** to succeed very easily, especially in a test, examination etc. *5*, *28*, *33*

**be sandwiched between sb/sth** *informal* to be in a small space in the middle of two people or things *7*

**scrape by** to manage to live when you do not have much money *36*

**scrape through (sth)** to manage with a lot of difficulty to succeed in something [e.g. exam] *33*

**screw up sb *or* screw sb up** *informal* to make someone feel confused or unhappy about themselves and their life *40*
**screw up sth *or* screw sth up** to make your eyes narrower, or to twist your face into a different shape, often in order to show an emotion *44*
**scroll down** to move text or other information on a computer screen, in order to view a different part of it *6, 9*
**scroll up** to move up your computer screen, in order to view a different part of the text or information on it *9*
**see about sth** to deal with something, or to arrange for something to be done *26*
**see sth through** to continue doing a job or activity until it is finished, especially when it is difficult *32*
**seize up** if part of your body or a machine seizes up, it stops moving or working in the normal way *54*
**sell up (sth) *or* sell (sth) up** *British & Australian* to sell your house or business in order to go somewhere else or do something else *6*
**send down sb *or* send sb down** *British informal* to send someone to prison *53*
**send in sb *or* send sb in** to send a group of people with special skills [e.g. police, troops] to deal with a difficult situation *1, 51*
**send out sth *or* send sth out** if a plant sends out something [e.g. roots, shoots], it grows *47*
**send out for sth** to telephone a restaurant and ask for food to be delivered to your home *55*
**separate off sth *or* separate sth off** to remove something from a large group of things *26*
**separate out sb/sth *or* separate sb/sth out** to divide a group of people or things into smaller groups *26*
**serve up sth *or* serve sth up** to put food on plates and in dishes for people to eat *55*
**set apart sth *or* set sth apart** to use something, especially time, for one purpose and no other purpose *17*
**set back sb/sth *or* set sb/sth back** to make something happen more slowly, or to make something happen later than it should happen *17*
**set sb back (sth)** *informal* to cost someone a particular amount of money, usually a large amount of money *36*
**be set back** if a building is set back, it is a little distance from the road *49*
**set in** if something unpleasant sets in, it begins and seems likely to continue *3, 12*
**set off sth *or* set sth off** to make something look attractive, usually by providing a very different colour *49*
**set (sth/sb) on/upon sb** to attack someone, or to make a person or animal attack someone *3, 22*
**set up sth *or* set sth up** to make arrangements so that something can happen or exist *16*
**set up sb *or* set sb up** to give someone the money that they need to start a business *35*
**set up (sth) *or* set (sth) up** to get all the necessary equipment ready for a particular activity *54*
**settle in (sb) *or* settle (sb) in** to begin to feel relaxed and happy in new surroundings *37*
**sex down sth *or* sex sth down** to make something less exciting *9*
**sex up sth *or* sex sth up** to make something more exciting than it really is *9*
**shake off sb *or* shake sb off** to succeed in escaping from someone who is following you *13*
**shake up sth *or* shake sth up** to make big changes to an organization in order to improve it *19*
**shake up sb *or* shake sb up** if an unpleasant experience shakes someone up, it makes them feel shocked and upset *41*
**shake-up** *n* when big changes are made to an organization in order to improve it *1*
**share out sth *or* share sth out** to divide something into smaller amounts and give one amount to each person or thing in a group *15*
**shine through (sth)** if a quality that someone has shines through or shines through something, that quality is very easily noticed *40*
**shoot down sb/sth *or* shoot sb/sth down** *informal* to criticize someone's ideas or suggestions and refuse to consider them *6*
**shoot down sb/sth *or* shoot sb/sth down** to destroy an aircraft or make it fall to the ground by firing bullets or weapons at it *51*
**shoot off** *British & Australian informal* to leave somewhere very quickly *42*
**shoot up** if the number, amount, or rate of something shoots up, it increases very quickly *7*
**shore up sth *or* shore sth up** to strengthen or improve an organization, agreement, or system that is not working effectively or that is likely to fail *16*
**shout down sb *or* shout sb down** to shout in order to prevent someone who is saying something that you disagree with from being heard *11*
**Shove off!** something that you say when you are angry to tell someone to go away *13*
**show in sb *or* show sb in** to lead a visitor into a room where they have arranged to meet or wait for someone *12*
**show off** to show someone or something that you are proud of to a group of people *13*
**show up** if something shows up, it can be seen clearly or easily *16*
**shrug off sth *or* shrug sth off** to not worry about something and treat it as unimportant *13*
**shut down (sth) *or* shut (sth) down** if a machine shuts down or someone shuts it down, it stops operating *11*

**shutdown** *n* when a factory or business closes and stops working *1*
**shut out sth or shut sth out** to prevent a sound or light from being heard or seen *23*
**shut (sb) up** to stop talking or making a noise, or to make someone do this *31*
**side against sb** to oppose a person or group in an argument *24*
**side with sb** to support a person or group in an argument *24*
**sift through sth** to examine a large collection of something, especially papers, usually in order to discover something or to decide what is important *26*
**sign over sth or sign sth over** to give someone else your property or legal rights to something by signing an official document *53*
**sign up sb or sign sb up** to arrange for someone to sign a document stating that they will work for you *35*
**single out sb/sth or single sb/sth out** to choose one person or thing from a large group in order to criticize or praise them *30*
**size up sb/sth or size sb/sth up** to carefully examine a situation or person in order to make a judgement *30*
**skill up sb or skill sb up** to provide or give someone the skills they need to do a particular job *9*
**skim through sth** to read quickly without studying the details *33*
**skirt around/round sth** to avoid discussing a difficult subject or problem *10*
**slam down sth or slam sth down** to put something down with a lot of force, especially the part of the telephone that you talk into *11*
**sleep off sth or sleep sth off** to sleep until you feel better, especially after too much alcohol *42*
**slice up sth or slice sth up** to cut or divide something into parts *55*
**slim down (sth) or slim (sth) down** to become smaller in size, often by employing fewer people, or to make something smaller *27*
**slip away** if a period of time slips away, it seems to pass quickly *17*
**slog away** *informal* to keep working very hard, usually for a long time *32*
**smarten up (sb/sth) or smarten sb/sth up** to make a person or a place look tidier *37*
**smash up sth or smash sth up** to badly damage or destroy something by hitting it many times *22*
**smooth down sth or smooth sth down** to press your hair or your clothes with your hands in order to make them flat *38*
**smooth over sth or smooth sth over** to make a disagreement or problem seem less serious or more easy to deal with, especially by talking to the people involved in it *29*
**snap out of sth** *informal* to force yourself to stop feeling sad and upset *41*
**be snowed under** *informal* to have so much work that you have problems dealing with it *33*
**soak up sth or soak sth up** to enjoy the effects of an experience *49*
**soak up sth or soak sth up** if a dry substance soaks up a liquid, it absorbs it *55*
**soldier on** to continue doing something, although it is difficult or unpleasant *7*
**sort out sth or sort sth out** to successfully deal with a problem or difficult situation *2, 15*
**sort out sth or sort sth out** to arrange or organize things which are untidy *15*
**sound out sb/sth or sound sb/sth out** to talk to someone in order to discover what they think about an idea or plan *45, 51*
**space out sth or space sth out** to arrange things so that there is enough space or time between them *17, 26*
**spill out (sth) or spill (sth) out** if you spill out an emotion or if emotion spills out, you express it, usually by talking in an uncontrolled way *41*
**spill over** if a bad situation or problem spills over, it begins to have an unpleasant effect on another situation or group of people *29*
**spill over (sth)** if the liquid in a container spills over, it flows over the edge of the container *55*
**spin out sth or spin sth out** to make something continue for as long as possible *17*
**split off** to stop belonging to a particular group or political party and form a separate one *13*
**split up (sth) or split (sth) up** to divide into smaller parts or groups, or to divide something into smaller parts or groups *16*
**spread out sth or spread sth out** to open something that is folded [e.g. map, towel] and put it down flat on a surface *15*
**spread out sth or spread sth out** if you spread out your arms, legs, or fingers, you stretch them so that there are wide spaces between them *44*
**spring sth on sb** to tell someone some news that surprises them *14*
**spring up** if something springs up, it suddenly appears or begins to exist *21*
**sprout up** if a large number of things sprout up, they suddenly appear or begin to exist *21*
**spur on sb or spur sb on** to encourage someone to try harder in order to achieve something *7*
**spy on/upon sb/sth** to watch secretly in order to discover information about them *52*
**square up** *informal* to pay someone the money you owe them *6, 36*
**squash (sb) in** to manage to get yourself or someone else into a very small space, or place that is full of people *12*
**squash up** if people who are sitting or standing together squash up, they move closer together in order to make space for someone else *46*
**stack up sth or stack sth up** to arrange things in a tall pile *26*

**stack up** if aircraft stack up, they fly over an airport at different heights waiting to be told they can land *50*

**stake sth on sth/doing sth** to risk losing money or harming something important [e.g. reputation] if a plan does not succeed *36*

**stake out sth *or* stake sth out** if the police or reporters stake out a building where someone is living or hiding, they watch the building continuously in order to see who is leaving or entering it *51*

**stamp on sth** to use force to get rid of something that you disapprove of *22*

**stand back** to move a short distance away from something or someone *46*

**stand by** to do nothing to prevent something unpleasant from happening *7*

**standby** *n* a person or thing that can be used if someone or something else is not available or cannot be used *1, 3*

**stand for sth** if a group of people stand for a set of ideas, they support those ideas, or if something stands for a particular idea, it represents that idea *24*

**stand up** to rise from a sitting or lying position to a standing position *1*

**stand up** if an idea or claim stands up, it is proved to be correct when it is examined carefully *16*

**start sb off** to help someone to start an activity, especially a piece of work *13*

**stand-off** *n* when two groups fail to reach an agreement in talks *3*

**start on at sb** to start complaining angrily to someone about something that they have done *21*

**start-up** *n* when a business or organization is created and starts to operate *3*

**steal away** to leave a place quietly without anyone knowing *46*

**steam up (sth) *or* steam (sth) up** if a glass surface steams up, or if something steams it up, it becomes covered with very small drops of water *48*

**be steeped in sth** to have a lot of (particularly tradition or history) *49*

**stem from sth** if a problem or difficult situation stems from something, it is caused by it *18*

**step aside** to leave a job or position, especially so that someone else can do it *32*

**stick by sth** to continue to support or use a decision, opinion, or plan *24*

**stick out sth *or* stick sth out** to push part of your body forward or out from the rest of your body *44*

**stick to sth** to limit yourself to doing or using one particular thing and not change to anything else *19*

**stick up** if part of something sticks up, it comes up above the surface of something, or it points upwards *16*

**stick up for sth** to defend or fight for something important [e.g. rights] *24*

**stick with sb** if something sticks with you, you remember it *20*

**stir up sth *or* stir sth up** if something stirs up memories, it makes you remember events in the past, usually ones that make you feel sad *20*

**stop up sth *or* stop sth up** to fill a hole so that nothing can pass through it *37*

**store up sth *or* store sth up** to remember things, usually so that you can tell people about them later *20*

**storm out** to leave a place in an angry way *48*

**stow away** to hide on a ship, aircraft, or other vehicle, in order to travel secretly or without paying *3, 50*

**stowaway** *n* a person who stows away *3, 50*

**straighten up sth *or* straighten sth up** to make a place tidy *37*

**stream into swh** to move continuously in one direction, especially if a lot of people do this at the same time *5*

**stretch out sth *or* stretch sth out** to hold a part of your body straight out in front of you *44*

**stretch out** if an area of land stretches out, it continues over a long distance *49*

**strike back (at)** to attack someone who has attacked you *22*

**strike out** to start doing something that you have not done before *7*

**strike up sth** to start a conversation or relationship with someone *39*

**stumble on/upon sth/sb** to find or meet by chance *46*

**succeed in sth/doing sth** to achieve something that you have been trying to get or do *28*

**suck up to sb** *informal* to try to make someone who is in a position of authority like you by doing and saying things that will please them *39*

**sum up (sth/sb) *or* sum (sth/sb) up** to describe briefly the most important facts or characteristics of something or someone *6*

**sum up sb/sth *or* sum sth/sb up** if something sums up someone or something, it represents the most typical qualities of that person or thing *34*

**summon up sth *or* summon sth up** if something summons up a memory or an image, it makes you remember something or think about something *20*

**summon up sth *or* summon sth up** to try hard to find a particular quality [e.g. courage, energy] in yourself because you need it in order to do something *41*

**swear by sth** to believe that something is very effective and that it will always work well *24*

**sweep aside sth *or* sweep sth aside** to refuse to think about something or let it affect your performance *7*

**swing around/round** to suddenly turn around so that you can see someone or something behind you *44*

**switch around/round** to move two or more things, so that each of them is now in the place that one of the others was in before *10*

**switch off** to stop giving your attention to something or someone *13*

**tail off** to decrease in amount or level *27*

**take sb aback** if something takes you aback, you are very surprised by it *60*

**take along sb/sth** *or* **take sb/sth along** to take someone or something with you when you go somewhere *60*

**take away sb** *or* **take sb away** to take someone with you when you stay somewhere for a short time *60*

**take away sth** *or* **take sth away** if you take away something [e.g. memory, impression, message] from an event or performance, you remember or think about that thing after the event or performance has finished *60*

**take away from sth** to make something seem less good or successful *60*

**take it away!** something that you say in musical contexts to tell someone to start playing or singing *31, 60*

**take down sth** *or* **take sth down** to remove a large temporary structure from a place by separating it into pieces and taking the pieces away *60*

**take down sth** *or* **take sth down** to remove a large temporary structure from a place by separating it into pieces and taking the pieces away *11*

**take down sth** *or* **take sth down** to write something, especially something that someone says *11*

**take off sth** *or* **take sth off** to spend time away from your work *60*

**take off** if an aircraft, bird, or insect takes off, it moves from the ground and begins to fly *60*

**take sb off sth** to stop giving someone a particular type of medical treatment or food *60*

**take-off** *n* imitation *60*

**take on sth** *or* **take sth on** to accept a particular job or responsibility and begin to do what is needed *6*

**take out sth** *or* **take sth out** to borrow a book from a library *60*

**take out sb/sth** *or* **take sb/sth out** to kill someone, or to destroy something *60*

**take out sb** *or* **take sb out** to go somewhere and do something with someone, usually something that you have planned or paid for *60*

**take sth out of sb** *informal* to make someone feel very tired *43*

**take over sth** *or* **take sth over** to get control of a company by buying most of its shares (= the equal parts into which the ownership of the company is divided) *6*

**take over sth** *or* **take sth over** to get control of an area of land or a political organization, usually by using force *47*

**take out sb** *or* **take sb out** to go somewhere and do something with someone, usually something that you have planned or paid for *42*

**take up sth** *or* **take sth up** to start doing a particular job or activity *33*

**take up sth** *or* **take sth up** to shorten a piece of clothing [e.g. skirt, trousers] *38*

**take up sth (with)** *or* **take sth up (with)** to discuss something or deal with something *60*

**take up sth** *or* **take sth up** to use a particular amount of time, space or effort *60*

**take the sting out of something** to make something that is unpleasant less so *8*

**talk at sb** to talk to someone without listening to them or allowing them to speak *45*

**talk through sth** *or* **talk sth through** to discuss all the details of something so that you can understand it or make a decision about it *25*

**tend towards sth** to be likely to choose a particular thing *30*

**tense up** if you tense up or your muscles tense up, your muscles stiffen because you are not relaxed *44*

**test out sth** *or* **test sth out** to test a theory or new idea by seeing how it works in a practical situation or by finding out what other people think of it *15*

**thaw out** if someone thaws out, they become warmer after they have been outside and have got very cold *44*

**thin out** if a large number of people or things thin out, they become fewer in number *27*

**think up sth** *or* **think sth up** to create an idea or plan by using your imagination and intelligence *25*

**thrash out sth** *or* **thrash sth out** to discuss a problem, idea, or plan in detail until you find a solution, reach an agreement, or make a decision *25*

**throw off** if you are thrown off the Internet, you lose your connection to it *9*

**throw off sth** *or* **throw sth off** to succeed in getting rid of a slight illness *43*

**throw out sth** *or* **throw sth out** if people in authority throw out a plan or idea [e.g. bill, proposal] they refuse to accept or use it *53*

**throw the baby out with the bathwater** to get rid of the good parts of something as well as the bad parts *8*

**tick off sb** *or* **tick sb off** *British & Australian* to tell someone that they have done something wrong and that you are angry about it *13*

**tie back sth** *or* **tie sth back** to fasten something that usually hangs down [esp. hair] so that it is fixed in position and not hanging down *2, 38*

**tie down sth/sb** *or* **tie sth/sb down** to fasten something or someone in a particular position, especially by using ropes *11*

**tie sb down** to stop someone from being free to do what they want to do *11, 30*
**tighten up sth** *or* **tighten sth up** to make rules more limiting and more difficult to avoid *53*
**tinker with sth** to make small changes to something, usually trying to improve or repair it *19*
**tire out sb** *or* **tire sb out** to make someone very tired *43*
**tired out** *adj* completely exhausted *4*
**top up** to pay money onto a top-up card which you spend when you use your mobile phone *9*
**toss (sb) for sth** to decide which person or team can do something or have something by throwing a coin in the air and guessing which side of the coin will be on top when it lands *30*
**toss-up** *n informal* a situation in which two people or things seem equally likely to be chosen or two possible results seem equally likely to happen *3*
**toughen up** to become stronger and more able to deal with problems, or to make someone become this way *40*
**toughen up sth** *or* **toughen sth up** to make rules more limiting and more difficult to avoid *53*
**trail off** to gradually become quieter and then stop *23*
**treat sb to sth** to buy or pay for something for someone else *42*
**trip over (sth)** to fall or almost fall because you have accidentally hit your foot against something while walking or running *46*
**tune into sth** to turn on the radio or television in order to listen to or watch a particular programme *54*
**turn (sb) against sth/sb** to decide not to like or agree with someone or something, or to make someone do this *41*
**turnaround** *n* a sudden improvement, especially in a business or the economy of a country *19*
**turn around/round (sb/sth)** *or* **turn (sth/sb) around/round** to turn so that you are facing the opposite direction, or to make someone or something do this *10, 44*
**turn around/round sth** *or* **turn sth around** change an unsuccessful business, plan or system so that it becomes successful *10, 19*
**turn out sth** *or* **turn sth out** if a company or business turns out something, they make or produce it *35*
**turn over sth** *or* **turn sth over** if a business or a company turns over an amount of money, it makes that amount in a particular period of time *6, 35*
**turn away sb** *or* **turn sb away** to refuse to allow someone to enter a place, usually because there is no more space *42*
**turn down sth** *or* **turn sth down** to reduce the amount of sound or heat that is produced by a device [e.g. television, radio, oven] *11*
**turn up the heat** to make a relationship more intense *8*
**turn (sb/sth) into sth/sb** to change and become something or someone different, or make something or someone do this *19*
**upkeep** *n* keeping a building in good condition, usually by providing money to repair it *59*
**uptake** *n* the number of people who have committed themselves to something *60*
**usher in sth** *formal* if an event ushers in a period of time in which new things or changes happen, it is at the beginning of that period or it causes those things to happen *12*
**vote on sth** to make a decision about something [e.g. proposal, motion] by counting the number of people for and against it *53*
**vouch for sb** to say that you know someone and that you can promise that they have a good character or good skills *40*
**Wake up!** *informal* something you say to tell someone to listen to what you are saying when they have not been listening *31*
**Wake up and smell the coffee!** *informal* to be realistic *8*
**walk away** to stop being involved in a situation that is difficult to deal with or that does not give you any advantages *29*
**walk in on sb** to go into a room and see what someone is doing when they did not want anyone to see them *46*
**walk out** to stop working because of a disagreement with your employer *3, 51*
**walkout** *n* when workers stop working because of a disagreement with their employer *3*
**walk-on** *adj* a walk-on part in a play is a very small part with no words for the actor to speak *3*
**want for** *formal* if someone does not want for anything, they have everything they need in order to have a satisfactory life *6*
**want out** *informal* to want to leave a place *15*
**warm to sb** to start to like someone *39*
**warm up sth** *or* **warm sth up** to heat food that has already been cooked *7*
**warm up sb** *or* **warm sb up** to make a group of people who are going to watch a performance start to enjoy themselves by entertaining them for a short time before the performance *7*
**warm up (sth)** *or* **warm (sth) up** if an engine or machine warms up, or if you warm it up, it starts working so that it becomes warm enough to work well *54*
**warm-up** *n* when a performer makes a group of people who are going to watch a performance start to enjoy themselves by entertaining them for a short time before the performance *3*
**wash away sth** *or* **wash sth away** if water [e.g. rain, flood] washes something away, it carries it away *47*

**wash down sth *or* wash sth down** to clean a large object or surface [e.g. floor, walls] with a liquid *37*

**wash down sth *or* wash sth down** to drink something while you are eating food or taking medicine in order to help you swallow it *55*

**washed out** *adj* if someone looks washed out, they look tired, pale and ill *43*

**waste away** to gradually get thinner and weaker, usually because of illness *44*

**Watch out!** something you say to tell someone to be careful so that they can avoid danger or an accident *31*

**watch over sb/sth** to protect or take care of a person or animal *47*

**water down sth *or* water sth down** to add water to a drink, especially an alcoholic drink *11, 55*

**water down sth *or* water sth down** to make an idea or opinion less strong in order to make more people agree with it, or to make a plan or suggestion more acceptable *11*

**watered-down** *adj* when something is made less strong in order to make people agree with it *4*

**wear out sb *or* wear sb out** to make someone very tired *1, 43*

**wear out (sth) *or* wear (sth) out** to use something so much that it becomes weak or damaged and cannot be used any more, or to become weak and damaged in this way *4*

**be weirded out** if you are weirded out by something, you feel uncomfortable about it or shocked by it *9*

**whip up sth** to try to make people feel strongly about something *51*

**whittle away sth *or* whittle sth away** to gradually reduce the size or importance of something until it does not exist any more *21*

**win back sb/sth *or* win sb/sth back** to persuade customers to return to using your company rather than competing companies because your company has improved *28*

**win out** if a particular emotion or type of behaviour wins out, it is stronger than other emotions or types of behaviour *28*

**win through** to finally succeed after trying hard to achieve something *28*

**wind up (sth) *or* wind (sth) up** to finish an activity *21*

**wipe out sth *or* wipe sth out** to destroy or get rid of something *22*

**wipe out sb *or* wipe sb out** *informal* to make someone extremely tired *43*

**wipe out sth *or* wipe sth out** to remove information stored on part of a computer [esp. memory, hard disk] *54*

**wire up sth/sb *or* wire sth/sb up** to connect something or someone to a piece of electrical equipment by using electrical wires *54*

**witter on** *British informal* to talk for a long time about unimportant things *45*

**wolf down sth *or* wolf sth down** to eat something very quickly because you are very hungry *55*

**work around/round sth** to organise activities to ensure that a problem does not prevent you from doing what you want to do *10*

**work yourself into sth** to make yourself become very angry or upset *41*

**work off sth *or* work sth off** to do something energetic to stop yourself becoming fat after eating a lot of food *13*

**work off sth *or* work sth off** to reduce the size of a debt, either by earning money to pay for it or by working for the person you owe money to *36*

**work out sth *or* work sth out** to think carefully about how you are going to do something and to make a plan or decision *1, 30*

**worked-up** *adj* if you are worked-up, you feel very upset, nervous or excited about something *4*

**worm sth out of sb** to manage to get information from someone which they are trying to keep secret *51*

**worn-out** *adj* weak and damaged through much use *4*

**wrap up sth *or* wrap sth up** to complete an activity, especially successfully *16*

**wring sth out of sb** to force or persuade someone to give you money or information *45*

**write up sth *or* write sth up** to write something on paper or on a computer in a complete or final form, often using notes you have made *16, 51*

**yell out (sth) *or* yell (sth) out** to suddenly shout something in a loud voice, especially to get someone's attention *15*

**zip up sth *or* zip sth up** to fasten a piece of clothing by using its zip (= a long metal or plastic fastener), or to help someone close the zip on a piece of clothing they are wearing *38*

**zone out** to stop thinking about anything *9*